Book Bands for Guided Reading

A handbook to support Foundation
and Key Stage 1 teachers

4th edition

Suzanne Baker

Shirley Bickler

Sue Bodman

Produced by the
UK Reading Recovery
National Network

First published 1998 by the Institute of Education, University of London,
20 Bedford Way, London WC1H 0AL
www.ioe.ac.uk/publications

4th edition, revised and expanded, 2007

British Library cataloguing-in-publication data
A catalogue record for this publication is available from the British Library

ISBN 978 0 85473 787 1

The paper used in this book is made from ECF Pulp procured from well managed, sustainable forests and is produced at a mill accredited by the Forestry Stewardship Council and ISO14001.

Designed by Peter Dolton
Production services by Book Production Consultants Ltd
25–27 High Street, Chesterton, Cambridge CB4 1ND
Printed in England by The Burlington Press, Foxton, Cambridge

Contents

Acknowledgements

Over the years, many publishers have provided material to be considered for inclusion in the band listings. Their continuing generosity is gratefully acknowledged. In particular, we would like to thank the following publishers for allowing us to reproduce the book covers for the 12 sample Guided Reading lessons that introduce each band:

Gardner Education for *Shimbir* and *Whales on the World Wide Web*
Harcourt Education for *What Shall I Wear?*, *Curly to the Rescue* and *The Perfect Present*
HarperCollins for *A Day at the Eden Project*
Kingscourt Publishing for *Pass the Pasta, Please* and *Diary of a Sunflower*
Nelson Thornes for *In our classroom*, *Father Bear Goes Fishing* and *Puss-in-Boots*
Oxford University Press for *The Wobbly Tooth*

We also wish to thank Deborah Wiles, the head teacher of Leys School, Dagenham, and Lisa Gurry, class teacher, for permission to photograph a Guided Reading lesson.

This listing is built on a database of titles used in Reading Recovery.

Introduction to the 4th edition

The choice of lovely books specifically written to provide valuable learning opportunities is pivotal for effective Guided Reading sessions. For this reason, we have created a new advisory section, **Series Reviews**, to assist with resourcing. In this section we have described and reviewed all the series in print commonly used for Guided Reading. Those that offer both fiction and non-fiction through Foundation Stage to Year 2 have received detailed treatment. There are briefer descriptions and recommendations of those that might be used to supplement your basic (core) sets of texts. **Is it worth a lesson?** investigates some of the characteristics that high quality Guided Reading texts offer. Also in this section is a discussion, **Fascinating facts**, about the delights and challenges of using the attractive, new non-fiction books written especially for young readers.

The **Exemplar sessions** and introductions to the colour-banded **Text listings** have been added to and updated for this 4th edition. They have been aligned with the Progression in Phonics suggested in *Letters and Sounds* (Primary National Strategy 2007) and with the reading strands of the *Primary Framework for Literacy 2006*. We have banded only those series produced by publishers specifically for Guided Reading. This excludes books intended for shared and independent use, and also all those series designed to provide practice with the decoding of certain phoneme-grapheme correspondences, and therefore more suited to a daily, discrete programme of phonic work. The Guided Reading books that we recommend in the Pink A, Pink B and Red listings already provide plenty of opportunities for children to flex their decoding skills on regular CVC words while still behaving as text readers.

In the past four years, hundreds of beautiful books especially designed for Guided Reading, many of them non-fiction, have come onto the market already colour banded. We have sifted through the listings again to remove titles now out of print, those with too few words at the beginner stages and too many at higher bands, and tedious texts lacking imaginative language, compelling plots or intriguing information. Unfortunately, we continue to receive requests for bands of books that have been out of print sometimes for decades, and material that was not specifically produced for Guided Reading.

Some publishers have involved us at the development stages of a new series, and we have helped to match the texts with our banding criteria. Others have undertaken the banding themselves, so there may well be a discrepancy between their published colour bands and our listings in this book. Where a title in a series is missing, we have judged that particular book unsuitable because of poor quality or too limited content. Titles considered too sophisticated for this age group may appear in *Bridging Bands for Guided Reading* (Institute of Education 2003). If you feel that a title has been inappropriately banded for the children you are working with, trust your own judgement.

We do urge schools not to spend their book budgets on inferior quality material of any kind. Children's early text reading experience will be best supported and enhanced as they read for themselves natural language sentences within beautifully illustrated, modern books that resonate with their prior experience of much-loved storybooks.

August 2007

PART 1

Text reading in the classroom

A balanced classroom text reading programme consists of a variety of text reading experiences, levels of support and methods of instruction.

Shared Reading, in which the whole class joins in the collaborative act of fluent, expressive text reading and re-reading. The teacher takes the lead, orchestrating responses, drawing attention to reading strategies and features at text, sentence and word levels appropriate to the age, experience and ability of the majority of the class. Sensitive questioning and prompting of individual children helps to ensure maximum participation and understanding. At Foundation Stage, two or three children will often work with an experienced reader to share a book, listening and commenting on the content, learning and responding to terms associated with books and print, supplying some of the words, and making links with what they know already.

Guided Reading, where children put into practice their developing expertise at an appropriate level in a structured situation. The teacher differentiates the instructional reading programme and guides a group of children who have reached a similar level of skill to develop independent reading strategies on new and increasingly challenging texts.

Independent Reading, where children read on their own a range of material, including:
- wall stories and personalised text and labels inside the classroom as a model for noticing print in the environment
- familiar texts to strengthen control over the reading process. Early behaviours become automatic and novice readers can devote more attention to print detail, phrasing and punctuation, as well as the message
- familiar or new books to locate information, print detail, spelling patterns and other features of text following Shared or Guided Reading sessions
- familiar or new books to use as a model for text layout such as a play or chart, paragraphing or punctuation
- at early bands, teacher-made caption books designed to provide a bridge between the reading of words and text reading. This personalised approach will encourage the application of skills taught in a systematic phonics programme.

Modelling text reading, where a skilled reader selects text from a wide range of literature and reads to children in formal or informal settings.

Some important distinctions between Shared, Guided and Independent Reading in a literacy lesson

	SHARED READING	GUIDED READING	INDEPENDENT READING
Grouping of pupils	WHOLE CLASS: mixed ability.	SMALL GROUP: usually 3–8 selected pupils at a similar stage of acquisition.	INDIVIDUALLY, in pairs or in small groups, e.g. for play reading.
Text	LARGE PRINT: One text for whole group (or copy of text per child). Text re-read aloud repeatedly until familiar.	SETS of texts with one copy for each group member. Lesson consists of unfamiliar book or a section of text.	VARIETY of texts from Shared and Guided Reading, library books, games, activities, book-tapes, environmental print, instructions, recipes, etc.
Text level	RICH CHALLENGING TEXT beyond the current ability of most of the class.	INSTRUCTIONAL LEVEL: i.e. each member of group able to read and readily comprehend text at or above 90 per cent accuracy.	EASY LEVEL: i.e. each child able to read and readily comprehend texts at or above 95 per cent accuracy.
Performance	HIGH LEVEL OF SUPPORT within a collaborative social framework of explicit teaching and oral response.	LOWER LEVEL OF SUPPORT: Teacher structures the task and then calls for individuals to apply strategies already introduced and practised in Shared Reading.	LITTLE/NO TEACHER SUPPORT: Pupils work independently or with others to practise reading in a variety of contexts, or respond to reading. Adults may organise and supervise certain activities.
Teaching style	TEACHER-LED, with formal, pre-planned teaching objectives.	PUPILS expected to take the initiative and read to themselves following an introduction, with TEACHER facilitating.	PUPILS monitor their own activities. They may assist and work with others within classroom organisation where expectations are clear and routines well established.
Focus	INTRODUCING AND PRACTISING planned objectives at the word, sentence and/or text levels.	REINFORCING AND EXTENDING strategies and/or objectives already taught in Shared Reading.	ACHIEVING FLUENCY AND FLEXIBILITY at current level of control. RESPONDING personally to text.

PART 2

The right book

Is it worth a lesson?

PRIOR EXPERIENCE OF BOOKS AND LETTERS

Small children will have listened to hundreds of storybooks if they are fortunate, learning by heart whole books and favourite refrains. The imagery and rhythmic flow of storybook language will have entered their oral language repertoire and developed their experience of what it is to be a reader. They will have pretended to read, turning the pages, adopting the voices of characters and capturing the mood of a story.

BEGINNING FORMAL LEARNING

Now in their reception classes, the new entrants will be joining in with reading books in a small group with a competent reader, and participating in whole-class Shared Reading. They'll be learning in more depth how books work by taking turns to help match the words spoken with the clusters of letters separated by spaces on the page, and becoming familiar with and using terms such as 'word', 'front cover', 'title', 'author' and 'full stop'.

In brisk daily sessions, as part of a systematic, high quality phonics programme, the children will be learning to distinguish and name letters, practising the phonemes they represent in a variety of activities, reading and writing them in left-to-right sequence to create words, and observing how a sequence of words represents complete ideas in sentences. They will know in detail their names and those of their families and friends, some words such as *cat*, *dog*, *I*, perhaps *zoo* plus other words that appear frequently in books, and begin to appreciate the flexibility of letters and letter sequences in the context of different words.

TEXTS THAT SUPPORT NOVICE TEXT READERS

Now it's time for a small group of children to have a go at the whole act of reading, all by themselves. The teacher has chosen just the right book and has planned his/her lesson carefully. The words are well-spaced on uncluttered pages, preferably opposite the main illustration. They form complete, repeated and punctuated sentences within a very simple story framework, in language that echoes children's natural speaking. The illustrations directly support the text without distracting the reader with unnecessary detail and over-colourful design. Introducing a new book in such a way that enables a group of novices to read it successfully is described in the section entitled *Implementing Guided Reading*. It is also played out in the *Exemplar sessions* preceding the colour banded listings.

When the children have read the whole book once or twice, the teacher will select one or two elements for detailed attention. At Pink, Red and Yellow Bands, at least, these will always include letter and word level aspects, e.g. locating and memorising, preferably by writing, high frequency words, or practising blending (synthesising) simple CVC words. At higher bands, this will include digraphs, trigraphs and multi-syllabic words. Often there will be opportunities to notice and use punctuation to re-read expressively any direct speech, discuss the use of capital letters and full stops to designate sentences, and explore further aspects of the story, characters or layout.

USING THE RIGHT BOOKS

Of course, if the sets of books selected by the school for Guided Reading do not offer at least three words in a complete punctuated sentence on each of a minimum of eight pages; if there is no repetition of at least one unfamiliar high frequency word and an absence of simple, decodable words; if the language structures and meaning are distorted to fit phonic requirements and have little resonance with the way young children speak or with their experience of favourite storybooks, then the children will be bewildered and discouraged, and the precious time put aside for those children to get to grips with continuous text reading will be squandered.

Single-form entry schools usually find it necessary to have at least 40 sets of Pink A Band books, and another 40 sets at Pink B Band, and at least 50 sets at Red Band. The need for so many books at the beginning stages is that children tend to spend more time at these levels, and the sets should remain in the classroom for several weeks to be re-read independently. Some children in Year 1 and even Year 2 may also be using these beginner books.

From Red Band up to Green, high quality fiction books tend to feature a character or characters with a problem, plot development that creates tension and involves the reader emotionally, and a happy resolution.

When children listen to [traditional tales and quality children's picture books] *in pindrop silence, it is because of the strength of the storyline that is holding them.*

Beverley Randell, 1998

This master of story-shaping for beginner text readers stresses the importance of books that provide a motivation for page-turning, opportunities for logical thought and problem-solving, the intrinsic reward of satisfying endings, and the experience of clear, precise language. Too many fiction books written for Guided Reading employ a cyclical formula, with the same sequence of words and ideas repeated without variation so that the reader's interest in the story wanes and full attention to the print is no longer necessary. There is clearly room for the type of story-telling repetition found in traditional tales, such as 'Run, run as fast as you can', but most effective stories for young readers will reflect their everyday routines, relationships and passions.

REVIEWS OF GUIDED READING SERIES

Other features that restrict children's reading experience are series of books that feature the same group of characters throughout their bands, the same types of sentence structures, the same authors and illustrators, and more or less the same placement of print on the page. A narrow range of Guided Reading books severely restricts children's learning opportunities. Because of the importance of selecting the very best books on the market, this edition of *Book Bands* includes reviews of all the Guided Reading series currently in print.

Fascinating facts

Non-fiction may be just the thing to get boys hooked on reading. There are those who feel that reading fiction is superior to reading non-fiction, and that information books are inherently boring. In the past, of course, many **have** been, and most were out of reach for learner readers. However, over the past decade, the updated English curriculum has elevated the reading of non-fiction to an essential taught strand throughout both primary key stages. Many publishers have responded enthusiastically with a wealth of well written accessible books with irresistible photographs and engaging layouts.

Now all the major Key Stage 1 Guided Reading series available in the UK either integrate non-fiction with fiction or produce parallel strands, so that we are one step closer to the possibility of topic-based literacy, with children reading around subject areas at the colour band that matches their reading skill.

A DIFFERENT KIND OF READING EXPERIENCE

As experienced readers, we certainly attend to the growing sophistication of vocabulary and literary style when we select texts for children who have mastered the basic reading process. Perhaps we under-estimate, though, the very different types of reading experience that fiction and non-fiction call for.

Fiction reading is a solitary pursuit requiring sustained concentration for ever-increasing periods of time. The fiction reader voluntarily suspends her/his habitual thinking and submits to the thought patterns, motives, sequences and values chosen by an unseen author. S/he must master the art of picking up the book hours or even days after the last reading session, re-entering an imaginary world by rapidly bringing to mind all the preceding events, emotions and complexities within the covers and also her/his own reactions. This act of faith in an author requires an enormous amount of concentration and practice, and often becomes addictive for children aged 8–12 as they graduate through short stories, more substantial paperbacks, and launch into Harry Potter and the like.

Non-fiction requires no suspended gratification and no strictures requiring the reader to start at the beginning and follow an author's path to the final page. Contents are ordered predictably and information is available in different forms. The reader is in control – free to choose which sections to read and in what order. It is not surprising, then, that some children prefer non-fiction.

VISUAL LITERACY

Whereas pace and fluency is an integral part of the enjoyment of fiction reading, the non-fiction reader must proceed more slowly in order to process new information, stopping to relate facts located in a variety of formats such as maps, charts, close-ups of insects, ingredients of the meal to be cooked, etc. and re-reading to check where necessary. The validity of this slower pace and pictorial presentation may well appeal to less able readers. Those whose English language skills are restricted certainly benefit from the direct illustrative support offered by non-fiction.

Non-fiction texts also provide an ideal basis for discussion and collaborative activity, particularly when accompanied by diagrams, maps and photographs. It's natural to read aloud particularly interesting snippets of information: 'Did you know that …?'; read aloud instructions as they're put into practice; and identify particular items of interest in reference books or directories and pause to note them down. Reading of this kind has immediate social relevance for young boys who observe and emulate the exchange of factual information that tends to be a major feature of adult male conversation, and the status that accrues from knowing facts. Non-fiction texts also tend to be less age-specific in terms of content and illustration than fiction, and have a generally 'adult' appearance.

WHAT CONSTITUTES 'NON-FICTION'?

Many of the texts at Pink Band could be classified as non-fiction. They consist of categories, e.g. different children playing in different places or taking different forms of transport to school, or the same child playing on, under, through and around. They may be written in the habitual present tense, e.g. 'Dogs like to eat …'; or in the simple present, 'This ball is soft. This ball is hard …', where the text together with the illustration forms an inseparable message. There may be a sketchy story format provided by the text or by the illustrations alone.

Layout conventions that are the classic hallmarks of non-fiction (e.g. a table of contents, headings, sub-headings and captions, an index and a glossary) can be found in simplified form even in Pink Band books. These organisational features are designed to support the reader's independence, and teachers need to adapt Guided Reading procedures to take this into account.

The title usually declares the topic area unambiguously. A quick flick through pages alive with informative photos reveals the range of subject matter. Chapter headings and the index enable readers to locate for themselves exactly what they want to read. This is in sharp contrast to fiction, where narrative imposes a rigid sequence, and the story often depends on unpredictable developments and a surprise ending.

Chronology is often a significant feature of non-fiction, and is found in diverse text types, e.g. diaries and logs, life cycles and timelines, programmes and timetables, procedures and instructions, and narrative sequence found in simple history and biography. Teachers need to bear this in mind when they teach children to distinguish non-fiction by noting layout features common in reports and explanations, e.g. maps, charts, cycles, fact boxes, question-and-answer formats of various types, and diagrams.

The recent widespread use of photographs has not only bestowed on non-fiction a glamour that beginner texts formerly lacked, but also creates an obvious link both with children's real-life experience and with screen-viewing.

USING NON-FICTION IN GUIDED READING

As in all Guided Reading, the teacher calls for the children to use the terms and understandings introduced during shared sessions. The literacy focus will be on non-fiction strategies such as:
- identifying the text type
- locating information using the contents table, index, headings, etc., and skimming and scanning the print
- summarising orally or note-taking
- interpreting information from a variety of formats to make decisions, carry out activities, etc.

- evaluating the effectiveness of the text in terms of language used, organisation and layout
- returning to the text and carrying out follow-up activities that will involve using specific layouts and specialised types of language.

Probably the biggest challenges for non-fiction readers involve understanding the rationales that determine the content and organisation of a book or piece of non-fiction writing; mastering new vocabulary and concepts; and developing a range of language registers that they can use appropriately in their own writing.

Most of us rarely, if ever, create poems, plays or stories in our adult lives, yet we earn our living from, and communicate with the world daily using the language and forms of non-fiction. Seen in this light, we need to cater effectively for such an important aspect of text reading and writing in Foundation and Key Stage 1 classrooms.

Reviews of Guided Reading series for Foundation and Key Stage 1

For Guided Reading sessions to be effective, it is crucial that teachers use high quality texts. However, no single publisher's materials will deliver the desirable variety and range for 4–7-year-olds as they graduate from beginners to fluency and relative independence. With so many Guided Reading books currently on the market, literacy co-ordinators cannot expect to be familiar with all the series or know their relative strengths and short-comings. With this in mind, we have written reviews of the main series currently in print with the aim of supporting schools to make the best use of their book budgets.

FULL REVIEWS

There are full reviews of what might be called 'core series'. These series offer a range of fiction and non-fiction from Foundation Stage through to the end of Year 2. It is not essential to have a core series, and many schools wisely use books from several. However, if a school is starting afresh to build up a resource of sets of texts, it makes good economic sense in terms of time and money to begin with an excellent series that has been **written specifically for Guided Reading**, and then build in variety.

BRIEF REVIEWS

Brief reviews are provided for other series. We have found that schools generally need far more Pink and Red Band books than one series can offer. Very few series fulfil our rigorous criteria at this important stage. Following the lead of several publishers, we have split the Pink Band listings in this edition into **Pink A** and **Pink B**. One-to-one matching left-to-right is the major text-reading challenge at this band, and many children need to start with just a single line of print, then slowly build up to two lines or more. (See further details on this in the introductory sections to each colour-banded listing.)

Areas that often need additional resourcing from Orange to White Bands are: non-fiction; brief fiction with imaginative language, and strong plot and characterisation; and well-written plays.

> If a prominent series used in your school does *not* appear in these reviews, it is out of print and/or was not produced for Guided Reading. We would recommend that the school urgently considers buying in more suitable and attractive books. Poor quality texts alone could be a source of disappointing teaching sessions, along with lack of motivation and poor pupil progress.

ALPHAKIDS; ALPHAKIDS PLUS; ALPHAWORLD

PUBLISHER
Gardner Education Ltd
Customer services tel no: 0845 230 0775
Website www.gardnereducation.com

PUBLISHER'S RECOMMENDATION
A Guided Reading programme for early years of schooling…
Alphakids is the ideal levelled reading resource.
*AlphaWorld is a non-fiction Guided Reading programme for the first three years of school … highly supportive of students as they **learn to read** and **read to learn**.*

TARGET AUDIENCE
Key Stage 1/P1–3

DESCRIPTION OF GUIDED READING SERIES
282 Alphakids titles

Alphakids; Alphakids Plus Emergent Levels 1–5	60 books
Alphakids; Alphakids Plus Early Levels 6–11	72 books
Alphakids; Alphakids Plus Transitional Levels 12–17	72 books
Alphakids Extending Levels 18–23	36 books
Alphakids Plus Extending Levels 18–24	42 books
70 AlphaWorld titles (non-fiction only)	
Book Bands 1–8	42 books
Levels 12–24 (Book Bands 5–10)	28 books

SUPPORT MATERIALS
Support Materials and Teacher Resource books for all titles
Alphakids Plus: also Teacher editions of all titles
AlphaWorld: Teacher editions of all titles
6 Big Book versions of pupil books
2 Literacy Learning Activities books with photo-masters
AlphaAssess package; 26 Alphakids Alphabet Books

REVIEW OF GUIDED READING MATERIALS

GENERAL COMMENTS
Series fits with the content of Primary Framework for Literacy, and Guided Reading methodology.
Books small in size. Content manageable in one lesson.
Alphakids contains a wide range of fiction and non-fiction.

STRENGTHS
- Contemporary appearance; clear typeface well separated from attractive illustrations. Quality of photography particularly high
- Text-rich at beginner bands; compact and manageable at advanced bands
- Broad range of text types and topics
- Sophisticated teaching support

LIMITATIONS
- Relatively small font and rather a lot of print in some Emergent and Early Level books

RECOMMENDATIONS
Highly recommended for use as a Key Stage 1 core Guided Reading series.
This could also be an excellent supplementary series, particularly at higher levels. Early non-fiction and other titles could be used with older readers.

BIG CAT

PUBLISHER
Collins Education
Customer services tel no: 0870 787 1610
Website www.collinseducation.com

PUBLISHER'S RECOMMENDATION
A brilliantly thought-out and well-planned reading series for Key Stage 1.

TARGET AUDIENCE
Key Stages 1 and 2 (Key Stage 1 only reviewed here)

DESCRIPTION OF GUIDED READING SERIES
136 titles

Lilac; Pink A and B; Red A and B	50 books
Yellow and Blue Bands	28 books
Green to Gold Bands	50 books
White Band	8 books

SUPPORT MATERIALS
4 Assessment and Support books
4 Big Book versions
3 CD-ROMs

REVIEW OF GUIDED READING MATERIALS

GENERAL COMMENTS
Produced in UK to fit content of the Primary Framework for Literacy and Guided Reading methodology.
Wide range of size, layout and illustrations.
Balanced provision of fiction and non-fiction.
Well-known authors have written some books at higher bands.

STRENGTHS
- Very high quality of production; modern and appealing illustrations, especially the non-fiction photography
- Generally well-written
- Strong focus on visual literacy

LIMITATIONS
- All Lilac and some Pink titles not included in banded listings as wordless or consist of brief captions
- Publisher has under-estimated challenge of some non-fiction titles at the higher bands
- Illustrations overwhelm the text at times throughout the series

RECOMMENDATIONS
Use as core series with the addition of stronger titles from another series, particularly at Pink and Red Bands.

KINGSCOURT READING CORE (STORY STEPS)

PUBLISHER
Kingscourt (McGraw-Hill)
Customer services tel no: 01628 502730
Website www.kingscourt.co.uk

PUBLISHER'S RECOMMENDATION
A whole-school Guided Reading programme.

TARGET AUDIENCE
Key Stages 1 and 2 (Key Stage 1 only reviewed here)

DESCRIPTION OF GUIDED READING SERIES
92 Core titles

Pink Band	8 titles
Red–Green Bands	48 titles
Orange–Purple Bands	24 titles
Gold and White Bands	12 titles

138 Extension Readers

Pink Band	13 titles
Red Band	26 titles
Yellow Band	15 titles
Blue Band	17 titles
Green Band	13 titles
Orange Band	16 titles
Turquoise Band	14 titles
Gold Band	16 titles
White Band	8 titles

SUPPORT MATERIALS
Core titles include 20 Benchmark Books for Assessment
Teacher's Guide with each band in both sets
Activity pads 150 titles in Phonic Strand

KINGSCOURT EXTENSION READERS (STORYTELLER)

REVIEW OF GUIDED READING MATERIALS

GENERAL COMMENTS
Fit with the content of the Primary Framework for Literacy, and the methodology of Guided Reading.
General quality of production is high.
All bands contain fiction and non-fiction.
Core Reading contains a Collection strand of Shared, Guided and Independent texts in Pink–Purple Bands.

STRENGTHS
- Contemporary appearance; clear typeface well separated from attractive illustrations; some particularly appealing Extension books
- Finely graded steps in Core Readers offer controlled challenge in a wide range of text types
- Assessment strand consists of a gradient of brief, unseen whole books for running records of text reading with teacher guidance

LIMITATIONS
- Content in the Collection books is in different strands which could be confusing for teachers
- Guided Reading texts in the Collection books are too brief, particularly at higher bands
- Some publisher's banding inconsistent

RECOMMENDATIONS
Use as core series supplemented by longer texts at Pink Bands from another series.

LIGHTHOUSE

PUBLISHER
Published by Ginn (Harcourt Education)
Customer services tel no: 01865 888000
Website www.myprimary.co.uk

PUBLISHER'S RECOMMENDATION
The backbone of your Key Stage 1 Guided Reading … offering step-by-step skills cover and the full range of genre.

TARGET AUDIENCE
Key Stage 1 into Year 3

DESCRIPTION OF GUIDED READING SERIES
90 books (plus Lime)

YR	Pink/Red Bands	26 titles
Year 1	Yellow–Orange Bands	32 titles
Year 2	Turquoise–White Bands	32 titles

SUPPORT MATERIALS
Each title accompanied by Teaching Notes on Guided Reading and 2 photocopiable masters per book
4 Programme Organisers
Programme Manager CD-ROM
Pupil Activity Software

REVIEW OF GUIDED READING MATERIALS

GENERAL COMMENTS
Developed in UK to fit with the content of the Primary Framework for Literacy, and the methodology of Guided Reading.
High quality paper and design features.

STRENGTHS
- Attractive contemporary appearance
- Clear typeface well separated from supportive illustrations including photographs
- Text-rich at beginner bands; compact and manageable in length at advanced bands
- Rich language at highest bands
- Non-fiction contains a range of text type and non-fiction features
- Sophisticated teaching support with each title

LIMITATIONS
- Relatively small number of books for the range covered.

RECOMMENDATIONS
Ideal as Key Stage 1 core Guided Reading series, but needs to be supplemented by other materials.

LITERACY LAND

PUBLISHER
Pearson Education (Longman Primary)
Customer services tel no: 0800 579579
Website www.longman.co.uk

PUBLISHER'S RECOMMENDATION
Ensuring reading enjoyment and success for all your children.

TARGET AUDIENCE
Key Stages 1 and 2   (Key Stage 1 only reviewed here)

DESCRIPTION OF PUPIL BOOKS
165 Story Street, Genre and Info Trail books
Story Street (Fiction)

Foundation Step 3	60 titles
Steps 4–6	27 titles
Genre range (fiction and poetry)	30 titles
Info Trail (non-fiction)	48 titles

SUPPORT MATERIALS
Literacy Land Co-ordinator's Handbook/Support Video
Story Street Teaching Notes steps F–6
Story Street Activity Sheets/CD-ROMs
Genre Range Teaching Notes and Activity Sheets
Info Trail Teaching Notes and Activity Sheets

REVIEW OF GUIDED READING MATERIALS

GENERAL COMMENTS
Not designed to fit NLS content or Guided Reading methodology in terms of natural language, high-frequency word repetition, tracking opportunities at beginner bands, and consistent gradient of challenge.

All books have a standardised appearance; illustrations limited in style, e.g. no photography in non-fiction.

STRENGTHS
- Genre range offers a variety of fiction
- Non-fiction covers a range of content and text type

LIMITATIONS
- Story Street Step 1 not included in *Book Bands* due to insufficient text, limited exposure to high-frequency vocabulary and difficult vocabulary for beginners at times
- Challenge in Genre range very uneven
- Non-fiction lacks clearly defined gradient of challenge
- Series generally lightweight in terms of content

RECOMMENDATIONS
Non-fiction and Genre titles could be used to supplement higher bands.

LITERACY LINKS PLUS

PUBLISHER
Kingscourt (McGraw-Hill)
Customer services tel no: 01628 502730
Website www.kingscourt.co.uk

PUBLISHER'S RECOMMENDATION
Provides a wide range of genre and text types for small group instruction on Guided Reading and writing.

TARGET AUDIENCE
Key Stages 1 and 2 (Key Stage 1 only reviewed here)

DESCRIPTION OF GUIDED READING SERIES
264 titles
24 each Emergent A/B/C/D titles
24 each Early A/B/C/D titles
18 each Fluent A/B/C/D titles

SUPPORT MATERIALS
Teaching Notes for all sets
Reading Records for each level
1 set of Comprehension Questions

REVIEW OF GUIDED READING MATERIALS

GENERAL COMMENTS
Series devised for Guided Reading and writing.
Each set contains both fiction and non-fiction.

STRENGTHS
- Provides a wide range of mostly well-written fiction and non-fiction at higher levels that are brief enough to be handled in one lesson
- Valuable teacher guidance includes running records for assessment

LIMITATIONS
- Beginner texts and some higher band titles tend to be too brief, at times contrived and offer little opportunity for high-frequency word learning, so these are not included in banded listings
- Text sometimes overwhelmed by illustrations

RECOMMENDATIONS
Use as a supplementary series, particularly at Fluent level.

OXFORD READING TREE

PUBLISHER
Oxford University Press
Oxford Literacy careline tel no: 01865 267881
Order hotline tel no: 01536 741171
Website www.oup.com/uk/primary

PUBLISHER'S RECOMMENDATION
The well-loved and widely used reading scheme for primary schools.

TARGET AUDIENCE
Key Stages 1 and 2 (Key Stage 1 only reviewed here)

DESCRIPTION OF PUPIL BOOKS
442 titles

Stage 1 First Words; Stage 1+ Patterned Stories (PS); More PS; First Sentences; and More First Sentences	42 books
Stage 2 PS; More PS A; Stories; More Stories A and B	30 books
Stage 3 Stories; More Stories A and B; Sparrows	24 books
Stages 4/5 Stories; More Stories A, B, C	60 books
Stage 6–9 Stories; More Stories	64 books
Stages 6–10 Robins Packs 1–3 (more able readers)	18 books
All Stars in 6 packs	30 books
Fireflies NF Stages 1+–10; More Fireflies 1–5	120 books
True Stories	12 books
Glow-worms Poetry Anthologies	42 books

SUPPORT MATERIALS
30 Big Books (large format of small books), Talkabout Cards, First Phonics Stage 1+–4 Rhyme and Analogy packs, Handbooks, Sequencing Cards, Extended Stories, Storytapes, Teaching notes, Guided Reading Cards, 4 Games Packs, Oxford Reading Tree Online, Talking Stories, 10 Woodpeckers Anthologies ORT stages 5–9 (phonics), Snapdragon independent readers; Reading and Spelling Tests

REVIEW OF GUIDED READING MATERIALS

GENERAL COMMENTS
Originally designed as independent readers, Oxford Reading Tree has grown and adapted to changing teaching practice. Fireflies non-fiction strand was produced more recently.

STRENGTHS
- Stories have appealing comic-style characters; realistic plots with humour
- Rhyme and analogy, and poetry anthologies of high quality
- Fireflies non-fiction attractively extends scope of series

LIMITATIONS
- Stories are very formatted with limited range of language
- Earliest storybooks brief and limited in tracking and HF word learning opportunities; books at advanced end often too wordy, and lack variety and language richness
- Challenge at stage 5 and above of Fireflies under-estimated

RECOMMENDATIONS
Select sparingly from the materials to supplement core series for Guided Reading.
Fiction is best in Yellow–Green Bands; non-fiction is best at Pink–Blue. Stories are useful for independent reading.

PATHWAYS TO LITERACY

PUBLISHER
Collins Primary
Customer services tel no: 0870 0100 441
Website www.collinseducation.com

PUBLISHER'S RECOMMENDATION
A diverse range of full texts that develop a wide range of reading and writing techniques.

TARGET AUDIENCE
Key Stages 1 and 2 (Key Stage 1 only reviewed here)

DESCRIPTION OF PUPIL BOOKS
125 books (excluding wordless texts)

YR Fiction and poetry	35 titles
YR Non-fiction	14 titles
Year 1 Fiction and poetry	37 titles
Year 1 Non-fiction	10 titles
Year 2 Fiction and poetry	25 titles
Year 2 Non-fiction	4 titles

SUPPORT MATERIALS
Big Books
YR, Year 1 and Year 2 Teachers' Notes
YR, Year 1 and Year 2 Activity Masters

REVIEW OF GUIDED READING MATERIALS

GENERAL COMMENTS
This series pre-dates the NLS, and pupil books were not specifically developed for Guided Reading.

STRENGTHS
- Books come in variety of size, shape and presentation
- Appealing illustrations
- Poetry anthologies particularly imaginative

LIMITATIONS
- Variable in quality and challenge
- Brief text in YR books offers very limited experience in one-to-one tracking, high-frequency word practice and story language
- Information books lack contents page, index and other non-fiction features

RECOMMENDATIONS
Poetry anthologies, alphabetically ordered books and others are suitable for Shared Reading with small groups. This series is good also for independent reading.

PM AND PM PLUS

PUBLISHER
Nelson Thornes
Customer services tel no: 01242 267280
Website www.nelsonthornes.com

PUBLISHER'S RECOMMENDATION
Building the skills for literacy success.
All PM stories are based on concepts children can grasp,
situations they can understand and plots they want to
resolve.

TARGET AUDIENCE
Key Stages 1 and 2 (Key Stage 1 only reviewed here)

DESCRIPTION OF GUIDED READING SERIES
740 books

PM; PM Plus Starters	60 titles
PM; PM Plus Storybooks Red–Green Bands	216 titles
PM; PM Plus Storybooks Orange–Silver Bands	190 titles
PM; PM Plus Non-fiction	120 titles
PM Traditional Tales and Plays Orange–Silver	30 titles
PM Photo Stories; PM Gems Magenta–Green Bands	100 titles
PM Maths Stages A and B	24 titles

SUPPORT MATERIALS
7 PM Teacher's Guides including Copymasters
Alphabet Starters (26 little books); Alphabet Blends (34)
PM Alphabet Big Book and small version
PM Benchmark Kits 1 and 2

REVIEW OF GUIDED READING MATERIALS

GENERAL COMMENTS
In line with the content of the Primary Framework for
Literacy, and Guided Reading principles.
Books small in size at early levels, A5 at higher levels.
Content manageable in one lesson at early levels, one –
two at higher levels.

STRENGTHS
- Pink Band Starters offer 16 pages of one-to-one
  tracking and development of sight vocabulary
- Storybooks use the natural rhythms of children's
  speech, a lot of direct speech and genuine story plots
- Story plots and early non-fiction based on familiar,
  age-appropriate situations; plots at higher bands deal
  with relevant social issues
- Traditional Tales and Plays very well written; layout of
  plays particularly clear
- Maths series pulls together language and concepts of
  maths in child-friendly situations

LIMITATIONS
- Some original PM books have an old-fashioned
  appearance
- A few titles betray Antipodean origin

RECOMMENDATIONS
This is an ideal core Guided Reading resource.
The starters are indispensable for every school. Traditional
Tales and Plays and higher levels of Storybooks are also
useful in Key Stage 2.
Benchmark Kits are particularly useful assessment tools
for text reading through Key Stages 1 and 2.

RIGBY STAR

PUBLISHER
Rigby (Harcourt Education)
Customer services tel no: 01865 888044
Website www.myprimary.co.uk

PUBLISHER'S RECOMMENDATION
Rich multi-layered stories for fiction Guided Reading.
Rigby Star Quest – making non-fiction really work.

TARGET AUDIENCE
Key Stage 1

DESCRIPTION OF GUIDED READING SERIES
117 Rigby Star fiction titles

YR Lilac Band	16 books
Pink and Red Bands	32 books
Year 1 Yellow, Blue and Green Bands	32 books
Year 2 Orange–White Bands	30 books
Star Plus (3 titles at Lime Band 11)	7 books

41 Rigby Star non-fiction titles

YR Pink and Red Bands	8 books
Year 1 Yellow–Green Bands	12 books
Year 2 Orange–White Bands	18 books
Star Plus (1 title at Lime Band 11)	3 books

SUPPORT MATERIALS
Each title in both series has its own teaching version
3 Rigby Star Planning and Assessment Guides
Rigby Star Pupil ICT Activity Software
Phonic and Rigby Rockets Independent readers

REVIEW OF GUIDED READING MATERIALS

GENERAL COMMENTS
Developed to fit with the content of Primary Framework for Literacy, and the methodology of Guided Reading. High quality illustrations and design features.

STRENGTHS
- Books have a glossy, appealing appearance
- Clear typeface, well separated from supportive illustrations including photographs
- Several fictional characters re-appear at different bands
- Attractive non-fiction covering a range of topic areas
- Most books are brief enough to read in one session
- Valuable Guided Reading versions of each book

LIMITATIONS
- Some early band fiction titles have limited number of words and weak storylines
- At highest bands, fiction titles lack language richness

RECOMMENDATIONS
This is a good core series but it needs to be supplemented by books with more text at Pink and Red Bands, and by fiction titles with greater literary challenge at higher bands.

STORYWORLDS; DISCOVERY WORLD

PUBLISHER
Heinemann (Harcourt Education)
Customer service tel no: 01865 888020
Website www.myprimaryco.uk

PUBLISHER'S RECOMMENDATION
Breadth and variety for guided or independent reading
(Storyworlds).
The proven way to make non-fiction work in the classroom
(Discovery World).

TARGET AUDIENCE
Key Stage 1

DESCRIPTION OF PUPIL BOOKS
156 Storyworlds titles
Stages 1–9 in 4 strands:

Our World (4 titles per stage)	36 books
Animal World	36 books
Fantasy World	36 books
Once Upon a Time World	36 books
Stages 10–12 Storyworlds Bridges	12 books

29 Discovery World titles (11 only currently in print)
6 stages A–F
20 Discovery World Links titles
4 levels C–F with 5 titles at each level

SUPPORT MATERIALS
Storyworlds: 28 Big Books; 4 Teaching Guides
24 Word Practice Books at stages 1–3
3 CD-ROMs: Pupil Activity Software
Word Skills Resource Book; Storyworlds Planning Guide
Discovery World: Guided Reading cards with each title
3 Planning and Teaching Guides
46 Big Books; 2 Writing Skills Big Books
2 Literacy Lesson Books
Young Discoverer Group Work Cards A–F

REVIEW OF GUIDED READING MATERIALS

GENERAL COMMENTS
Both series produced prior to NLS apart from Discovery
World Links.

STRENGTHS
- Some attractive individual titles, especially in the Once
  Upon a Time fiction strand, and in the Discovery World
  and Discovery World Links ranges

LIMITATIONS
- Storyworlds have a somewhat old-fashioned formatted
  appearance
- Earliest Discovery World are too challenging/formal for
  beginners, and few titles still in print

RECOMMENDATIONS
Selected sets could be used to supplement core series.
Some titles could be used at Foundation Stage to share
with a small group of children.

WEB GUIDED READING

PUBLISHER
Oxford University Press
Oxford Literacy careline tel no: 01865 267881
Order hotline tel no: 01536 741171
Website www.oup.com/uk/primary

PUBLISHER'S RECOMMENDATION
Carefully controlled progression of reading skills and strategies.

TARGET AUDIENCE
Key Stages 1 and 2/P1–7 (Key Stage 1 only reviewed here)

DESCRIPTION OF GUIDED READING SERIES
174 fiction and non-fiction books
Web fiction:

Duck Green Stories stages 1–9	60 titles
Variety Stories stages 1–9	60 titles
Web Weavers non-fiction:	
First Words non-fiction stages 1–2	18 titles
Web non-fiction 6 packs	36 titles

SUPPORT MATERIALS
Guided Reading cards for every title
2 Fiction Teacher's Guides: Starter, Stage 3; Stages 4–5
Duck Green Teacher's Guide Stages 6–9
Variety Teacher's Guides 6–9
6 First Non-Fiction Big Books
Web Anthology (fiction, poetry, non-fiction)
Web Poetry Anthologies: 6 for Year 1; 6 for Year 2
Web Phonics Programme

REVIEW OF GUIDED READING MATERIALS

GENERAL COMMENTS
Previously known as Oxford Literacy Web.
Duck Green Stories feature a group of children.

STRENGTHS
- Variety Stories offer a range of settings and characters
- Non-fiction books attractively illustrated

LIMITATIONS
- Texts in early stages tend to be very brief, and in later stages, especially Duck Green stories, very wordy
- Books lack variety in language, vocabulary, print layout, and general presentation
- Challenge in non-fiction titles rather variable

RECOMMENDATIONS
The series is more suitable for independent rather than Guided Reading.

CRUNCHIES

PUBLISHER
Orchard Books
Customer service tel no: 01235 827729
Website www.orchardbooks.co.uk

DESCRIPTION
70+ slim paperback fiction titles in different sets, Bands 7–10.

SUITABILITY FOR GUIDED READING

STRENGTHS
- Cleverly written by well-known authors
- Humorous stories and raps to appeal to a wide age range
- Great fun and good link into full-length paperbacks for young able readers

LIMITATIONS
- Niche series only

RECOMMENDATIONS
Valuable addition to Guided Reading resource, and for adults and able readers to read aloud to others.

DRAGONFLIES

PUBLISHER
Gardner Education
Customer services tel no: 0845 230 0775
Website www.gardnereducation.com

DESCRIPTION
46 fiction titles Pink–Gold Bands. Further titles to follow.

SUITABILITY FOR GUIDED READING

STRENGTHS
- Mostly well-written stories with good plotlines

LIMITATIONS
- Covers and layout lack variety

RECOMMENDATIONS
Useful supplement to core series, particularly at higher bands.

ENJOY GUIDED READING

PUBLISHER
Badger Publishing
Customer services tel no: 01438 356907
Website www.badger-publishing.co.uk

DESCRIPTION
4 sets of picture books and paperback fiction for Year 2
1 set of 10 banded non-fiction books for Year 1
2 sets of banded non-fiction books for Year 2.

SUITABILITY FOR GUIDED READING

STRENGTHS
- Fiction books by well-known authors, but unbanded
- Attractive banded non-fiction relating to National Curriculum areas

LIMITATIONS
- Sets tend to be expensive

RECOMMENDATIONS
Useful addition to specific sections of Guided Reading provision.

FIRST EXPLORERS

PUBLISHER
Kingscourt (McGraw-Hill)
Customer services tel no: 01628 502730
Website www.kingscourt.co.uk

DESCRIPTION
First Explorers comprises two sets of 12 books each covering a range of non-fiction topics and layouts for Year 2 readers.

SUITABILITY FOR GUIDED READING

STRENGTHS
- Written especially for this age group on relevant topics

LIMITATIONS
- Language and concepts at times need teacher mediation

RECOMMENDATIONS
Attractive and useful to provide challenge at Bands 8–10 for able pupils in Year 2.

FIRST FACTS

PUBLISHER
Badger Publishing
Customer services tel no: 01438 356907
Website www.badger-publishing.co.uk

DESCRIPTION
48 non-fiction books in four sets, each concentrating on a specific non-fiction feature or skill Bands 1–9.

SUITABILITY FOR GUIDED READING

STRENGTHS
- Very attractive photo books designed for small children
- Cover a wide range of National Curriculum topic areas

LIMITATIONS
- All books follow similar layout
- Content at higher bands tends to be rather thin

RECOMMENDATIONS
Could provide an inexpensive and worthwhile boost to non-fiction resources at lower bands.

FIRST STORIES

PUBLISHER
Gardner Education
Customer services tel no: 0845 230 0775
Website www.gardnereducation.com

DESCRIPTION
60 little fiction and non-fiction Pink Band books organised according to high frequency words featured.

SUITABILITY FOR GUIDED READING

STRENGTHS
- Designed to appeal to Foundation Stage children
- Clear print layout and attractive supporting illustrations

LIMITATIONS
- A few weaker titles

RECOMMENDATIONS
Very useful boost to Guided Reading provision at Pink Bands A and B.

FOUR CORNERS

PUBLISHER
Longman Primary (Pearson Education)
Customer services tel no: 0800 579579
Website www.longman.co.uk

DESCRIPTION
60 non-fiction books designed for YR, Year 1 and Year 2. Variety of text-types. Links to wide range of National Curriculum topics.

SUITABILITY FOR GUIDED READING

STRENGTHS
- Beautiful photography
- Some excellent books in Year 1 and 2 sets

LIMITATIONS
- 20 Year R books slim in content with formal language for beginners, and very variable in challenge

RECOMMENDATIONS
Select titles in Year 1/2 collections to supplement non-fiction range.

I LOVE READING

PUBLISHER
Ticktock Media Ltd
Customer services tel no: 0870 3812223
Also available from Gardner Education

DESCRIPTION
12 non-fiction photo books at Blue Band, six of which are also enriched for both Orange and Purple Bands. Further titles to follow.

SUITABILITY FOR GUIDED READING

STRENGTHS
- Very attractive, child-friendly books, carefully worded

LIMITATIONS
- Original approach but could be considered costly to buy three versions of the same book

RECOMMENDATIONS
Could provide an engaging addition to non-fiction provision.

NATIONAL GEOGRAPHIC

PUBLISHER
Ginn (Harcourt Education)
Customer services tel no: 01865 888044
Website www.myprimary.co.uk

DESCRIPTION
40 books in 10 colour bands, Pink–White (40 independent books in parallel).

SUITABILITY FOR GUIDED READING

STRENGTHS
- Attractive illustrations
- Some good topics especially at higher bands

LIMITATIONS
- Beginner texts are too brief
- Books lack variety of format, tables of contents, indexes and glossaries

RECOMMENDATIONS
For independent or supported reading.

SAILS

PUBLISHER
Heinemann (Harcourt Education)
Customer services tel no: 01865 888044
Website www.myprimary.co.uk

DESCRIPTION
96 Pink Band titles designed around 24 high-frequency words.

SUITABILITY FOR GUIDED READING

STRENGTHS
- High-frequency word practice in a range of sentence structures

LIMITATIONS
- Heavily formatted appearance
- Pink A1–3 (12 books) unbanded – 2-word captions only

RECOMMENDATIONS
A few sets could add variety to book provision at Pink Band A.

SKYRIDER LM CHAPTERS

PUBLISHER
Gardner Education
Customer services tel no: 0845 230 0775
Website www.gardnereducation.com

DESCRIPTION
48 fiction and non-fiction books in 2 sets, Bands 7–9.

SUITABILITY FOR GUIDED READING

STRENGTHS
- Large range of text types with attractive illustrations
- Compact, lively books on contemporary topics

LIMITATIONS
- Niche series only

RECOMMENDATIONS
Very useful Guided Reading supplement for Year 2. Ideal independent reading for Years 2 and 3.

SPOTTY ZEBRA

PUBLISHER
Nelson Thornes
Customer services tel no: 01242 267280
Website www.nelsonthornes.com

DESCRIPTION
60 fiction and non-fiction books for Foundation Stage:
Pink A, B, Red Band books, each with two packs of mixed fiction/non-fiction organised in topic areas: *Ourselves* and *Changes*.

SUITABILITY FOR GUIDED READING

STRENGTHS
- Child-friendly
- Paired fiction and non-fiction titles

LIMITATIONS
- Pink B Band books tend to be very variable in challenge

RECOMMENDATIONS
More suitable for sharing and discussion in conjunction with topic areas than for Guided Reading.

STORYCHEST

PUBLISHER
Kingscourt (McGraw-Hill)
Customer services tel no: 01628 502730
Website www.kingscourt.co.uk

DESCRIPTION
146 fiction books.

SUITABILITY FOR GUIDED READING

STRENGTHS
- Some enduring favourites

LIMITATIONS
- Heavily formatted books that look old-fashioned
- Many early books are too brief, and lack opportunities for tracking and high-frequency word learning
- Some storylines weak

RECOMMENDATIONS
Use selectively for Guided or independent reading.

SUNSHINE READERS

PUBLISHER
Gardner Education
Customer services tel no: 0845 230 0775
Website www.gardnereducation.com

DESCRIPTION
36 fiction books in Orange, Turquoise and Purple Bands.

SUITABILITY FOR GUIDED READING

STRENGTHS
- Well written and attractively presented
- Contemporary themes

LIMITATIONS
- Niche series only

RECOMMENDATIONS
Excellent for supplementing fiction provision; also good for older readers.

PART 3

Children and text

Assessing text reading

Success motivates and empowers children to work at new challenges. In Key Stage 1, the teacher carefully selects the membership of each Guided Reading group so that children are working at a similar level of control of the reading process. Each lesson is structured to minimise the risk of children making too many errors without robbing them of problem-solving opportunities. To achieve this, individuals are assessed regularly and the groups adjusted from time to time to reflect different rates of progress and to take into account group dynamics.

INITIAL LITERACY ASSESSMENT

Assessing alphabet and phonic knowledge, word reading and word writing, and a child's awareness of how books work and the terms associated with texts and print provides essential information as a basis for decisions involving children's initial placement in groups and their early progress. Increasingly, decisions will depend on the information gained through regular running records of text reading linked with the colour banded gradient of challenge listed in this book.

CAPTURING TEXT READING PERFORMANCE

A teacher unaccustomed to the recording conventions of a running record will need to practise with a range of readers and texts before running records can be used as a reliable assessment technique. Once these are well rehearsed, the teacher can devote full attention to each child, chatting briefly about the procedure and establishing a relaxed relationship.

It is not necessary for the recorder to have a printed copy of the text, although it can be helpful when recording very rapid, able readers. It is essential, of course, to write down the name of each child, the title of the book and page numbers of the text on which the child's performance is to be recorded, and, crucially, the recording date. Running record information only has validity for a week or so: children regularly engaging with a wide variety of new texts can make rapid progress, requiring running record information to be collected frequently, so that learning objectives reflect what each child is currently able to do.

GETTING GOING

Choose a relatively easy text to start with. If a child's previous records are available, they may indicate the current band at which the child is working. An alternative method of establishing a starting point at the higher bands is to ask the child to read a passage of about 100 words silently and then ask for a paraphrase. If the child reads quite rapidly and is able to give a number of accurate details, repeat this procedure at a higher band. If it is apparent that the child cannot manage the text, repeat at a lower band until it is clear that the passage can be read and some facts recalled.

Supply the title of the book, and then make a detailed record without interrupting the reading or giving the child any clues or prompts. It may be necessary to urge him/her to 'have a go' at an unfamiliar word, particularly if the child should be able to blend known graphemes to read the word. Tell the child the word if the reading has come to a standstill, and count this as an error.

A full discussion of the rationale, administration and analysis of running records may be found in the NLS document entitled *Guiding Reading: Supporting transition from KS1 to KS2* (London: DfES 2003); and in *An Observation of Early Literacy Achievement* by M.M. Clay (Heinemann Education 2002).

Many teachers select banded books from their resources, keep their own range of favourite assessment texts or make use of commercial packs aligned with the colour gradient, e.g. The PM Benchmark Kits 1 and 2 (Nelson Thornes), AlphaAssess (Gardner Education) and the Benchmark Books that accompany the Story Steps series (Kingscourt).

ESTABLISHING AN INSTRUCTIONAL LEVEL

When a child makes only one uncorrected error in every 10–20 words (i.e. reads at 90–94 per cent accuracy), we say that this book is at an **instructional level** for the child. This indicates that the challenge is not so great that s/he loses control, and not so easy that there are few learning opportunities. Other texts listed within the same band should provide similar teaching and learning opportunities, although there is always individual variation in terms of prior experience and preference.

It is important to take a running record on a book from the next band up to establish the highest possible instructional level. More than ten errors in 100 words indicates a hard level for the child and the likely need for further experience at the band below.

Accuracy rate

Step 1	Count the number of words in the passage, excluding the title.
Step 2	Count the uncorrected errors.
Step 3	Express errors as a ratio of total number of words (e.g. 6 errors in a total of 120 words: 1:20).
Step 4	Convert to accuracy rate (e.g. 95%).

Conversion table

Error rate	Accuracy	
1:100	99%	
1:50	98%	Texts read at an instructional-to-easy level.
1:35	97%	
1:25	96%	
1:20	95%	
1:17	94%	Observation of reading pace and control, together with
1:14	93%	analysis of errors, provides teachers with the most valuable
1:12.5	92%	information at this accuracy rate.
1:11.75	91%	
1:10	90%	
1:09	89%	
1:08	87.5%	The reader tends to lose control and is unable to use of
1:07	85.5%	balance of print information, syntax and comprehension.
1:06	83%	
1:05	80%	

Self-corrections indicate that the reader is monitoring his/her own reading carefully as well as using a balanced range of information from the print detail, from the sentence structure and from the meaning of the passage. However, too much self-correction may indicate impulsive guessing using insufficient print information, and may break the flow of phrases and sentences. A child who has established this style of reading may need to work with guidance on easier texts until more fluency is established.

ANALYSING READING STRATEGIES

Accuracy rates alone do not provide sufficient information about a pupil's reading. A full analysis of running records should indicate whether a child is getting carried away by meaning and syntax without taking sufficient account of print detail; or is becoming over-reliant on the look or sounds of words and neglecting to check for meaning. This analysis informs a teacher to acknowledge the positive aspect of the child's performance while urging closer attention to the areas of neglect.

OBSERVING PHRASING AND FLEXIBILITY

The pace and quality of reading should be noted on every running record, along with ability of a child to adjust to different text types. A fictional text usually needs to flow quite rapidly, with careful attention to punctuation to support longer phrasing, and direct speech. Non-fiction demands a slower, more deliberate pace with pauses to check information and refer to illustrations, maps and diagrams. Poetry may require rehearsal while the reader explores metre, rhyme and alliterative elements, and decides on a tone to fit humour, melancholy or metaphorical language. The same exploratory approach may be necessary with plays and texts that use dialect and vocabulary unfamiliar to the reader.

Skilled text selection ensures that each book provides neither too little nor too much challenge for an inexperienced reader. Where the accuracy rate falls consistently below 90 per cent (more than one error in every ten words), the reader may lose control of the reading process. When this happens, fluency and phasing, comprehension and enjoyment are sacrificed.

ORGANISING CHILDREN FOR GUIDED READING

Teachers who use running records regularly to monitor progress are able to establish and adjust the composition of groups sensitively. Over time, patterns of progress may emerge. Early in the acquisition stage, a teacher will need to monitor and assess progress more frequently – at least monthly. Pupils reading at higher bands will need to be monitored less often, and the teacher will concentrate more on those who are experiencing problems in order to pinpoint difficulties and adjust their teaching accordingly.

Guided Reading, then, enables all children to enjoy books and work at solving problems for themselves, taking pleasure in their own progress as readers, and benefiting from the interaction of others facing similar challenges.

A GRADIENT OF TEXT CHALLENGE

Where a school has set up a rich range of resources using a common gradient of challenge across different types of books and different series related to National Curriculum levels, a teacher is able to establish the appropriate band both for assessment and for subsequent lessons. **A child or group's position on this gradient, then, becomes a short-hand description for their level of processing, a valid guide to their progress in text reading, and valuable information about class and school standards.**

Useful reading

Clay, M.M. (2002) *An Observation Survey of Early Literacy Achievement*, 2nd edition. Auckland, NZ: Heinemann Education.

Implementing Guided Reading

	Prior to the lesson

PLANNING

- A new text is chosen which the teacher anticipates will be within the control of the group, but contains some challenge and suitable learning opportunities. Wherever possible, a copy of the text is provided for each child.
- The teacher decides on specific learning outcomes for a particular group.
- The teacher prepares the whole text, planning the introduction, key teaching points, and any follow-up activities.

	During the lesson

Introducing the new book
See: Clay, M.M. (1998) 'Introducing story books to young readers' in *By Different Paths to Common Outcomes* (Maine: Stenhouse).

TEXT INTRODUCTION

- The teacher usually reads the title and gives a very brief overview of how the text had been written, e.g. 'In this book, Jan is telling us what happened when she fell off her bike.' Able readers can check the blurb for themselves and predict the content from the title and illustrations on the cover.
- The children are invited to contribute their own experience and understanding to a **brief** discussion based on illustrations and the main ideas in the text. The teacher guides their language and observations as they leaf through the book so that each child is prepared to read this particular text independently, and at times with a specific feature in mind.
- Inexperienced readers will need more detailed introductions than competent readers. It is important to 'debug' each book appropriately, leaving a certain amount of challenge for the children.
- In the case of non-fiction, the group will explore with the teacher the layout of the book as well as the range of content. Each member of the group may then be directed to read different sections in preparation for further discussion. Alternatively, pairs of children may work together.

READING THE NEW BOOK INDEPENDENTLY

- **Each child then reads independently all or part of the book quietly or silently.**
- After a satisfactory introduction, pupils will have a sense of how the text is structured and be familiar with the main ideas, unpredictable vocabulary, difficult names and usual sentence patterns.
- The teacher may listen in to monitor and/or work with one child and then another, supporting where necessary. If the child is reading silently, the teacher will signal to the child to read aloud from the point reached in the text.

PRAISING AND PROMPTING

The teacher's role in Guided Reading is to prompt a child to use print information together with prior knowledge, following spoken language syntax as s/he re-constructs the author's meaning. Prompts and confirmation of useful responses may help children to use a fuller range of information and keep track of their own reading, for example:

- Did that match? Well done – you went back and pointed carefully to make your reading fit the words. Is that right now?
  You said, 'Bess banks at everyone.' Does that make sense? Try sounding all the phonemes, and then check the meaning.
- You were thinking about the story, but does that word ('glad') look like 'happy'? What would 'happy' begin with? Sound the phonemes, then read the sentence again and check if it makes sense.

RETURNING TO THE TEXT

The first reading is usually followed by a brief teaching session to reinforce the lesson focus, e.g. deepening comprehension, making full use of punctuation, and linking with other appropriate word, sentence and text level work already introduced in Shared Reading or in the discrete phonics teaching. Children may be asked to return to specific parts of the text to justify their responses or to frame questions for each other arising from the text.

After the lesson

FOLLOW-UP

An independent activity based on the text may follow this first reading. Many publishers provide follow-up activities and tasks that provide opportunities for children to apply their reading skills. The best of these involve them in thinking actively, making decisions, and working without assistance.

Teachers may prefer to devise activities that require children to search the text for specific information, e.g. make a simple map to show a sequence of events; locate the first/last words of paragraphs in a book; make a note of words with a particular spelling or grammatical feature; create questions from information in the text or locate answers.

Writing can also be a valuable follow-up to a Guided Reading session, because the text will provide support for words that the child needs. Well-written stories, poems, plays and various non-fiction text types may provide a valuable springboard for children's own creative writing, or further recreational reading. Composing a different ending, putting an episode into direct speech, writing a letter from one of the characters, or imagining a character's thoughts or reactions can all provide opportunities to develop literacy skills.

RE-READING

Copies of books used in Guided Reading now join those in the book basket designated for a particular group to be re-read independently or to classmates, classroom assistants, parents, volunteers, carers, brothers and sisters in and out of the classroom.

Fluent and expressive re-reading in a variety of settings increases enjoyment and establishes the identity and relaxed control of the novice as a 'real reader'. Regular practice assists automatic recognition of commonly occurring words or clusters of letters. It fosters a fluent reading process that pulls together print information and comprehension without undue conscious effort, freeing attention to appreciate the subtleties of meaning or detail and enabling further learning to take place.

However, this control and impetus will not develop if over-familiarity with a very few early books leads to a child paying scant attention to the words. Children may think that the task is to memorise rather than to read, or use unreliable strategies such as guessing what would fit without attending to information in print. A teacher may avoid this by introducing a larger variety of texts within the same band in order to present familiar words and phrases in new contexts and lots of opportunities to apply phonic skills and knowledge in text reading. For some children, moving to books in a higher band so that they need to attend more closely to the print detail will increase visual attending.

PART 4

School management and staff development

Tracking text reading throughout Foundation and Key Stage 1

Investigating disappointing progress in text reading

Professional development and school management

Setting up and maintaining resources

Tracking text reading throughout Foundation and Key Stage 1

The chart opposite maps the expected progress in successful text reading by most children from school entry through to the end of Key Stage 1 and beyond in relation to the National Curriculum for English.

Head teachers, language post-holders and class teachers may find it a useful reference when resourcing, planning and delivering Guided Reading, assessing the effectiveness of teaching, and targeting and monitoring the progress of individuals and groups of children.

TRACKING YOUR PUPILS' PROGRESS

Successful reading and comprehension of unfamiliar text at Level 2B (Gold Band) or above in the SATs assessment is the goal for most pupils in Key Stage 1. As they normally spend between one and three terms in Year R, three terms in Year 1 and two terms in Year 2 prior to SATs administration, most children will have between six and eight terms to work through nine bands, Pink to Gold, to reach a satisfactory standard of text reading. Some children, of course, enter school as text readers, and many will reach Level 3 (White Band) and beyond.

However, progress through the bands is not automatic, and it is important to ensure that children who are slow to make progress have frequent group or individual sessions (three to five per week), have access to a wide range of simple texts and work consistently at the instructional and easy levels. This is particularly important for those children:
- with limited literacy experience before and during Foundation Stage
- at the early stages of learning English as an additional language
- experiencing difficulties learning letters and words, pronouncing words distinctly, etc.

All these children are entitled to a full allocation of Guided Reading lessons carried out by the class teacher. However, they may require a more structured and richer introduction to each text, along with opportunities during and after the lessons.

Progress through the text reading bands should not be held back to satisfy a teacher's need for every child to read every book with 100 per cent accuracy. Active monitoring and self-correction, and fluent, expressive reading is the goal.

Progression of successful text reading through Key Stage 1

Band	National Curriculum level	Colour	Year R/P1	Year 1/P2	Year 2/P3	Year 3/P4
1	Working towards Level 1	PINK	■ (secure)			
2	Working towards Level 1	RED	■ (secure)	□ (normal range)		
3	Working within Level 1	YELLOW	■ (secure)	■ (secure)		
4	Working within Level 1	BLUE	□ (normal range)	■ (secure)		
5	Working within Level 1	GREEN		■ (secure)	□ (normal range)	
6	Working towards Level 2	ORANGE		■ (secure)	■ (secure)	
7	Working towards Level 2	TURQUOISE		□ (normal range)	■ (secure)	
8	Working within Level 2	PURPLE			■ (secure)	□ (normal range)
9	Working within Level 2	GOLD			■ (secure)	■ (secure)
10	Working towards Level 3	WHITE			□ (normal range)	■ (secure)

■ Majority of pupils secure at these levels

□ Normal range of achievement

A wider range of achievement in text reading may well occur within a class. The challenge for schools is to make provision for children falling above and below the ranges indicated, if necessary, on an individual basis.

Investigating disappointing progress in text reading

There are many reasons why children may not make satisfactory progress in reading. The following notes provide a starting point for reflection, discussion with colleagues and classroom observation.

TEXTS	Poor quality texts with too little print at early bands and too much at higher bands; limited variety of books from a narrow range of series and very little non-fiction; too few sets of books particularly in Pink Band; poor choice of texts for a particular group – too easy or too hard; known rather than new texts selected for each session.
GROUPING	Range of ability within the group too wide so that some children become bored and others frustrated; little challenge, variety and breadth offered to high progress readers; slow progress children faced with books that are too hard.
LETTER AND WORD KNOWLEDGE	Children unable to recognise upper- and lower-case letters and the sounds they represent quickly and use this knowledge to track words from left to right; insecure knowledge of high frequency words that can be written automatically as well as read.
LESSON FREQUENCY	Too few Guided Reading sessions, particularly at the early stages (recommended minimum three lessons per week for Year R, EAL pupils, and slow progress children); too much time spent at each band.
LACK OF PLANNING	Books plucked off the shelf immediately prior to a session; no clear focus for the lesson; book introductions too brief and/or distracting at the early stages and too detailed later; no return to the text to teach specific aspects; no follow-up word work.
TEACHER'S ROLE	Too much teacher-talk during Guided Reading sessions allowing too little time for children to read complete texts for themselves; pace of session languid and unfocused.
PACE OF READING	Slow pace with finger-pointing persisting for too long; unphrased, expressionless, word-by-word reading accepted as satisfactory.
PROMPTING	Partially correct responding ignored and errors highlighted; lack of balanced prompting; insistence on error-free first reading of new books; children immediately supplied with unknown words rather than prompted to 'have a go' for themselves.
LESSON FOCUS	Teaching focused on delivering the curriculum rather than fostering an independent initial read for enjoyment.
RE-READING BOOKS	Too few opportunities for children to re-read Guided Reading books and other familiar texts independently throughout Key Stage 1, especially at the early bands.

CHILDREN'S PROGRESS THROUGH READING LEVELS AT KEY STAGE 1

SCHOOL: **CLASS:** **YEAR:**

Names	Sept	Oct	Nov	Dec	Jan	Feb	Mar	Apr	May	Jun	Jul

NATIONAL CURRICULUM READING LEVELS: Colour Key

PINK A	PINK B	RED	YELLOW	BLUE	GREEN
Working towards Level 1	Working towards Level 1	Working towards Level 1	Level 1	Level 1	Level 1

ORANGE	TURQUOISE	PURPLE	GOLD	WHITE
Working towards Level 2	Working towards Level 2	Level 2C	Level 2B	Level 2A–3

EXTRA TEACHING

If individual children continue to make disappointing progress after these areas have been addressed, consideration should be given to providing intensive support to prevent long-term literacy difficulties developing. For struggling readers, additional group lessons and, where necessary, a one-to-one intervention such as Reading Recovery should be provided.

For more information about Reading Recovery and training courses for teachers, contact the Reading Recovery National Network (see p. 44).
For more information about the Early Literacy Support programme for Year 1 children, contact the Primary National Strategy.

Professional development and school management

Book Bands for Guided Reading can be used to inform and stimulate professional development. Individual teachers and school teams may find the suggestions below helpful as they review their organisation and practice in teaching literacy, and reflect on children's learning and the effectiveness of class teaching.

1. Tracking the progress of Individual Key Stage 1 pupils in text reading

OBSERVING AND ASSESSING READING PROGRESS

The combination of *Book Bands for Guided Reading* as a reliable gradient of difficulty, and running records as an objective record of children's control of the reading process, can enable schools and individual teachers to organise, carry out assessment and monitor children's progress very effectively.

Learning how to make and interpret running records of text reading should enable teachers to be more accurate and detailed observers.
(See Clay, M.M. (2002) *An Observation Survey of Early Literacy Achievement*, 2nd edition, Auckland, NZ: Heinemann Education)

For children in the early stages of learning to read, a more comprehensive assessment including letter knowledge and high-frequency word reading and writing, may help to identify children for special support. These procedures are also fully described in *An Observation Survey of Early Literacy Achievement*.

REVIEWING AND REFINING MONITORING PROCEDURES AT THE SCHOOL AND CLASSROOM LEVELS

The gradient of difficulty in *Book Bands for Guided Reading* can provide a baseline for identifying the starting point of individuals or groups of pupils at the beginning of each school year. Children's progress can be tracked throughout Key Stage 1 to provide formative assessment of the effectiveness of classroom teaching and school policies.

2. Extending staff knowledge of Key Stage 1 texts

USING THE BANDING RATIONALE

Descriptions introducing each band can be used as a starting point to explore ways in which texts vary as their challenge increases, and new opportunities for learning are introduced. Enhanced judgement may be applied to new materials to enable teachers to select and use the most appropriate texts to achieve specific learning goals.

ORGANISING AND AUDITING KEY STAGE 1 TEXTS

Book Bands for Guided Reading forms an effective basis for organising texts throughout Key Stage 1, ensuring continuity and consistency across years and classes. See section on **Setting up and maintaining resources** on p. 44.

Information in Part 2, **The Right Book** (pp. 6–28) can be used as an auditing tool to ensure range of text type, variety of appeal, satisfactory representation of race and gender, replacement of battered books and incomplete sets, and an injection of attractive up-to-date materials. Schools may also use it to identify themes within different bands in order to support class topic work through Guided Reading.

3. Empowering children to read independently

DEEPENING THEORETICAL UNDERSTANDING

Book Bands for Guided Reading can provide a stimulus and a context for discussion about the challenges that children face when they are learning to read text. Teachers may benefit from practice in taking running records of children reading text and help in learning how to analyse errors and self-corrections.

Examples of teaching at each band can stimulate reflection about praise for a child's attempts to read a new text attending to certain cues, and prompts to alert a child to use neglected information at particular points in the reading, in order to foster balanced, independent problem-solving. Self-monitoring and self-correction are significant evidence of this independence.

4. Reviewing and enhancing the effectiveness of Guided Reading

Descriptions and charts in this handbook may be useful in raising awareness of distinctions between Guided Reading and other learning experiences. Descriptions of procedures and examples of teaching can stimulate discussion about book introductions, the teacher's role during independent reading, and ways to return and respond to text after an initial reading.

Suggested independent activities in the end of the Guided Reading sessions introducing each colour band in this book may form an introduction to discussions around the quality and effectiveness of this aspect of the classroom literacy programme.

Book Bands for Guided Reading is designed to work alongside the Primary Framework for Literacy to enable teachers to explore the relationship between appropriate learning opportunities and progress in text reading.

Setting up and maintaining resources

A central resource area gives all teachers access to a full range of texts to cater for the range of ability found in Foundation and Key Stage 1 classes.

SHELVING

- Locate a convenient area to install shelving for rows of magazine files or plastic baskets for sets of books and accompanying teaching notes, activity sheets or ideas for relevant extension work.
- Provide shelf space for teachers' handbooks, assessment materials and other professional texts; and stands for hanging or storing Big Books and poem cards.

SELECTING

- Gather together all suitable texts already in the school. Organise into sets of six or more and refer to **Series Reviews** (pp. 11–28) to decide which are worth using for Guided Reading or other purposes, or should be discarded.
- Decide on one or two core series and supplement with titles from other recommended series for diversity, breadth and relevance to specific topics. **To prevent novice readers becoming over-dependent on the vocabulary and structures of any one series, include a range of series and publishers within each band.**
- Place orders, preferably through a publisher's representative.

BANDING

- Armed with coloured stickers (see below) and a copy of *Book Bands for Guided Reading*, check each title in the alphabetic listing and label sets of books according to colour bands.
- Label plastic or cardboard magazine files with titles of several sets of books in the same band and ideally in the same reading series. Number each file within each colour band, and each book to match its file for quick access. Rank the files on the shelves in order of bands.
- Supply a guide to the banding system. Set up a system that ensures resources can be accessed and returned easily, regularly and reliably.

AUDITING

- Review books regularly. Remove those that are rarely used or in poor condition.
- Supplement weaker bands with modern, well-written titles. Check **Series Reviews** or the colour-banded listings for additional fiction and non-fiction titles and publishers. More titles will usually be needed at the lower bands and a greater variety of text types at the higher bands.

USEFUL ADDRESSES

To order coloured labels for banding books:
Sato UK Limited, Valley Road, Harwich, Essex CO12 4RR
Tel: 01255 240000   Fax: 01255 252840
Email: enquiries@satouk.com

Reading Recovery National Network
Institute of Education, 20 Bedford Way, London WC1H 0AL
Tel: 020 7612 6585   Fax: 020 7612 6828
Email: Readrec@ioe.ac.uk
Website: www.ioe.ac.uk/readrec.html

PART 5

Colour-banded listings
with introductions and examplar
Guided Reading sessions

Band 1 PINK A

Reading Recovery Level 1
FOUNDATION STAGE

**WORKING TOWARDS
LEVEL 1: LEARNING
OPPORTUNITIES**
Aligned to Phase 2
Progression in Phonics

- Locate title.

- Open front cover.

- Turn pages appropriately.

- Understand that left page comes before right.

- Understand that we read print from left to right.

- Use meaning together with repeated language patterns (syntax) to predict the storyline.

- Start to match spoken word to printed word (one-to-one correspondence).

- Use a few known words to assist own reading.

TEXT CHARACTERISTICS

- natural language following children's speech patterns

- simple, highly predictable text of about 24–60 words involving familiar objects and actions

- one repetitive whole sentence structure that includes at least one high-frequency word

- reasonably large font size with clear spaces between words

- illustrations that provide full and direct support for the text and are well separated from it

- fully punctuated text in the same position on each page

GUIDED READING

PINK BAND

SIMPLE EXPOSITORY TEXT

IN OUR CLASSROOM
PM Plus Starters Level 1

Text by Beverley Randell,
Jenny Giles, Annette Smith

Published by Nelson Thornes (2000)

ISBN 0 17 009531 2

LEARNING OUTCOMES

Most children:
- know that print carries meaning and is read from left to right
- attempt and practise one-to-one correspondence
- read a range of familiar and common sentences independently
- read and write a high-frequency word.

TEXT SELECTION NOTES

In this simple 16-page book, a girl is showing a new boy in her class where things are put. The text is an example of the earliest non-fiction where different types of objects are presented in a sequence of four-word repeated sentences: 'The … go here.' On the last page, the word 'up' is inserted, adding a small tracking challenge. Clearly spaced print and uncluttered photos on two-page spreads making this an ideal beginner's book.

LINK TO WHOLE-CLASS WORK

Shared Reading sessions provide opportunities for discussion about stories. Repeated unison reading with full phrasing and expressiveness enriches comprehension and helps to set a model for children's own reading in a guided situation.

The conventions of text placement on the page, and formal terms such as 'title', 'front cover', 'word', 'letter', 'full stop' are taught, and one-to-one matching is modelled and practised in Shared Reading. In Guided Reading, the teacher calls for the use of this knowledge and can observe whether each child really understands these terms and can track reliably.

Children should be called on to use their high frequency word and letter knowledge only to the extent that this does not break the flow of their first text-reading efforts.

TEXT INTRODUCTION

Teacher gives a book to each child and reads the title. S/he gives a carefully prepared, brief overview of the book using the verb in the same form as in the book, establishing the sentence structure, and then engaging the children in a focused discussion:

*In this book, a girl tells a boy who's just joining the class where all the things **go**. We'll look at the pictures and talk about the book first, and then you can read it all by yourselves.*

p. 2 *The girl says, 'The bags go here.'*
p. 4 *What do you think she says now? Yes, the books go here.*

Carry on through the book with the children looking at the photos and modelling the language expressively.

p. 6 *Yes, they are bricks but in this book they're called blocks.*
p. 16 *Now the teacher is talking. She says, 'The paintings go **up** here.' Now you say it.*

STRATEGY CHECK

Now it's time for you to read the book pointing carefully underneath all the words. Let's read the title together.

INDEPENDENT READING

Teacher ensures that all the children read the first page correctly. As each child reads their own book, the teacher works with one and then another.

I like the way you put your finger (or a pen with a retractable nib) *underneath the words. Did that fit? Try again and make the pointing fit. Check the picture and then try again. That makes sense now, doesn't it?*

RETURN TO THE TEXT

Let's turn to page 2. Read the words and stop when you come to 'go'. Now find 'go' on all the pages in the book. Tell us about that word. (It has two letters: **g** is the first letter; **o** is the second letter.) *Here are some letters. Make **go**. Now check **go** with the book. Which letter is first? Here's a whiteboard and pen. Write **go** lots of times, and leave a space between each word you write.*

What's this word you've written? What good spaces!

Now re-read the book, making it sound like the girl talking.

INDEPENDENT ACTIVITY

Pretend you are showing someone around our classroom. Draw a picture about where some things go.

Teacher writes the child's dictated sentence/s, leaving a space for the child to write 'go'. For example, 'The pencils _____ here.'

SERIES	PUBLISHER	SET (OR AUTHOR)	TITLE	BAND
Alphakids	Gardner	Emergent Level 1	Can You See Me?	1A
			Dogs	1A
			Fruit Salad	1A
			Glasses	1A
			Ice Cream	1A
			Playing	1A
		Emergent Level 2	I'm Brave	1A
Alphakids Plus	Gardner	Emergent Level 1	At the Zoo	1A
			Chairs	1A
			Circus	1A
			Face Painting	1A
			Look at Me	1A
		Emergent Level 2	Making Music	1A
			My Dinner	1A
AlphaWorld	Gardner	Band 1A: Pink	My Toys	1A
			Playing Outside	1A
Big Cat	Collins	Pink B	Cats	1A
			Come to the Circus	1A
			Fly Away Home	1A
			Pond, The	1A
			See-saw, The	1A
			Wheels	1A
		Red A	Beach, The	1A
			In the Dark	1A
Dragonflies	Gardner	Pink	Lunch Boxes	1A
			My Best Bear	1A
First Facts	Badger	Level 1	Me	1A
			Pets	1A
First Stories	Gardner	Emergent A	Crash!	1A
			Going Places	1A
			I Wash	1A
			My Painting	1A
			Present, The	1A
			Puppy, The	1A
			Sandcastle, The	1A
			Snails	1A
			Up the Tree	1A
			We Get Squashed!	1A
		Emergent B	Clown, The	1A
			Fair, The	1A
			Here I Am!	1A
			Line Dancing	1A
			Max Comes Home	1A
			Mitt For Me, A	1A
			My Cat	1A
			My Family	1A
		Emergent C	Box, The	1A
			Friend for Me, A	1A
			I Like Rice	1A
			My Friend	1A
			Picnic, The	1A

SERIES	PUBLISHER	SET (OR AUTHOR)	TITLE	BAND
First Stories	Gardner	Emergent C	Play, The	1A
			Thanksgiving	1A
		Emergent D	Dog on Holiday	1A
			Fish Picture, A	1A
		Emergent E	My Balloon Man	1A
			Party, The	1A
			That Cat	1A
		Emergent F	Hide-and-Seek	1A
			My School Bag	1A
			Stew for Dinner	1A
Kingscourt Reading, Core	Kingscourt	Level 1 Benchmark Bk	My Place	1A
		Level 1 Collection	Two Little Birds	1A
		Level 1 Little Books	Patterns	1A
			Who Lives on a Farm?	1A
Kingscourt Reading, Extension	Kingscourt	Set 1	Big and Little	1A
			Helping Dad	1A
			Things I Like	1A
			What Can I See?	1A
Lighthouse	Ginn	Pink A: 1	Traffic	1A
		Pink A: 2	Look at Me!	1A
		Pink A: 3	My Cat	1A
		Pink A: 4	Up, Up and Away	1A
		Pink A: 5	Washing the Elephant	1A
		Pink A: 6	For My Birthday	1A
		Pink A: 7	Me and My Dog	1A
		Pink A: 8	Look What I Found!	1A
Literacy Links Plus	Kingscourt	Emergent A	Miss Popple's Pets	1A
			What Are You?	1A
			Who's Coming For a Ride?	1A
		Emergent B	What Has Spots?	1A
		Emergent C	Climbing	1A
National Geographic	Rigby	Pink Level	Animal Hospital, The	1A
			Look at the Tree	1A
			What Can a Diver See?	1A
			Who Looks After Me?	1A
Oxford Reading Tree	OUP	Fireflies Stage 1+	Maya's Family	1A
			This is Me	1A
		Fireflies, More – Stage 1+	Animal Faces	1A
			Clothes For Rain	1A
			Fire Engine, The	1A
			On The Beach	1A
		Stage 1 First Words	Floppy Floppy	1A
			Good Trick, A	1A
			Pancake, The	1A
		Stage 1+ Patterned Stories	Pet Shop, The	1A
PM Plus	Nelson Thornes	Starters One	Baby	1A
			Balloons	1A
			Going on Holiday	1A
			I Am Running	1A
			In Our Classroom	1A
			In the Garden	1A

SERIES	PUBLISHER	SET (OR AUTHOR)	TITLE	BAND
PM Plus	Nelson Thornes	Starters One	Look at the House	1A
			Play, The	1A
			Up in the Sky	1A
			We Dress Up	1A
PM Plus Non-fiction	Nelson Thornes	Starters One	Making a Bird	1A
			Making a Dinosaur	1A
			Making a Rabbit	1A
PM Storybook Starters	Nelson Thornes	Set 1	At the Zoo	1A
			Big Things	1A
			Climbing	1A
			Dad	1A
			Dressing Up	1A
			Go Cart, The	1A
			House, A	1A
			In the Trolley	1A
			Little Things	1A
			Look at Me	1A
			Me	1A
			Mum	1A
			Mums and Dads	1A
			Pets	1A
			Playing	1A
			Shopping Mall, The	1A
			Skier, The	1A
			Way I Go to School, The	1A
			We Go Out	1A
Rigby Star	Rigby	Pink Level	Catch It!	1A
			Dog Show, The	1A
			Fancy Dress	1A
			Home for Curly, A	1A
			Josie and the Junk Box	1A
			Juggling	1A
			Ned's Noise Machine	1A
			New Pet, The	1A
		Red Level	Animal Presents	1A
			Guess Who?	1A
			Monster Meal	1A
			Next Door Pets	1A
Rigby Star Non-fiction	Rigby	Pink Level	Friends	1A
			Wings	1A
Sails Foundation	Heinemann	Pink A – Am	I Am Jumping	1A
			I Am Working	1A
			Monkeys	1A
			Sailors	1A
		Pink A – Can	Animals, The	1A
			I Can	1A
			I Can Laugh	1A
			I Can Swim	1A
		Pink A – He	Family, The	1A
			Goat, The	1A
			I Am a Bee	1A

SERIES	PUBLISHER	SET (OR AUTHOR)	TITLE	BAND
Sails Foundation	Heinemann	Pink A – He	I Am a Painter	1A
		Pink A – Is	Here is a Bird	1A
			Party, The	1A
			Show, The	1A
			Water Park, The	1A
		Pink A – Like	I Like Birds	1A
			I Like Elephants	1A
			I Like Hats	1A
			I Like Riding	1A
		Pink B – And	Hats	1A
			I Like Boxes	1A
			I Like Jam	1A
			Rainbow Town	1A
		Pink B – For	Dinner	1A
			New House, The	1A
			Presents, The	1A
			Wheels	1A
		Pink B – Look	Look at the Animals	1A
			Look at the Robot	1A
			Pets, The	1A
			Shopping	1A
		Pink B – On	My Hat	1A
			Rally Car, The	1A
			Snowman, The	1A
			Spy, The	1A
		Pink B – See	Balloon Ride, The	1A
			Boat, A	1A
			House, A	1A
			Moon, The	1A
		Pink B – This	Hole, The	1A
			In the Garden	1A
			Monster Town, The	1A
			Shoe, A	1A
		Pink B – Was	Bird, The	1A
			In the Mud	1A
			My Trip	1A
			Snake, The	1A
		Pink B – Went	Bears, The	1A
			Holiday, The	1A
			Mice, The	1A
			Our Day	1A
		Pink C – Are	Going Shopping	1A
			Silly Tricks	1A
			Spies, The	1A
			Tunnel, The	1A
		Pink C – Come	Come	1A
			Come in the Grass	1A
			Market, The	1A
			Turkey, The	1A
		Pink C – Get	Cooking	1A
			I Can Help	1A

SERIES	PUBLISHER	SET (OR AUTHOR)	TITLE	BAND
Sails Foundation	Heinemann	Pink C – Get	Rides, The	1A
			Zoo Dinners	1A
		Pink C – Go	Ants, The	1A
			Bike Race, The	1A
			Mice	1A
			Water, The	1A
		Pink C – Going	Balloons, The	1A
			Birthday, The	1A
			Going to Bed	1A
			Kites, The	1A
		Pink C – Me	Bumper Cars, The	1A
			Snow, The	1A
			Spider, The	1A
			This Is for Me	1A
		Pink C – Said	Grass for Dinner	1A
			I Am Here	1A
			Naughty Monkey	1A
			Robot, The	1A
		Pink C – You	Can You See?	1A
			Elephant Trick	1A
			Ice Cream	1A
			Trucks, The	1A
Spotty Zebra	Nelson Thornes	Pink A – Change	Ama's Blanket	1A
			What's Inside?	1A
			What's That Sound?	1A
		Pink A – Ourselves	At the Market	1A
			Flat Shapes, Fat Shapes	1A
			Getting Ready For Football	1A
			Messy Hands	1A
			What Alice Makes	1A
		Pink B – Change	Bed For David, A	1A
Story Chest	Kingscourt	Get-ready Set A	Ghost, The	1A
		Get-ready Set BB	Gotcha Box, The	1A
			Mrs Wishy-Washy's Tub	1A
			Salad	1A

Band 1 PINK B

Reading Recovery Level 2
FOUNDATION STAGE

**WORKING TOWARDS
LEVEL 1: LEARNING
OPPORTUNITIES**
**Aligned to Phase 2
Progression in Phonics**

- Locate title, open front cover, and turn pages appropriately.

- Understand that left page comes before right.

- Use the meaning together with repeated language patterns (syntax) and some letters to read simple text.

- Match spoken word to printed word (one-to-one correspondence).

- Use known words to check own reading.

- Read a simple CVC word in the text from left to right.

TEXT CHARACTERISTICS

- natural language following children's speech patterns

- simple, highly predictable text of about 35–100 words involving familiar objects and actions

- one or two repetitive whole-sentence structures with at least two high-frequency words, often with a change of structure on the last page

- illustrations that provide full and direct support for the text

- reasonably large font size with clear spaces between words

- fully punctuated text in the same position on each page

Children are ready to move to Red Band when one-to-one correspondence is secure and they can write quickly and accurately about 15 high-frequency words. They should be able to link their knowledge of phonemes and graphemes with some words in the text.

GUIDED READING

PINK BAND

SIMPLE NON-FICTION

WHAT SHALL I WEAR?
Lighthouse

Text by Penny Lee

Published by Ginn (2001)

ISBN 0 602 30042 8

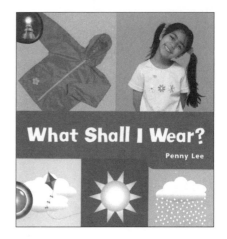

LEARNING OUTCOMES

Most children:
- know that print carries meaning and is read from left to right, top to bottom
- master one-to-one correspondence
- read some high-frequency words and use phonic knowledge to work out some simple words
- show an understanding of the sequence of events
- show an understanding of how information can be found in non-fiction text.

TEXT SELECTION NOTES

In this accumulative text, a young girl puts on more and more clothing in response to changes in the weather. The language used is the habitual present 'I wear …', which is common in simple non-fiction.

Two lines of well-spaced print on page 2 swell to six lines on page 10, each line supported by an illustration. It is unusual to have so many lines of print on a page at Pink Band. However, with each line starting with 'and', there is a fun element that children seem to respond to easily. A chart on the final page summarises the weather changes and there is a simple index on the back cover.

LINK TO WHOLE-CLASS WORK

Weather is a familiar topic of discussion in Foundation Stage. This beautifully illustrated book, a mix of photography and computer-generated setting, creates a powerful link between the observation of daily weather changes and adjustments in clothing we make in response to them.

Children will be developing a repertoire of known words and consolidating their knowledge of graphemes and their link phonemes in left-to-right sequence. They should be encouraged to use this knowledge to blend some simple, unfamiliar words in the book.

TEXT INTRODUCTION

Teacher reads the title and asks the group to use the front cover to predict how the book will work. It is important that once the teacher talks about the book, s/he uses the verb tense in the book.

*Yes, the girl has different clothes to **wear** in different weather. Let's look through the book and talk about the weather each day. She says, 'On a sunny day, I wear my T-shirt.' What does she say on the next page?*

The children supply the text orally, guided by the illustrations and sentence format.

STRATEGY CHECK

Now it's your turn to read. Read the title again, and remember to point carefully underneath each word.

INDEPENDENT READING

As each child reads their own book, the teacher works with one and then another, praising careful monitoring and prompting children to correct their own reading.

*I like the way you blended **o** … **n** to read on. Well done. Was that right?*
*How did you know? Yes, there's a picture of a coat and the word starts with **c**.*
Try again and make the pointing fit.
*It could be 'jersey' because it starts with **j**, but in this book it's called a 'jumper'.*

RETURN TO THE TEXT

Ask the children to turn to page 12 and talk about the layout. *Yes, it's a chart of the different weather. Let's read the captions. Why is the girl wearing her hood up here? … her gloves here? … just a T-shirt here?*

Talk about the capital letters, and ask the children to find lower-case letters on page 10 to correspond with each one.

Find all the 'ands' in the book. What do you notice about 'and'? (It's a word; it has three letters; first letter is **a**, first and last letters are round like **a**, **c**; last is tall.) *Now write 'and' on the table/carpet with your finger: first **a**, then **n** then **d**. Run your finger underneath and sound **a-n-d**.*

Check/correct formations of **a** and **d**.

INDEPENDENT ACTIVITY

Ask children to draw the items of clothing they have on, writing: 'My (picture) and my (picture) and …'

SERIES	PUBLISHER	SET (OR AUTHOR)	TITLE	BAND
Alphakids	Gardner	Emergent Level 2	Grandpa's House	1B
			Living and Non-living Things	1B
			My Baby Sister	1B
			What's This? What's That?	1B
Alphakids Plus	Gardner	Emergent Level 1	Big and Small	1B
		Emergent Level 2	Balls	1B
			My Fish Bowl	1B
			My Hats	1B
			Painting	1B
		Emergent Level 3	Cats	1B
AlphaWorld	Gardner	Band 1A: Pink	Flowers	1B
		Band 1B: Pink	At the Aquarium	1B
			In My Family	1B
			Soft and Hard	1B
			We Go Shopping	1B
Big Cat	Collins	Pink B	Robot, The	1B
		Red A	Day Out, A	1B
			Tec and the Cake	1B
			Tec and the Hole	1B
			Up, Up and Away	1B
			What's Inside?	1B
		Red B	Let's Go Shopping	1B
			Pirates	1B
Discovery World	Heinemann	Stage A	Seasons	1B
		Stage B	My History	1B
Dragonflies	Gardner	Pink	In the Garden	1B
			Look at Me	1B
			Off Goes the Hose!	1B
			Too Big!	1B
First Facts	Badger	Level 1	Caring For Pets	1B
			Dogs and Cats	1B
			My Five Senses	1B
			Pets With Fur	1B
			Plants Have Leaves	1B
First Stories	Gardner	Emergent B	Apple Star, The	1B
			My Little Sister	1B
		Emergent C	In the Car	1B
			Ruff and Me	1B
			Who Took the Cake?	1B
		Emergent D	I Like That Horse	1B
			My New Truck	1B
			Snowman Day	1B
			Toast	1B
			Too Big for Me!	1B
			Toys' Picnic, The	1B
			Traffic Jam	1B
			Wind Blows, The	1B
		Emergent E	Bear Wakes Up	1B
			Is It an Insect?	1B
			Little Ducklings	1B
			Little Seeds	1B

SERIES	PUBLISHER	SET (OR AUTHOR)	TITLE	BAND
First Stories	Gardner	Emergent E	Lunchtime at the Zoo	1B
			My Snowman	1B
			Playing	1B
		Emergent F	Buttons	1B
			Edmond Went Splash!	1B
			Follow the Leader	1B
			Look at My Weaving	1B
			Look at This Mess!	1B
			Looking Down	1B
			Poor Puppy!	1B
Four Corners	Pearson	Year 1	Small and Large	1B
Kingscourt Reading, Core	Kingscourt	Level 1 Little Books	I Spy	1B
		Level 2 Benchmark Bk	Snowman, The	1B
		Level 2 Little Books	Birthday Bug, The	1B
			Off to School	1B
			Patterns are Fun!	1B
Kingscourt Reading, Extension	Kingscourt	Set 1	Chalk Talk	1B
			Fun With Fruit	1B
			I Made a Picture	1B
			Look at the Ball	1B
			My Special Book	1B
			Nest, The	1B
			Our Week	1B
			Puzzle, The	1B
			We Ski	1B
Lighthouse	Ginn	Pink B: 1	Down the Side of the Sofa	1B
		Pink B: 2	Look Out Fish!	1B
		Pink B: 3	When I Grow Up	1B
		Pink B: 4	I Can Fly	1B
		Pink B: 5	We Love the Farm	1B
		Pink B: 6	What Shall I Wear?	1B
		Pink B: 7	Too Hot!	1B
		Pink B: 8	What Jessie Really Likes	1B
Literacy Links Plus	Kingscourt	Emergent C	Yellow	1B
National Geographic	Rigby	Red Level	My Bed is Soft	1B
			Our New Puppy	1B
Oxford Reading Tree	OUP	Fireflies Stage 1+	Dogs	1B
			Making Muffins	1B
		Fireflies Stage 2	Is This Too Much?	1B
		Fireflies, More – Stage 1+	Hop, Skip and Jump	1B
			Put On a Clown Face	1B
		Fireflies, More – Stage 2	Making Prints	1B
		Stage 1 First Words	Fun at the Beach	1B
			Six in a Bed	1B
			Who is it?	1B
		Stage 1+ First Sentences	Hide and Seek	1B
			Kipper's Diary	1B
			Look at Me	1B
PM Gems	Nelson Thornes	Magenta 2/3	Big Hole, The	1B
			Boat Ride, The	1B
PM Maths	Nelson Thornes	Stage A	Big Shapes and Little Shapes	1B

SERIES	PUBLISHER	SET (OR AUTHOR)	TITLE	BAND
PM Maths	Nelson Thornes	Stage A	Counting Down	1B
			One Picture	1B
			Picnic For Two	1B
PM Photo Stories	Nelson Thornes	Magenta 2/3	Meg's Messy Room	1B
			Zac's Train Set	1B
PM Plus	Nelson Thornes	Starters Two	Big and Little	1B
			Big Sea Animals	1B
			Going Out	1B
			My Clothes	1B
			My Little Cat	1B
			My Sandcastle	1B
			Parade, The	1B
			Party Hats	1B
			Playing Outside	1B
			Toy Box, The	1B
PM Plus Non-fiction	Nelson Thornes	Starters Two	On and Off	1B
			Round and Round	1B
			Up and Down	1B
PM Storybook Starters	Nelson Thornes	Set 2	At The Library	1B
			Ball Games	1B
			Ben's Red Car	1B
			Can You See The Eggs?	1B
			Cat and Mouse	1B
			Farm in Spring, The	1B
			Fishing	1B
			Four Ice Creams	1B
			Looking Down	1B
			My Accident	1B
			My Little Dog	1B
			Out in the Weather	1B
			Packing My Bag	1B
			Pencil, The	1B
			Rock Pools, The	1B
			Sally's New Shoes	1B
			Stop!	1B
			We Can Run	1B
			We Like Fish!	1B
			Where are the Babies?	1B
Rigby Star	Rigby	Pink Level	Curly is Hungry	1B
			Moving Day	1B
			New Hat, The	1B
			Play, The	1B
			Scaredy Cat	1B
			Where is Patch?	1B
Rigby Star Non-fiction	Rigby	Pink Level	Our Five Senses	1B
Spotty Zebra	Nelson Thornes	Pink A – Change	Leela's Tree	1B
			Look at the Painting	1B
			Matt's Socks	1B
		Pink A – Ourselves	Ellie and Sam	1B
			Out of Milk	1B
		Pink B – Change	Enzo in the Park	1B

SERIES	PUBLISHER	SET (OR AUTHOR)	TITLE	BAND
Spotty Zebra	Nelson Thornes	Pink B – Change	Getting Bigger	1B
			Just Like You	1B
			Where Do These Go?	1B
		Pink B – Ourselves	Happy Diwali	1B
		Red – Change	We Like Weddings	1B
Story Chest	Kingscourt	Get-ready Set A	In the Mirror	1B
			Tree-House, The	1B
		Get-ready Set AA	Escalator, The	1B
			Shoo, Fly!	1B
			Snowman	1B
			Waiting	1B
		Get-ready Set B	Bicycle, The	1B
		Get-ready Set C	Clown and Elephant	1B
			Going to School	1B
		Get-ready Set CC	Halloween	1B
			Mouse Train	1B
		Get-ready Set DD	Tick-Tock	1B
		Ready-set-go Set B	Bee, The	1B
			Copy-Cat	1B
Storyworlds	Heinemann	Stage 2 Animal World	Big Surprise, The	1B
Web Guided Reading	OUP	Stage 1 (Duck Green)	Getting Ready	1B
			Windy Day, A	1B
Web Weavers Non-fiction	OUP	Stage 1 First Words NF	Animal Homes	1B
			Changes	1B
			Fierce Creatures	1B
			How Many Legs?	1B
			Things That Go	1B
			Wrong Colours	1B

Band 2 RED

Reading Recovery Levels 3–5
FOUNDATION STAGE

WORKING TOWARDS LEVEL 1: LEARNING OPPORTUNITIES
Aligned approximately with Phase 3 Progression in Phonics

- Locate and recall title.

- Consolidate secure control of one-to-one matching on a wide range of texts.

- Use known words to check and confirm reading.

- Solve simple (CVC) words by blending phonemes from left to right and check for meaning, and correct syntax – i.e. does it make sense and sound right?

- Start to read more rhythmically or use phrasing while maintaining track of the print.

- Repeat words, phrases or sentences to check, confirm or modify own reading.

TEXT CHARACTERISTICS

- slightly longer, highly predictable text involving familiar objects and actions

- some repeated sentence/phrase patterns that include high-frequency words and simple (CVC) words that children can solve by blending phonemes

- sentences short, clear and straightforward that follow children's speech patterns

- illustrations provide full and direct support for the text

- simple story development (fiction text)

- non-fiction texts that may have more than one type of layout

- reasonably large print with obvious spaces between words and a full range of punctuation

Children are ready to move to Yellow Band when one-to-one correspondence no longer requires much attention, they can read and write quickly and accurately about 30 high-frequency words, and can sound out some simple, unfamiliar words in the text. Results from running records on briefly introduced, unseen texts are invaluable from Red Band onwards.

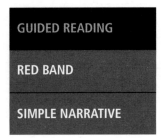

GUIDED READING

RED BAND

SIMPLE NARRATIVE

FATHER BEAR GOES FISHING
PM Story Books

Written by Beverley Randell
Illustrated by Isabel Lowe

Published by Nelson Thornes (1994)

ISBN 0 17 422948 8

LEARNING OUTCOMES	Most children:

Most children:
- use syntax and context when reading for meaning
- read simple words by sounding out and blending phonemes left to right
- locate, read and write high-frequency words
- show an understanding of the elements of stories
- retell narratives in the correct sequence.

TEXT SELECTION NOTES

Beverley Randell, master of appealing and accessible stories for beginner readers, has produced a classic using familiar storybook characters. In a limited range of vocabulary, the story unfolds through simple sentence structures repeated in different contexts, and supported by expressive illustrations. Pages consisting of 1–5 lines of well-spaced print offer a variety of tracking challenges, and most pages contain direct speech.

LINK TO WHOLE-CLASS WORK

In the enjoyable re-reading of large-print storybooks, children work with their teacher to deepen their understanding of the elements of stories such as plot and character. They are learning to recognise readily what direct speech looks like written down, and respond to punctuation together with an understanding of different characters in order to bring their own reading to life.

By now, the children will be able to recognise automatically a growing bank of high-frequency words, and be eager to put into practice their developing phonic skills to read some CVC words.

TEXT INTRODUCTION

Give a book to each child, and read the title. *Can you find the graphemes **th** and **sh** in the title?* Then ask: *Do you think Father Bear catches some fish? What makes you think that? Let's look at illustrations and see if you're right.*

Look through the pictures ensuring the children can identify the river (p. 2); know that Father Bear was talking to himself and said, 'Where are the fish?' (p. 4); can identify Mother and Baby Bear (p. 10) and understand why Mother Bear looked at her watch; and hear Father Bear's reassuring 'Here I come' modelled.

STRATEGY CHECK

*Now you can read the book yourself. Think about the story while you are sounding out words you don't know. Check that you are using **sh** and **th**.*

INDEPENDENT READING

Listen in on individual children, praising their attempts to work out unfamiliar words and check their own reading.

p. 3 *You said 'water'. That makes sense but does that word look like 'water'? Try saying the phonemes from left to right.*
p. 5 *Well done. 'Were are the fish' doesn't make sense, so you changed it.*
p. 8 *'said' makes sense, but check the sound of the first two letters and the middle part, and have another try ('shouted').*
pp. 11/15 *I like the way you made that part of the story sound like the bears talking.*

RETURN TO THE TEXT

I want you to tell me this story in your own words. You can use the pictures to help you. Would you like to start. ...?

Work with the children to put the story into context and explain Father Bear's feelings when there were no fish, and then he started to catch them, etc.

Let's practise the talking parts in the story. Turn to page 5. Put your left pointing finger on the first speech marks, and your right one on the ones at the end of the line. Do you see the question mark? Let's read it together making it sound like Father Bear asking a question.

Repeat using speech on pages 7, 8, 9, 11, 15 and 16.

INDEPENDENT ACTIVITY

Draw or photocopy page 14 and insert a speech bubble for Baby Bear. Ask the children to write what Baby Bear said ('Look at the fish').

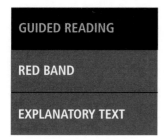

GUIDED READING

RED BAND

EXPLANATORY TEXT

PASS THE PASTA, PLEASE
Kingscourt Reading – Extension

Written by Dorothy Avery
Photographed by Mary Walker

Published by Shortland (1998)
Distributed by Kingscourt Publishing Ltd

ISBN 0 7699 0229 4

LEARNING OUTCOMES

Most children:
- read a range of simple sentences independently
- read simple words by sounding out and blending phonemes
- locate, read and write high-frequency words
- find information in non-fiction texts.

TEXT SELECTION NOTES

This is a colourful and imaginative little non-fiction book with an artistic layout and photographs illustrating many ideas for the use of pasta beyond satisfying the appetite. The text uses simple, impersonal language structures – 'can be' and 'is fun' – and photos of cooking procedures provide opportunities for the oral use of instructional language.

LINK TO WHOLE-CLASS WORK

The class will have been reading and writing some non-fiction enlarged texts, discussing how these are organised and illustrated, and answering relevant questions about where to find out facts. They may have had the opportunity to discuss features of book design and how they link up with the topics.

Through their writing, children will have been using their knowledge of grapheme–phoneme correspondences, and teachers will be encouraging them to apply this skill in their text reading.

TEXT INTRODUCTION	*This book is called* **Pass the Pasta, Please**. *This girl on the cover tells us about pasta and the fun we can have with it.*
	Let's look at the title page. What's the lady doing? Can you see what they've got around their necks? I wonder what this book is going to tell us about. Any ideas?
	pp. 2/3 *Look at all the colours pasta can be.* pp. 4/5/6/7 *What shape can pasta be? Yes, it can be thin, fat, long, short.* pp. 8/9 *Look. Pasta can be all sorts of shapes. Try saying that: 'All sorts of shapes.'* p. 10 *The girl thinks pasta is fun to sort. Now she's poking some string through the middle of the pasta. She thinks pasta is fun to thread.* pp. 12/13/14/15 *What kind of fun are they having now?*
STRATEGY CHECK	*Look at the words and check the pictures carefully to make sure what you read makes sense.*
INDEPENDENT READING	p. 2 Check that each child has established the sentence structure 'Pasta can be …'. Encourage the children to sound out the colours if necessary (red, yellow, green, black). p. 4 *Remember to work from left to right across that word. Can you see a little word you know (**in** in 'thin')?* p. 6 *Well done for sounding out 'long'.* (Phase 3) p. 8 *Do you remember we said 'All sorts of shapes'?* p. 10 *The hard words here are 'sort' and 'thread'. Which one do you think this is? Has it got **s/th** at the beginning?*
RETURN TO THE TEXT	Discuss the cooking procedure on pages 12 and 13.
	Now go through the book and notice all the different shapes pasta can be. Choose one and we'll take turns to show the group what one kind of pasta is like just with our hands. No speaking. See if the others can guess.
	Write each correct answer on a whiteboard ('long', 'short', 'thin', 'wide', 'shell-shaped', 'wiggly', 'curly', 'bow-shaped'), inviting the children to help with the spelling.
INDEPENDENT ACTIVITY	Provide pasta of various colours and shapes for children to stick onto card to make a picture, or create jewellery.

SERIES	PUBLISHER	SET (OR AUTHOR)	TITLE	BAND
Alphakids	Gardner	Emergent Level 2	Sandwiches	2
		Emergent Level 3	Butterfly	2
			Monsters	2
			Parcel, The	2
			Party, The	2
			Too Busy	2
			What's for Dinner?	2
		Emergent Level 4	Birthday Cakes	2
			Rain	2
			Tickling	2
			Twins	2
			What's That Noise?	2
		Emergent Level 5	I Can't Find My Roller Skates	2
			Making Lunch	2
			Plants	2
Alphakids Plus	Gardner	Emergent Level 3	Hamburger	2
			Helping in the Garden	2
			Milk Shake	2
			My Dog	2
			Sniffs	2
		Emergent Level 4	Follow Me	2
			Goat, The	2
			In a Cold, Cold Place	2
			In the Ocean	2
			Making Pizza	2
		Emergent Level 5	Pond, The	2
			Sebastian Learns to Fly	2
			Shut the Gate!	2
			Signs	2
		Early Level 6	Run, Rabbit, Run!	2
AlphaWorld	Gardner	Band 1A: Pink	Stripes	2
		Band 2: Red	Big Brother	2
			Leaves	2
			Tails	2
			Water Moves	2
		Band 3: Yellow	Pets	2
Big Cat	Collins	Red A	Shapes on the Seashore	2
		Red B	At the Dump	2
			Tec and the Litter	2
			What Do You Like?	2
			Where is the Wind?	2
			Woody's Week	2
Dragonflies	Gardner	Red	Happy Birthday	2
			Time For Bed	2
			Training Ruby	2
			Walking the Dog	2
			What's in the Cake Tin?	2
			Where Is Sam?	2
First Facts	Badger	Level 1	Caring For Plants	2
			Flower Petals	2
			Keeping Healthy	2

SERIES	PUBLISHER	SET (OR AUTHOR)	TITLE	BAND
First Facts	Badger	Level 1	Living or Not?	2
			My Face	2
		Level 2	City, Farm and Sea	2
			Clothes	2
			In the Garden	2
			Let's Eat!	2
			Make a Zoo	2
			My Toys	2
Four Corners	Pearson	Year 1	Then and Now	2
Genre Range	Pearson	Beginner Letters	Better Letter, A	2
			Pip's Thank-You Letter	2
Kingscourt Reading, Core	Kingscourt	Level 2 Collection	Bake a Cake	2
		Level 3 Benchmark Bk	Seagull, The	2
		Level 3 Collection	Paws and Claws	2
		Level 3 Little Books	Growing	2
			Hungry Hedgehog	2
			Wake Up!	2
		Level 4 Benchmark Bk	When the Tide Goes Out	2
		Level 4 Collection	Blow, Wind, Blow!	2
		Level 4 Little Books	Cheese, Please!	2
			Look Out of the Window	2
			Make a Kite	2
		Level 5 Benchmark Bk	Fly, The	2
		Level 5 Collection	Stop!	2
		Level 5 Little Books	Boxes of Fun	2
			Come and Play	2
			What Am I?	2
Kingscourt Reading, Extension	Kingscourt	Set 2	Balloons!	2
			Before I Go to School	2
			Black and White	2
			Breakfast on the Farm	2
			Burrows	2
			Face in the Dark, The	2
			Homes	2
			Looking After Baby	2
			My Baby	2
			My Bike	2
			Our Chore Chart	2
			Pass the Pasta, Please	2
			Pass the Present	2
			Picture, A	2
			Presents	2
			Puppet Play, A	2
			Scissors	2
			Shopping	2
			Strings	2
			Tea Party, The	2
			What Can it Be?	2
			What is it?	2
			What Lays Eggs?	2
			Who?	2

SERIES	PUBLISHER	SET (OR AUTHOR)	TITLE	BAND
Lighthouse	Ginn	Red: 1	Stop, Look and Listen	2
		Red: 2	My Breakfast	2
		Red: 3	They All Ran Away	2
		Red: 4	Three Bears, The	2
		Red: 5	You Can't Catch Me	2
		Red: 6	Kenji's Haircut	2
		Red: 7	In Ravi's Den	2
		Red: 8	Stuck in the Mud	2
		Red: 9	Please Mum!	2
		Red: 10	Whose Footprints?	2
Literacy Links Plus	Kingscourt	Contemporary Stories	Waves	2
		Early A	Legs	2
		Emergent B	Hat Trick, The	2
		Emergent C	Dear Santa	2
			In My Bed	2
			In My Room	2
			Our Dog Sam	2
			Sunrise	2
			Woof!	2
		Emergent D	What Did Kim Catch?	2
National Geographic	Rigby	Red Level	Up, Down and Around	2
			Weather in the City	2
		Yellow Level	This is an Island	2
Oxford Reading Tree	OUP	Fireflies Stage 1+	Big and Little	2
		Fireflies Stage 1+	Wheels	2
		Fireflies Stage 2	Over and Under	2
			Shopping for a Party	2
			Transport	2
		Fireflies Stage 3	Going Somewhere	2
		Fireflies, More – Stage 2	Boots and Shoes	2
			Diggers	2
			Push and Pull	2
			Sorting	2
			What is This?	2
		Fireflies, More – Stage 3	Mirrors	2
		Stage 1+ First Sentences	Reds and Blues	2
		Stage 1+ More First Sentences	Top Dog	2
		Stage 1+ More Patterned Stories	Shopping	2
			Who Did That?	2
		Stage 1+ Patterned Stories	At the Park	2
			Good Old Mum!	2
		Stage 2 More Patterned Stories	Band, The	2
			Little Dragon, The	2
			Lost Puppy, The	2
			New Trees	2
			Up and Down	2
			What is it?	2
		Stage 2 Patterned Stories	Creepy Crawly	2
			Hey Presto!	2
			It's the Weather	2
			Monkey Tricks	2

SERIES	PUBLISHER	SET (OR AUTHOR)	TITLE	BAND
Oxford Reading Tree	OUP	Stage 2 Patterned Stories	Naughty Children	2
			Sinking Feeling, A	2
		Stage 2 Storybooks	New Dog, A	2
			Toy's Party, The	2
		Stage 3 Storybooks	Nobody Wanted to Play	2
Pathways	Collins	Year 1	What's There?	2
PM Gems	Nelson Thornes	Magenta 2/3	Bubbles in the Sky	2
			Dad's Ship	2
			Hello, Bingo	2
			Jack's Road	2
			Matthew and Emma	2
			Sally and the Elephants	2
			Sally and the Leaves	2
			Sun and the Moon, The	2
		Red 3	Holiday Time	2
			Little Teddy and Monkey	2
			Raccoon Wakes Up	2
			Sally's Snowman	2
		Red 4	Balloons Go Pop!	2
			Hungry Squirrel, The	2
			Kitty Cat and the Bird	2
		Red 5	Ben's Jigsaw Puzzle	2
			Little Chimp is Brave	2
			Presents for Jack and Billy	2
PM Maths	Nelson Thornes	Stage A	Five Birds and Five Mice	2
			Four Cars	2
			Game With Shapes, A	2
			Long and Short	2
			Making a Butterfly	2
			Red Block, Blue Block	2
			Sorting Leaves	2
			We Can See Three	2
PM Photo Stories	Nelson Thornes	Magenta 2/3	Josh and Scruffy	2
			Josh and the Big Boys	2
			Josh and the Kite	2
			Lily and the Leaf Boats	2
			Little Duck for Lily, A	2
			Meg Goes to Bed	2
			Meg's Tiny Red Teddy	2
			Zac and Puffing Billy	2
		Red 3	Little Giraffe, The	2
			Zac and Chirpy	2
		Red 4	Jake's Car	2
			Lily's Play House	2
			Present For Karl, A	2
			Zac and the Ducks	2
		Red 5	Erin Meets Tiffy	2
			Jake Kicks a Goal	2
			Puzzle for Scruffy, A	2
			Tiny Teddies' Picnic, The	2
PM Plus	Nelson Thornes	Red Level	Baby Panda	2

SERIES	PUBLISHER	SET (OR AUTHOR)	TITLE	BAND
PM Plus	Nelson Thornes	Red Level	Baby Wakes Up	2
			Bedtime	2
			Big Hill, The	2
			Billy is Hiding	2
			Bingo's Ice-Cream	2
			Here Comes Little Chimp	2
			Jack and Billy	2
			Jack's Birthday	2
			Kitty Cat	2
			Kitty Cat and Fat Cat	2
			Kitty Cat and the Fish	2
			Let's Pretend	2
			Little Chimp	2
			Little Chimp and Big Chimp	2
			Lucky Dip, The	2
			Monkey on the Roof	2
			Mother Bird	2
			My Book	2
			My Tower	2
			Photo Time	2
			Red Puppy	2
			Run, Rabbit, Run!	2
			Sam and Bingo	2
			Sam's Balloon	2
			Sam's Picnic	2
			Sam's Race	2
			Teddy Bears' Picnic	2
			Toytown Helicopter, The	2
			Toytown Rescue, The	2
PM Plus Non-fiction	Nelson Thornes	Red Level	At the Toyshop	2
			Making a Cat and a Mouse	2
			Playing with Dough	2
PM Storybooks	Nelson Thornes	Red Set A	Baby Lamb's First Drink	2
			Ben's Teddy Bear	2
			Ben's Treasure Hunt	2
			Big Kick, The	2
			Father Bear Goes Fishing	2
			Hedgehog is Hungry	2
			Lazy Pig, The	2
			Lizard Loses His Tail	2
			Merry Go Round, The	2
			Photo Book, The	2
			Pussy and the Birds	2
			Sally and the Daisy	2
			Sausages	2
			Tiger, Tiger	2
			Tom is Brave	2
			Wake Up, Dad!	2
		Red Set B	Baby Owls, The	2
			Birthday Cake For Ben, A	2
			Bumper Cars, The	2

SERIES	PUBLISHER	SET (OR AUTHOR)	TITLE	BAND
PM Storybooks	Nelson Thornes	Red Set B	Flower Girl, The	2
			Hide and Seek	2
			Home For Little Teddy, A	2
			Little Snowman, The	2
			Where is Hannah?	2
Rigby Star	Rigby	Red Level	Den, The	2
			Elephant Walk	2
			I Like to Jump	2
			Josie and the Parade	2
			Max Gets Ready	2
			My Camera	2
			Nature Trail	2
			Shopping	2
			Snake is Going Away!	2
			What is He?	2
		Yellow Level	Grandpa	2
			Josie and the Baby	2
Rigby Star Non-fiction	Rigby	Blue Level	What's it Made Of?	2
		Pink Level	Big, Bigger, Biggest	2
		Yellow Level	Baby Animals	2
			Funny Ears	2
Spotty Zebra	Nelson Thornes	Pink B – Change	I Am Hot!	2
			I Spy in the Garden	2
			Rain in the Park	2
		Pink B – Ourselves	Babies	2
			Check-up, The	2
			Hello Baby	2
			Playing Together	2
		Red – Change	Birthday Surprise	2
			Chicks Hatching	2
			Dad's Coming Home	2
			Little Duckling	2
			Mum's Photo Album	2
			Spiders	2
		Red – Ourselves	Artist, The	2
			What is it?	2
			Who Lives Here?	2
Story Chest	Kingscourt	Get-ready Set AA	New Pants	2
		Get-ready Set B	Houses	2
			Monster Sandwich, A	2
			Mouse	2
			Night-time	2
		Get-ready Set BB	Bridge, The	2
			Fishing	2
			Green Grass	2
			Rat's Funny Story	2
		Get-ready Set C	Hello	2
			I Am Frightened	2
			Little Brother	2
			One, One is the Sun	2
			Silly Old Possum	2

SERIES	PUBLISHER	SET (OR AUTHOR)	TITLE	BAND
Story Chest	Kingscourt	Get-ready Set C	What's For Lunch?	2
		Get-ready Set CC	Dan Gets Dressed	2
			Jump, Jump, Kangaroo	2
			Look Out, Dan!	2
			Nest, The	2
		Get-ready Set DD	Boogie-Woogie Man, The	2
			Gifts, The	2
			Happy Birthday, Frog	2
			How to Make a Hot Dog	2
			Microscope	2
		Ready-set-go Set A	Where Are They Going?	2
		Ready-set-go Set AA	Bears' Picnic, The	2
			Chicken For Dinner	2
			Little Hearts	2
			Skating	2
			Umbrella	2
			Valentine's Day	2
			Who Can See the Camel?	2
		Ready-set-go Set B	Little Pig	2
			Lost	2
			My Home	2
			Plop!	2
		Ready-set-go Set BB	Barn Dance	2
			Ducks	2
			Ebenezer and the Sneeze	2
			I Love Chickens	2
			My Brown Cow	2
		Ready-set-go Set C	Horace	2
			Look For Me	2
			Night Train, The	2
			Too Big For Me	2
		Ready-set-go Set CC	Fantastic Cake	2
		Ready-set-go Set D	No, No	2
			Two Little Dogs	2
Story Street	Pearson	Step 2	Ben Gets a Hat	2
			In the Hen House	2
			Pet for Sam, A	2
			Save Our Baby!	2
			Secret Room, The, Part 1	2
			Secret Room, The, Part 2	2
			Shopping	2
			Wet! Wet! Wet!	2
Storyworlds	Heinemann	Stage 2 Animal World	Bingo and the Bone	2
			Bingo Wants to Play	2
			Yum! Yum!	2
		Stage 2 Fantasy World	Monty and the Ghost Train	2
			Monty at McBurgers	2
			Monty at the Party	2
			Monty at the Seaside	2
		Stage 2 Once Upon a Time	Bears and the Honey, The	2
			Fox and the Rabbit, The	2

SERIES	PUBLISHER	SET (OR AUTHOR)	TITLE	BAND
Storyworlds	Heinemann	Stage 2 Once Upon a Time	Fox and the Stork, The	2
			Old Woman and the Hen, The	2
		Stage 2 Our World	Clever Joe	2
			Dinner Time	2
			Helpers	2
			Naughty Joe	2
		Stage 3 Animal World	Frisky and the Cat	2
			Frisky and the Ducks	2
			Frisky plays a Trick	2
			Frisky Wants to Sleep	2
		Stage 3 Fantasy World	Mr Marvel and the Cake	2
			Mr Marvel and the Car	2
			Mr Marvel and the Lemonade	2
			Mr Marvel and the Washing	2
		Stage 3 Once Upon a Time	Boy Who Cried Wolf, The	2
			Hare and the Tortoise, The	2
			Selfish Dog, The	2
			Three Billy Goats, The	2
		Stage 3 Our World	Empty Lunchbox, The	2
			Lost Coat, The	2
			Robots, The	2
			See-saw, The	2
		Stage 4 Animal World	Max and the Apples	2
Web Fiction	OUP	Stage 1 (Variety)	Animals at the Zoo	2
			Can I Have a Pet?	2
			Magic Paintbrush, The	2
			Nama's Hats	2
			Nelly Paints a Monster	2
		Stage 2 (Variety)	Big Bear's Bad Day	2
			Big Bear's Party	2
			Hermit Crab's New Shell	2
			Where's Daddy Bear?	2
Web Guided Reading	OUP	Stage 1 (Duck Green)	Oh No, Jo, No!	2
			Two the Same	2
		Stage 2 (Duck Green)	Box, The	2
			Lost and Found	2
		Stage 3 (Duck Green)	Big Puddle, The	2
			Choose the Shoes	2
			Pets	2
			String's the Thing	2
Web Weavers Non-fiction	OUP	First Non-fiction: Pack B	Which Animals Lay Eggs?	2

Band 3 YELLOW

Reading Recovery Levels 6–8
NATIONAL CURRICULUM LEVEL 1

**WORKING WITHIN LEVEL 1:
LEARNING OPPORTUNITIES**
Aligned with Phases 3/4
Progression in Phonics

- Follow print with eyes, finger-pointing only at points of difficulty.

- Take more note of punctuation to support the use of grammar and oral language rhythms.

- Cross-check all sources of information more quickly while reading.

- Note familiar words and phonemes and use these to get to unknown words, e.g. look, took.

- Search for information in print to predict, confirm or attempt new words while reading.

- Notice relationships between one text and another.

- Predict in more detail.

TEXT CHARACTERISTICS

- some repetition of phrase patterns, ideas and vocabulary

- more variation of sentence structure

- storylines include more episodes following a time sequence

- some literary conventions along with familiar oral language structures

- stories may involve imaginary happenings in framework of familiar experiences

- non-fiction texts still use personal experience and children's language patterns

- illustrations still support the text quite closely

GUIDED READING

YELLOW BAND

NARRATIVE FICTION

CURLY TO THE RESCUE
Rigby Star

Written by Tony Mitton
Illustrated by Jo Brooker

Published by Rigby (2000)

ISBN 0 433 02767 3

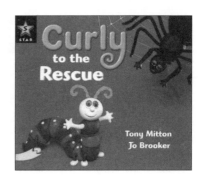

LEARNING OUTCOMES

Most children:
- use language to imagine, and to recreate roles
- read more challenging texts using their phonic knowledge along with automatic recognition of high-frequency words
- use syntax and context when reading for meaning
- interpret a text by reading aloud with some variety of pace and emphasis.

TEXT SELECTION NOTES

Curly is a colourful caterpillar who features in a number of Rigby Star titles. In this one, he comes to the rescue of several insect friends who have been beguiled into the web of the wicked black spider! The story follows the accumulative pattern of traditional tales such as Chicken Licken, with each insect accompanied by an alliterative adjective: little ladybird, green grasshopper, big beetle.

The superb illustrations consist of photographed dioramas of each 'scene' featuring models of the insects whose dramatic expressions reflect the storyline.

LINK TO WHOLE-CLASS WORK

This story builds on children's experience of stories including the main character, sequence of events and satisfactory endings.

During Shared Reading sessions, children will be taking part in fluent, expressive reading, learning to respond appropriately to punctuation, including speech marks that feature prominently in this text.

They will be investigating words with adjacent consonants and practising blending phonemes to read unfamiliar words in text, and be able to recognise an increasing number of high-frequency words.

Read the title and ask the children to look at the characters on the front cover.

Which one do you think is Curly? Does anyone know what 'rescue' means?
What do you think happens in the story?
Let's see if you're right.

Look through the book, using the names of the insects and ensuring the children get the general idea, but leaving the dialogue for them to read for themselves. The exceptions to this may be:

p. 4 *Look! Along came Curly. They all wanted him to help them, didn't they?*
p. 16 *'Hurray!' they all said.*

There's a lot of talking in this story. When you're reading, pretend you're the spider who's talking, and then pretend you're the other insect talking. Make it sound exciting.

While each child reads their own book, the teacher works with one individual and then another, acknowledging their efforts especially where there are difficulties, and prompting for additional information.

p. 2 *You sounded just like the spider talking.*
p. 4 (**green**) *Sound all the phonemes. Now carry on reading. Does 'green grasshopper' make sense? Good!*
p. 8 (**smiled**) *Start sounding out the word. Good. Now look at his mouth. He's happy, isn't he?*
p. 10 (**help**) *Well done. You sounded all the phonemes, and you noticed the darker print and used a shouting voice.*

Let's practise the talking parts in the story. Turn back to page 2. Who's going to be the spider?

When the children have taken turns to read the direct speech, help them to turn the story into a little play to perform to the class. The sixth child in the group could be the narrator who introduces Spider and each insect in turn.

Ask the children to draw all the characters in the story and label them. Alternatively, they can write their own version of the story.

SERIES	PUBLISHER	SET (OR AUTHOR)	TITLE	BAND
Alphakids	Gardner	Emergent Level 4	Making Butter	3
		Emergent Level 5	Going Shopping	3
			Looking for Fang	3
			Tadpoles and Frogs	3
		Early Level 6	Lost Mother, The	3
			Sleeping Animals	3
			Springs	3
			Taking Photos	3
			Tree, The	3
			Where's the Baby?	3
		Early Level 7	Shadow Puppets	3
			Snake's Dinner	3
			Too Many Animals	3
			Video Game	3
			Washing Our Dog	3
			Who is the Tallest?	3
		Early Level 8	Animal Skeletons	3
			Growing Tomatoes	3
			Pet for Me, A	3
			Show and Tell	3
			Thomas Had a Temper	3
			Three Little Pigs, The	3
Alphakids Plus	Gardner	Emergent Level 4	Dinosaurs	3
		Emergent Level 5	Best Pizza in the World, The	3
			Riding My Bike	3
		Early Level 6	Dress-ups	3
			Making a Picture	3
			Mighty Machines	3
			My Farm	3
			Pasta Party	3
		Early Level 7	Alphabet Party	3
			Fancy That!	3
			Fishing	3
			Gymnastics	3
			My Brother's Birthday	3
			Working with Dad	3
		Early Level 8	Lizard's Tail	3
			Mammals	3
		Early Level 11	Picnic, The	3
AlphaWorld	Gardner	Band 3: Yellow	Favourite Places	3
			Hurry Up!	3
			Ice and Snow	3
			One Step, Two Steps	3
			When I Was Sick	3
		Band 4: Blue	Our Favourite Food	3
			Stay Away!	3
			Using Rocks	3
Big Cat	Collins	Green	Worm Looks for Lunch	3
		Yellow	Dance to the Beat	3
			Hands	3
			How to Have a Party	3

SERIES	PUBLISHER	SET (OR AUTHOR)	TITLE	BAND
Big Cat	Collins	Yellow	New Kite, The	3
			Percy and the Rabbit	3
			Rat-a-tat-tat	3
			Rebecca at the Funfair	3
			Sam, the Big, Bad Cat	3
			Wind, The	3
Bright and Early Books	Collins	Le Seig, Theo	Eye Book, The	3
Discovery World	Heinemann	Stage C	Materials	3
Dragonflies	Gardner	Yellow/Blue	Don't Throw That Out	3
			Keep Trying	3
			My Sister	3
			Off Went the Light	3
First Facts	Badger	Level 2	Drums and Shakers	3
			Families Help Each Other	3
			Let's Pretend	3
			My Family Tree	3
			Spiders	3
			Toys and Games	3
		Level 3	Hot Places	3
Four Corners	Pearson	Year 1	Guide to Growing	3
Genre Range	Pearson	Beginner Comics	Cats and Dogs	3
			Looking for Lucky	3
			Nuts	3
		Beginner Traditional Tales	Mouse and the Bull, The	3
Info Trail	Pearson	Beginner Geography	Addressing a Letter	3
			What Shall We Have For Tea Tonight?	3
		Beginner History	Emma's Photo Album	3
			It's Best to be Five!	3
			When Grandad Was at School	3
		Emergent History	How to Dress a Knight	3
Kingscourt Reading, Core	Kingscourt	Level 6 Benchmark Bk	Pete Paints a Picture	3
		Level 6 Collection	Wilbur's Wild Ride	3
		Level 6 Little Books	Cake, The	3
			Family Tree, The	3
			Look What You Can Make!	3
		Level 7 Benchmark Bk	Bears, Bears, Bears	3
		Level 7 Collection	Shoo, Shoo, Shoo!	3
		Level 7 Little Books	Pet Day at School	3
			Surprise!	3
			Whose Egg is This?	3
		Level 8 Benchmark Bk	Trip into Space, A	3
		Level 8 Collection	Sam, Sam	3
		Level 8 Little Books	Absolutely Not!	3
Kingscourt Reading, Extension	Kingscourt	Set 3	Bus Ride, The	3
			Butterfly Net, The	3
			Camping	3
			Clever Little Bird	3
			Make a Glider	3
			Monster at the Beach, The	3
			Rhyme Game, The	3
			Say Cheese!	3

SERIES	PUBLISHER	SET (OR AUTHOR)	TITLE	BAND
Kingscourt Reading, Extension	Kingscourt	Set 3	Skeletons	3
			Snake's Sore Head	3
			Stella	3
			Three Goats, The	3
			Up and Down	3
			Wet Paint	3
Lighthouse	Ginn	Yellow: 1	Cecil the Caterpillar	3
		Yellow: 2	Jenny in Bed	3
		Yellow: 3	Charlie's PE Kit	3
		Yellow: 4	What Do You Want That For?	3
		Yellow: 5	Our Camping Trip	3
		Yellow: 6	Bear Hunt	3
		Yellow: 7	Carnivals Around The World	3
		Yellow: 8	Meg's Cat	3
Literacy Links Plus	Kingscourt	Early B	In the Garden	3
			Roll Over	3
		Emergent C	Ben the Bold	3
		Emergent D	Boogly, The	3
			Go Back to Sleep	3
			Timmy	3
National Geographic	Rigby	Yellow Level	Baby Shark, The	3
			New Clothes	3
			Now and Then	3
Oxford Reading Tree	OUP	Fireflies Stage 2	Hot and Cold	3
			Our Class	3
		Fireflies Stage 3	Choices	3
			Football, Football!	3
			How to be Healthy	3
			How to Draw Yourself	3
			My Week	3
		Fireflies, More – Stage 3	Building a Road	3
			Floating Boats	3
			Jumpers	3
			School Band, The	3
		Fireflies, More – Stage 4	Animal Feet	3
		Stage 2 More Stories A	Baby-sitter, The	3
			Floppy's Bath	3
			Kipper's Balloon	3
			Kipper's Birthday	3
			Spots	3
			Water Fight, The	3
		Stage 2 More Stories B	Biff's Aeroplane	3
			Chase, The	3
			Foggy Day, The	3
		Stage 3 More Stories A	At the Seaside	3
			Jumble Sale, The	3
			Kipper the Clown	3
			Snowman, The	3
			Strawberry Jam	3
		Stage 3 More Stories B	At the Pool	3
			Book Week	3

SERIES	PUBLISHER	SET (OR AUTHOR)	TITLE	BAND
Oxford Reading Tree	OUP	Stage 3 More Stories B	Bull's-eye	3
		Stage 3 Sparrows	Joe and the Bike	3
			Midge in Hospital	3
			Roy and the Budgie	3
		Stage 3 Storybooks	By the Stream	3
			Dolphin Pool, The	3
			On the Sand	3
			Rope Swing, The	3
		Stage 4 More Stories A	Poor Old Mum!	3
		Stage 4 More Stories B	Everyone Got Wet	3
			Flying Elephant, The	3
			Swap!	3
			Wet Paint	3
		Stage 4 More Stories C	Stuck in the Mud	3
			Tug of War	3
		Stage 4 Sparrows	Adam Goes Shopping	3
			Adam's Car	3
			Mosque School	3
			Yasmin's Dress	3
Pathways	Collins	Year 1	Luke's First Day	3
			My New Bike	3
			Waste	3
PM Gems	Nelson Thornes	Yellow 6	Big Helicopter, The	3
			Bingo and the Ducks	3
			Ella and the Toy Rabbit	3
			Sandy Gets a Lead	3
		Yellow 7	Flowers for Grandma	3
			Kitty Cat Runs Up a Tree	3
			Toytown Bus Helps Out, The	3
		Yellow 8	Bad Day For Little Dinosaur, A	3
			Mother Bear's Scarf	3
			Speedy Bee's Dance	3
PM Maths	Nelson Thornes	Stage B	As Heavy As	3
			Boxes, Tins and Balls	3
			Days of the Week	3
			Five and Five Are Ten	3
			From One to Eight	3
			Making Party Hats	3
			Nine Children at the Pool	3
			Seven in a Line	3
			Shapes with a Rope	3
			Six Under the Sea	3
PM Non-fiction	Nelson Thornes	Red Level	Eggs For Breakfast	3
			Look Up, Look Down	3
			Red and Blue and Yellow	3
			Roof and a Door, A	3
			Tall Things	3
			Two Eyes, Two Ears	3
PM Photo Stories	Nelson Thornes	Yellow 6	Hiding from Bella	3
			Josh Rides a Skateboard	3
			Lamby's Breakfast	3

SERIES	PUBLISHER	SET (OR AUTHOR)	TITLE	BAND
PM Photo Stories	Nelson Thornes	Yellow 7	Dino at the Park	3
			Jake and the Big Fish	3
			Zac's Train Ride	3
		Yellow 8	Birthday Kitten, The	3
			Erin Rides Tiffy	3
			Jake's Plane	3
			Rani Comes to Stay	3
PM Plus	Nelson Thornes	Yellow Level	Big Hit, The	3
			Big Yellow Castle, The	3
			Billy Can Count	3
			Bingo's Birthday	3
			Bread for the Ducks	3
			Clever Fox	3
			Crocodile and a Whale, A	3
			Dilly Duck and Dally Duck	3
			Here Come the Shapes	3
			Jolly Roger and the Treasure	3
			Jumbo	3
			Katie's Caterpillar	3
			Kitty Cat Plays Inside	3
			Leaf Boats, The	3
			Little Chimp Runs Away	3
			Little White Hen, The	3
			Look Out For Bingo	3
			Max and the Little Plant	3
			Max Goes Fishing	3
			Max Rides His Bike	3
			Mother's Day	3
			New Boots	3
			Party for Brown Mouse, The	3
			Red Squirrel Hides Some Nuts	3
			Roar Like a Tiger	3
			Sam and the Waves	3
			Sam Goes to School	3
			Speedy Bee	3
			Toytown Fire Engine, The	3
			Walk, Ride, Run	3
PM Plus Non-fiction	Nelson Thornes	Red Level	Time For Play	3
			Toys and Play	3
			Where is it Safe to Play?	3
		Yellow Level	It is Raining	3
			Making a Caterpillar	3
			Rain is Water	3
PM Storybooks	Nelson Thornes	Yellow Set A	Baby Bear Goes Fishing	3
			Ben's Dad	3
			Blackberries	3
			Brave Father Mouse	3
			Fire! Fire!	3
			Friend for Little White Rabbit, A	3
			Hermit Crab	3
			Hungry Kitten, The	3

SERIES	PUBLISHER	SET (OR AUTHOR)	TITLE	BAND
PM Storybooks	Nelson Thornes	Yellow Set A	Little Bulldozer	3
			Lucky Goes to Dog School	3
			Mumps	3
			New Baby, The	3
			Sally's Beans	3
			Seagull is Clever	3
			Where Are the Sun Hats?	3
		Yellow Set B	Baby Hippo	3
			Choosing a Puppy	3
			Football at the Park	3
			Jolly Roger, the Pirate	3
			Lucky Day for Little Dinosaur, A	3
			Sally and the Sparrows	3
			Snowy Gets a Wash	3
			Tiny and the Big Wave	3
Rigby Star	Rigby	Yellow Level	At Last!	3
			Be Quiet!	3
			Computer Game, The	3
			Curly to the Rescue	3
			Dentist, The	3
			Have You Got Everything, Colin?	3
			I Can't Open it!	3
			Lion's Dinner, The	3
			Pop! A Play	3
			Rush Hour	3
			Super Shopping	3
			What a Week!	3
			Where is Curly?	3
			Where's Our Car?	3
Rigby Star Non-fiction	Rigby	Blue Level	I Take Care of My Dog	3
		Red Level	My Chinese New Year	3
		Yellow Level	From Seedling to Tree	3
Spotlight on Fact	Collins	Y1 Toys and Games	Choosing Toys	3
Spotty Zebra	Nelson Thornes	Pink B – Ourselves	Night of Light	3
			Wiggle! Woggle	3
		Red – Change	Making Muffins	3
			Matt's Big Day	3
		Red – Ourselves	Food For Fred	3
			How Does it Work?	3
			How to Look After a Rabbit	3
			Round and Round	3
			Staying at Nan's	3
			Swimmer's Day, A	3
Story Chest	Kingscourt	Get-ready Set DD	Ice-Cream Stick	3
			Sunflower Seeds	3
		Ready-set-go Set AA	Little Meanie's Lunch	3
		Ready-set-go Set BB	Doctor Boondoggle	3
			How to Make Can Stilts	3
			Roberto's Smile	3
		Ready-set-go Set C	Pumpkin, The	3
			Sleeping Out	3

SERIES	PUBLISHER	SET (OR AUTHOR)	TITLE	BAND
Story Chest	Kingscourt	Ready-set-go Set C	What a Mess!	3
		Ready-set-go Set CC	My Mum and Dad	3
			Pet Shop	3
			Roy G. Biv	3
			Teeth	3
		Ready-set-go Set D	Danger	3
			Fizz and Splutter	3
			Grumpy Elephant	3
			Oh, Jump in a Sack	3
			Stop!	3
		Ready-set-go Set DD	Best Children in the World, The	3
			Hungry Giant's Lunch, The	3
			We'd Better Make a List	3
Story Street	Pearson	Step 2	Doctor Ravi	3
		Step 3	Aha!	3
			Ben and the Boxes	3
			Brave Mouse Part 1	3
			Brave Mouse Part 2	3
			Jojo and the Football	3
			Lost	3
			Magic Button, The	3
			Sam's Zoo	3
Storyworlds	Heinemann	Stage 4 Animal World	Max and the Cat	3
			Max and the Drum	3
			Max Wants to Fly	3
		Stage 4 Fantasy World	Pirate Pete and the Monster	3
			Pirate Pete and the Treasure Island	3
			Pirate Pete Keeps Fit	3
			Pirate Pete Loses His Hat	3
		Stage 4 Once Upon a Time	Ant and the Dove, The	3
			Little Rabbit	3
			Sun and the Wind, The	3
			Town Mouse & the Country Mouse, The	3
		Stage 4 Our World	Lucy Loses Red Ted	3
			Red Ted at the Beach	3
			Red Ted Goes to School	3
			Sam Hides Red Ted	3
		Stage 5 Animal World	Dipper and the Old Wreck	3
Web Fiction	OUP	Stage 1 (Variety)	Anansi Traps a Snake	3
		Stage 2 (Variety)	Lunch for Tig	3
			Tig	3
			Tig's Pet	3
		Stage 3 (Variety)	At the Fair	3
			Late For School	3
			Octopus's Legs	3
			Shark's Tooth	3
			Who Made This Mess?	3
		Stage 4 (Variety)	Billy Beetle	3
			Ned the Fighting Donkey	3
			Rabbit's Trick	3
Web Guided Reading	OUP	Stage 2 (Duck Green)	Baby Bird, The	3

SERIES	PUBLISHER	SET (OR AUTHOR)	TITLE	BAND
Web Guided Reading	OUP	Stage 2 (Duck Green)	Big Books and Little Books	3
			Poppy's Puppets	3
			What's in Your Lunchbox?	3
		Stage 3 (Duck Green)	Best Fish, The	3
			Little Angels	3
		Stage 4 (Duck Green)	Fly Away, Cheep	3
			Mr Jelly's Surprise	3
			That Cat!	3
Web Weavers Non-fiction	OUP	First Non-fiction: Pack A	Make a Milkshake	3
		First Non-fiction: Pack B	Growing Mr Greenhead	3
		Stage 2 First Words NF	Festivals	3
			My Pet	3
			What Do You Want to Be?	3

Band 4 BLUE

Reading Recovery Levels 9–11

NATIONAL CURRICULUM LEVEL 1

WORKING WITHIN LEVEL 1: LEARNING OPPORTUNITIES
Aligned with Phases 4/5 Progression in Phonics

- Move through text attending to meaning, print and sentence structure flexibly.

- Self-correct more rapidly on-the-run.

- Solve new words using print information and understanding of the text to try alternative pronunciations.

- Re-read to enhance phrasing and to clarify precise meaning.

- Identify constituent parts of unfamiliar two-syllable words to read correctly.

- Manage a somewhat greater variety of text genre.

- Discuss content of the text in a manner that indicates precise understanding.

TEXT CHARACTERISTICS

- greater variation in sentence patterns and content

- literacy language integrated with natural language

- any repeated language patterns are longer or act as refrains

- more lines of text on page, sometimes up to 6–8 lines

- stories have more events

- non-fiction texts include some abstract terms and impersonal sentence structures

- pictures support storyline rather than convey precise meaning so closely

- more similar-looking words appearing in text calling for flexible word-solving

THE WOBBLY TOOTH
Oxford Reading Tree

Written by Roderick Hunt
Illustrated by Alex Brychta

Published by Oxford University Press (1989)

ISBN 0 19916090 2

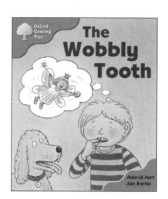

LEARNING OUTCOMES

Most children:
- read more challenging texts which can be decoded using their phonic knowledge along with automatic recognition of high-frequency words
- use syntax and context when reading for meaning
- interpret a text by reading aloud with some variety of pace and emphasis
- comment on events, characters and ideas, making imaginative links to their own experience.

TEXT SELECTION NOTES

The experience of losing teeth is particularly pertinent to 5- and 6-year-olds, and they can readily identify with the emotional interchange between family members in this story. Kipper's door sign and imaginary note from the Tooth Fairy, the unfamiliar text layout on pages 14 and 15, and the rhymed ending to the story all offer new but accessible reading experiences to young children.

LINK TO WHOLE-CLASS WORK

There is strong graphic support for the storyline, and for the social and emotional responses between the characters in this story. Prediction followed by confirmation or modification is part of being a skilled reader, and there is scope here for children to work actively between their own experience linked with the illustrations, and the print on the page. There is a range of different yet short and simple sentence constructions that offer 'real reading' opportunities.

This story, with its well-defined beginning, development and denouement, can also serve as a model for children's simple narrative writing.

TEXT INTRODUCTION

The teacher introduces the main character and asks the children to predict the title from the front cover illustration.

Yes, Kipper's got a wobbly tooth. Some children get money from the Tooth Fairy when their tooth falls out. They put it by their bed at night, and in the morning there is £1 there instead of the tooth. I wonder if Kipper gets money from the Tooth Fairy.

p. 1 *Who do you think this is in the thought bubble?*
pp. 2/3 *What do you think mum wanted to do?*
pp. 4/5 *His dad's teasing him, isn't he?*
pp. 6/7 *Here's Biff on the swing.*
pp. 8/9 *Oh! What happened?*
p. 11 *He's swallowed his tooth!*

Continue briskly page by page, encouraging children to respond, comment and relate the story to their own experience.

pp. 14/15 *How much money has Kipper got now? Do you think he's still sad?*

STRATEGY CHECK

Think about the story and check the speech marks, and try to make your reading sound like the characters talking.

INDEPENDENT READING

Teacher prompts children to check the print more closely if necessary, and attend to meaning and syntax.

p. 6 *Yes, Biff **was** on the swing. That makes sense and this word (**went**) does start with **w**. Sound all the phonemes from left to right.*
Now read it again and see if 'went' fits.
p. 11 Supply 'swallowed' if necessary. *Say 'swallowed' slowly and run your finger under that word to check the phonemes.*
p. 12 'Never mind': *Can you make that sound like Mum/Dad talking?*
p. 16 *Kipper **was** very happy, but does that word ('glad') look like **happy**? Try sounding through that word. Now start with the sentence on the page before and read the story to the end and see if it's right. Yes, they rhyme.*

RETURN TO THE TEXT

p. 14 *Let's look at all the talking. Put your left finger on the first speech mark and your right finger on the other. Now read the words in between, pretending you are Biff and Chip.*
pp. 14/15/16 Ask the children to re-read the story in pairs, taking different roles.

INDEPENDENT ACTIVITY

Ask the children to generate other words using the phoneme **oo** as in '**too**th': 'shoo', 'roof', 'proof', 'broom', 'spoon', 'droop'.

Suggest that the children write another story based on the same illustrations. Alternatively they can write their own story about losing a tooth.

SERIES	PUBLISHER	SET (OR AUTHOR)	TITLE	BAND
Alphakids	Gardner	Early Level 9	Concrete	4
			Fox and the Crow, The	4
			Giant Gingerbread Man, The	4
			Mr Wolf Tries Again	4
			Scare and Dare	4
			Sebastian	4
		Early Level 10	Great Day Out	4
			Rainforest Plants	4
			Revenge of the Three Little Pigs	4
			Sarah and Will	4
			Socks Off!	4
			Worm Song	4
		Early Level 11	Floating and Sinking	4
			Little Monkey	4
Alphakids Plus	Gardner	Early Level 8	Cat and the Mouse, The	4
			Hiding in the Sea	4
			Tidy Your Room!	4
			Train Race, The	4
		Early Level 9	Camping	4
			Fox and the Snail, The	4
			Goldilocks and the Three Bears	4
			Making Spaghetti	4
			Two Snakes	4
		Early Level 10	Baby Bear Goes Visiting	4
			Reptiles	4
			Sebastian's New Sister	4
			Who's That Knocking at My Door?	4
		Early Level 11	Billy Banana	4
		Transitional Level 12	Mice in Space	4
AlphaWorld	Gardner	Band 4: Blue	After School	4
			Dog School	4
			Our Market	4
		Level 12 (trans)	Life Cycles	4
Badger NF Guided Reading	Badger	First Facts	Friends	4
	Franklin Watts	Let's Read About Pets	Goldfish	4
	Raintree	Read and Learn	Green Foods	4
Big Cat	Collins	Blue	Bert's Band	4
			Fantastic Flying Squirrel, The	4
			Funny Fish	4
			Mojo and Weeza and the Funny Thing	4
			Percy and the Badger	4
			Robots	4
			Sounds	4
			Talk, Talk, Talk	4
			Top Dinosaurs	4
Discovery World	Heinemann	Stage C	My Bean Diary	4
		Stage D	Fun Things to Make and Do	4
Discovery World Links	Heinemann	Stage C	Tractors	4
			What Can be Recycled?	4
Dragonflies	Gardner	Blue	Don't Forget Grandma	4
			Gardener and the Scarecrow, The	4

SERIES	PUBLISHER	SET (OR AUTHOR)	TITLE	BAND
Dragonflies	Gardner	Blue	Greedy Cat's Door	4
			Halfmoon Bay	4
			Lunch for Greedy Cat	4
			My Brother	4
		Yellow/Blue	Miss Pool Is Cool	4
			Purr-fect!	4
First Facts	Badger	Level 3	Farm Animals	4
			Farm Day	4
			Friends	4
			My School	4
			Our School Week	4
			School Rules	4
			What Do I Need?	4
Four Corners	Pearson	Year 1	Matsumura's Ice Sculpture	4
			Oscar's Day	4
Genre Range	Pearson	Beginner Letters	Postcards	4
		Beginner Plays	I am Miss Cherry	4
			Poor Sam	4
		Beginner Traditional Tales	Frog Prince, The	4
			Hare and the Tortoise, The	4
		Emergent Plays	Jumbo	4
I Love Reading	Ticktock	Blue Level	Airline Pilot	4
			Animal Hospital	4
			Bug Watch	4
			Busy Trucks	4
			Dinosaur Hunters	4
			Dinosaur Plant-eaters	4
			My Cat Has Had Kittens	4
			My Dog Has Had Puppies	4
			Orang-utan Baby	4
			Scary Snakes	4
			Tiger Cub	4
			To the Rescue	4
Info Trail	Pearson	Beginner Geography	Have You Seen My Bag?	4
			Pick Up That Crisp Packet!	4
			Up the Big Hill	4
		Beginner History	This House is Too Small!	4
			Were the Old Days the Best?	4
		Beginner Science	I Grew a Sunflower Big as My Dad	4
		Emergent Geography	Don't Throw it Away	4
			Pigeon Patrol, The	4
		Emergent History	How to Dress a Queen	4
		Emergent Science	From an Acorn to an Oak Tree	4
Kingscourt Reading, Core	Kingscourt	Level 8 Little Books	Colour it My Way	4
			Polar Bears	4
		Level 9 Benchmark Bk	Tug of War, The	4
		Level 9 Collection	Bugs	4
		Level 9 Little Books	Good Morning, Who's Snoring?	4
			Hippos	4
			What's This Spider Doing?	4
		Level 10 Benchmark Bk	Ladybird, Ladybird	4

SERIES	PUBLISHER	SET (OR AUTHOR)	TITLE	BAND
Kingscourt Reading, Core	Kingscourt	Level 10 Collection	Ten Little Ducks	4
		Level 10 Little Books	Flock Watch	4
			How the Geese Saved Rome	4
			Owls	4
		Level 11 Benchmark Bk	Cow Up a Tree	4
		Level 11 Collection	Runaway Engine	4
		Level 11 Little Books	Bees and the Bear, The	4
			Down the Track	4
Kingscourt Reading, Extension	Kingscourt	Set 3	Big Bear's Socks	4
		Set 4	Balcony Garden	4
			Frogs	4
			Goldilocks and the Three Bears	4
			Grandpa's Lemonade	4
			Horse's Hiccups	4
			Jeremy's Cake	4
			Lili's Breakfast	4
			Mr Smarty Loves to Party	4
			Night Noises	4
			Pond Where Harriet Lives, The	4
			Recycle Michael	4
			Robot Crash	4
			Sky is Falling, The	4
			Swimming Lessons	4
			Tom's Trousers	4
			Who Lives Here?	4
			Wibble-Wobble	4
Lighthouse	Ginn	Blue: 1	Answer the Phone, Fiona!	4
		Blue: 2	Quiet Morning for Mum, A	4
		Blue: 3	Stop the Car!	4
		Blue: 4	Hullabaloo at the Zoo	4
		Blue: 5	It's a Gift	4
		Blue: 6	Lion's Lunch	4
		Blue: 7	No Running!	4
		Blue: 8	Sports Dictionary	4
Literacy Links Plus	Kingscourt	Contemporary Stories	Royal Dinner, The	4
			Who's in the Shed?	4
		Early A	Can I Play Outside?	4
			Just Like Grandpa	4
			Sleepy Bear	4
		Early B	Family Photos	4
			Mrs Bold	4
			Printing Machine, The	4
			Skin	4
			T J's Tree	4
			What's Around the Corner?	4
			Wobbly Tooth, The	4
			Woolly, Woolly	4
		Early C	BMX Billy	4
			Buffy's Tricks	4
			Ten Little Caterpillars	4
		Early D	Barnaby's New House, The	4

SERIES	PUBLISHER	SET (OR AUTHOR)	TITLE	BAND
Literacy Links Plus	Kingscourt	Emergent D	Noses	4
		Traditional Tale	Goldilocks and the Three Bears	4
			Little Red Hen, The	4
National Geographic	Rigby	Blue Level	Cooking Dinner	4
			Hairy Harry	4
			Night Sky, The	4
			Park, The	4
New Way	Nelson Thornes	Green Core Book	Bad Cow & other stories	4
		Green Easy Start Set A	Film Star, The	4
			Hello	4
			Postcard, The	4
			Rob Goes to Hospital ...	4
			Tim and Tom & Who Will Push Me?	4
		Green Easy Start Set B	New Tie, The	4
Oxford Reading Tree	OUP	Fireflies Stage 4	Night Animals	4
			Shells	4
		Fireflies, More – Stage 3	Patterns	4
		Fireflies, More – Stage 4	Ballet	4
			Big Cats	4
			Hello!	4
			How to Make a Fruit Salad	4
			How to Make a Puppet Theatre	4
		Stage 2 More Stories B	Floppy the Hero	4
			Kipper's Laces	4
			Wobbly Tooth, The	4
		Stage 2 Storybooks	Dream, The	4
		Stage 3 More Stories A	Kipper's Idea	4
		Stage 3 More Stories B	Barbecue, The	4
			Carnival, The	4
			Cold Day, The	4
		Stage 3 Sparrows	Midge and the Eggs	4
			Pip and the Little Monkey	4
			Pip at the Zoo	4
		Stage 3 Storybooks	Cat in the Tree, A	4
		Stage 4 More Stories A	Nobody Got Wet	4
			Weather Vane, The	4
			Wedding, The	4
		Stage 4 More Stories B	Dragon Dance, The	4
			Scarf, The	4
		Stage 4 More Stories C	Dad's Jacket	4
			Den, The	4
			Important Case, An	4
			Look Smart	4
		Stage 4 Sparrows	Lucky the Goat	4
			Yasmin and the Flood	4
		Stage 4 Storybooks	Come In!	4
			House for Sale	4
			New House, The	4
			Play, The	4
			Secret Room, The	4
			Storm, The	4

SERIES	PUBLISHER	SET (OR AUTHOR)	TITLE	BAND
Oxford Reading Tree	OUP	Stage 5 More Stories A	Monster Mistake, A	4
		Stage 5 Storybooks	Magic Key, The	4
		Traditional Tales 5-7	Goldilocks and the Three Bears	4
			Three Billy Goats Gruff, The	4
Pathways	Collins	Year 1	Animal House	4
			Five Little Men	4
			Grandad's Ears	4
			Mrs Barmy	4
			Red Bird	4
			Room Full of Light, A	4
			Sam's Bus	4
Pelican Big Bks	Pearson	Body, Wendy	One, Two, Three ... Off to the Sea!	4
			What Can You See?	4
PM Gems	Nelson Thornes	Blue 9	Beach Boat, The	4
			Fat Cat's Chair	4
			Playing Skittles	4
			Playing with Milly	4
		Blue 10	Eggs and Dandelions	4
			Fussy Heron	4
			Harry's New Hat	4
		Blue 11	Jolly Roger and the Spyglass	4
			Little Chimp Finds Some Fruit	4
			Sandy Goes to the Vet	4
PM Maths	Nelson Thornes	Stage B	Animal Graphs	4
			Ten Frogs in the Pond	4
PM Non-fiction	Nelson Thornes	Yellow Level	My Big Brother	4
			My Dad	4
			My Gran and Grandad	4
			My Little Sister	4
			Our Baby	4
			Our Mum	4
PM Photo Stories	Nelson Thornes	Blue 9	Bath-time Goggles	4
			Best Dancer, The	4
			Scary Masks, The	4
		Blue 10	Long Bike Ride, The	4
			Scruffy Runs Away	4
			Shopping with Grandma	4
		Blue 11	Apples for Tiffy	4
			Berry Cake, The	4
			Crab Hunt, The	4
			Party Clown, The	4
PM Plus	Nelson Thornes	Blue Level	Baby Bear Climbs a Tree	4
			Baby Bear's Hiding Place	4
			Beach House, The	4
			Best Hats, The	4
			Billy at School	4
			Bingo Goes to School	4
			Birthday Presents	4
			Broken Flower Pot, The	4
			Brown Mouse Gets Some Corn	4
			Brown Mouse Plays a Trick	4

SERIES	PUBLISHER	SET (OR AUTHOR)	TITLE	BAND
PM Plus	Nelson Thornes	Blue Level	Bugs for Breakfast	4
			Down by the Sea	4
			Fire on Toytown Hill, The	4
			House on the Hill, The	4
			Jack and Billy and Rose	4
			Joe Makes a House	4
			Kitty Cat and the Paint	4
			Little Chimp and Baby Chimp	4
			Little Chimp and the Bees	4
			Lost Socks	4
			Max and the Bird House	4
			Mother Tiger and Her Cubs	4
			Rabbits' Ears	4
			Sam Plays Paddle Ball	4
			Sam's Painting	4
			Swan Family, The	4
			Tom's Ride	4
			Toytown Racing Car, The	4
			Treasure Island, A	4
			Two Little Ducks Get Lost	4
PM Plus Non-fiction	Nelson Thornes	Blue Level	Making a Toy House	4
			Our House is a Safe House	4
			Our New House	4
		Yellow Level	Hot Sunny Days	4
			Sun, the Wind and the Rain, The	4
			Where Did All the Water Go?	4
PM Storybooks	Nelson Thornes	Blue Set A	Baby Bear's Present	4
			Best Cake, The	4
			Christmas Tree, The	4
			Come On, Tim	4
			Cows in the Garden	4
			Honey for Baby Bear	4
			House in the Tree, The	4
			Jane's Car	4
			Late For Football	4
			Lion and the Rabbit, The	4
			Magpie's Baking Day	4
			Mushrooms for Dinner	4
			Sally's Friends	4
			Tabby in the Tree	4
		Blue Set B	Birthday Balloons	4
			Chug the Tractor	4
			Duck With the Broken Wing, The	4
			Little Bulldozer Helps Again	4
			Lost at the Fun Park	4
			Teasing Dad	4
			Tiger Runs Away	4
			Tim's Favourite Toy	4
		Red Set A	Sally's Red Bucket	4
Rigby Star	Rigby	Blue Level	Ball Called Sam, A	4
			Bully Bear	4

SERIES	PUBLISHER	SET (OR AUTHOR)	TITLE	BAND
Rigby Star	Rigby	Blue Level	Josie and the Play	4
			Josie's New Coat	4
			Mrs Mog's Cats	4
			Space Ant	4
			Terrible Tiger, The	4
			Vroom!	4
Rigby Star Non-fiction	Rigby	Green Level	How to Make a Bird Feeder	4
Spotlight on Fact	Collins	Y1 Toys and Games	Let's Play Board Games!	4
			Telling Prog	4
			Toys and Games Around the World	4
			Toys and Games from A to Z	4
			Toys and Games in Art	4
			What Makes Toys Move?	4
Story Chest	Kingscourt	Ready-set-go Set CC	How Many Hot Dogs?	4
			Lift, The	4
			Where is Skunk?	4
		Ready-set-go Set D	Haunted House, The	4
		Ready-set-go Set DD	Blueberry Muffins	4
			Clown in the Well	4
			Fire and Water	4
			Giggle Box, The	4
			Gulp!	4
Story Street	Pearson	Step 3	Strange Street Again	4
		Step 4	Ben Gets Cross	4
			Billy's Baby	4
			Missing Shoes, The, Part 1	4
			Missing Shoes, The, Part 2	4
Storyworlds	Heinemann	Stage 5 Animal World	Dipper Gets Stuck	4
			Dipper in Danger	4
			Dipper to the Rescue	4
		Stage 5 Fantasy World	Bag of Coal, The	4
			Big Snowball, The	4
			Creepy Castle, The	4
			Fire in Wild Wood	4
		Stage 5 Once Upon a Time	Lake of Stars, The	4
			Ugly Duckling, The	4
		Stage 5 Our World	Mango Tree, The	4
			Presents	4
			Who Did it?	4
		Stage 7 Animal World	Duma and the Lion	4
Web Fiction	OUP	Stage 4 (Variety)	Alex the Ant	4
			Gordon the Clever Goat	4
		Stage 5 (Variety)	Sir Ben and the Dragon	4
			Stupid Ogre, The	4
Web Guided Reading	OUP	Stage 4 (Duck Green)	Flying Footballs	4
			I'm Not Scared	4
			Twins, The	4
		Stage 5 (Duck Green)	Hiccups!	4
			Leela's Secret Plan	4
			Snow Surprise	4
			Where's Cheep?	4

SERIES	PUBLISHER	SET (OR AUTHOR)	TITLE	BAND
Web Weavers Non-fiction	OUP	First Non-fiction: Pack A	Why Do You Need to Read?	4
			Writing	4
		First Non-fiction: Pack B	Fruit	4
			Heating Food	4
			My Diary of an Oak Tree	4
		Stage 2 First Words NF	Building Site, The	4
			Emergency!	4
			How to Make a Party Hat	4

Band 5 GREEN

Reading Recovery Levels 12–14
NATIONAL CURRICULUM LEVEL 1

WORKING WITHIN LEVEL 1: LEARNING OPPORTUNITIES
Aligned with Phase 5 Progression in Phonics

- Read fluently with attention to punctuation.

- Solve new words using print detail while attending to meaning and syntax.

- Track visually additional lines of print without difficulty.

- Manage effectively a growing variety of texts, including non-fiction.

- Discuss and interpret character and plot more fully.

- Use contents page and glossary in non-fiction books, and locate information.

TEXT CHARACTERISTICS

- varied and longer sentences

- little repetition of phrases, but unfamiliar words usually repeated

- more varied and larger number of characters involved

- events sustained over several pages

- may have larger number of words on page

- less familiar and some specialised vocabulary used

- illustrations may provide only moderate support for fiction texts

- print may be located in captions, fact boxes and diagrams in non-fiction

GUIDED READING
GREEN BAND
NON-FICTION RECOUNT

A DAY AT THE EDEN PROJECT
Big Cat

Written by Kate Petty
Photographs by Ley Honor Roberts

Published by Collins Education (2005)

ISBN 0 00 718593 6

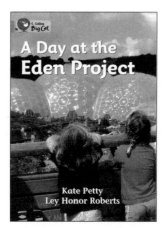

LEARNING OUTCOMES

Most children:
- make predictions using the cover and an understanding of text type
- read more challenging texts
- use meaning and syntax when reading for meaning
- read two- and three-syllable words making full use of phonic knowledge
- distinguish between fiction and non-fiction texts.

TEXT SELECTION NOTES

This modern recount written in the present tense can be found in a Guided Reading series developed by Collins in collaboration with Cliff Moon. It is lavishly illustrated with photographs that invite children to share in the family's visit and observe the plants and setting closely.

There are some key non-fiction layout features including a simple table of contents and headings, labelled photographs and a pictorial project map. The text uses children's language and responses combined with more formal language. 'Guided Reading ideas' are provided on the last two pages of the book.

LINK TO WHOLE-CLASS WORK

Simple recounts form many of the first texts that are written in infant classrooms, both by teachers and by children. Most are written in the past tense, and there is a basic level of organisation. Children are often involved in writing up a class visit or experience in simple sentences, using connectives such as 'next' and 'then', and recognise features such as contents tables, captions and maps.

Compound words and unusual vocabulary in this book provide opportunities for children to apply their knowledge of graphemes to make plausible attempts to read unknown words.

TEXT INTRODUCTION

Read the title to the group and locate Cornwall on a map.
Explain that the Eden Project is located in a vast old tin mine. Ask the children to examine the front cover and discuss what the project might be, and the reason for photos of the two girls in the foreground.

Now look through the book to see if you're right about the book being a report by the two girls of some of things they saw.

Go through the book quite quickly, checking that the children read and say the word 'biomes', and understand that the temperature changes in each one to suit different types of plants.

STRATEGY CHECK

This is a non-fiction book, so check the illustrations carefully as you read, and look out for the compound words.

INDEPENDENT READING

*Read to page 13 and try to remember all the different kinds of plants in the first **biome**.*

Listen in on individual children as they read aloud, commenting on their work-solving and the information they discover.

*Close your books. What type of climate was in the first **biome**? That's right – warm and wet. So, how many plants can you remember? I'll write them up on the whiteboard.*

Now turn to the contents page, find the section after 'The jungle', and read the rest of the book.

RETURN TO THE TEXT

Turn to pages 22 and 23. I want you to use the map to remind yourselves what happened during the visit. Talk about it first with your partner.

Ask the children to report back and write up the connectives that indicate the sequence of events: 'they started', 'then', 'next', 'after that', 'now', 'finally'.

INDEPENDENT ACTIVITY

Ask the children to hunt through the text and write
- all the words with **er**: 'over', 'bigger', 'flowers', 'closer', 'water', 'rubber', 'cooler'
- all the compound words: 'Cornwall', 'greenhouses', 'pineapples'.

SERIES	PUBLISHER	SET (OR AUTHOR)	TITLE	BAND
Alphakids	Gardner	Early Level 11	Beaks and Feet	5
			Roads and Bridges	5
			Stubborn Goat, The	5
			Tarantula	5
		Transitional Level 12	Hungry Bear, The	5
			I'm on the Phone	5
			Kim's Lunch	5
			Making Bread	5
			Sooty	5
			Sun in the Sky, The	5
		Transitional Level 13	Early One Morning	5
			Last One Picked	5
			Sebastian Gets the Hiccups	5
		Transitional Level 14	Duckling, The	5
			Paint My Room	5
			Trash or Treasure	5
		Transitional Level 15	Dragon, The	5
Alphakids Plus	Gardner	Early Level 10	My Trip	5
			Spiders	5
		Early Level 11	Circus Boy	5
		Transitional Level 12	Don't Worry	5
			Let's Make Pancakes	5
			My Pet Lamb	5
			Treasure Hunt	5
		Transitional Level 13	Busy Bird	5
			Grizzlegrots, The	5
			Growing Strawberries	5
		Transitional Level 14	Fantastic Frog Facts	5
			Hungry Baby, The	5
			Our Classroom Pet	5
			Snip! Snap!	5
		Transitional Level 16	Stop That Dog!	5
AlphaWorld	Gardner	Band 5: Green	Dangerous Plants	5
			In the Playground	5
			Kitchen Garden	5
			Rough and Smooth	5
			Wheels	5
			Wings	5
		Level 12 (trans)	At the Weekend	5
			Land Around Us, The	5
			Shadows and Shade	5
		Level 13 (trans)	Children's Farm, The	5
			Going Swimming	5
			Pushing and Pulling	5
			Tree House, The	5
		Level 14 (trans)	River, The	5
Badger NF Guided Reading	Badger	First Facts	Seasons	5
	Walker Books	Peep-hole Books	Guess What I Am?	5
	Raintree	Read and Learn	Seeds	5
Big Cat	Collins	Blue	What's Underground?	5
		Green	Day at the Eden Project, A	5

SERIES	PUBLISHER	SET (OR AUTHOR)	TITLE	BAND
Big Cat	Collins	Green	I Want a Pet!	5
			Jodie and Juggler	5
			Magic Pen, The	5
			Spines, Stings and Teeth	5
		Orange	Arthur's Fantastic Party	5
			Brave Baby, The	5
			Morris Plays Hide and Seek	5
Bright and Early Books	Collins	Seuss, Dr	Foot Book, The	5
Discovery World Links	Heinemann	Stage C	Animal Skeletons	5
			Victorian Seaside Holiday, A	5
		Stage D	Toys	5
Dragonflies	Gardner	Green	Gardener's Maze, The	5
			Hissing Bush, The	5
			Ling Lee's Surprise	5
			Me and My Dog	5
			School Band, The	5
			Skipper's Happy Tail	5
First Facts	Badger	Level 3	Seasons	5
			Stormy Weather	5
			Working Dogs	5
Four Corners	Pearson	Year 1	Beatrix Potter	5
			Dig In	5
			Fins, Wings and Legs	5
Genre Range	Pearson	Beginner Plays	What a Mess!	5
		Beginner Poetry	Nursery and Action Rhymes	5
			Songs and Riddles	5
		Emergent Comics	Bad Bert and the Bully	5
			Fatcat and the Mouse	5
			Frog Goes on Holiday	5
		Emergent Letters	Haircut Letters, The	5
			My Diary	5
		Emergent Plays	Duck Pond	5
			Sunita and the Wishing Well	5
		Emergent Traditional Tales	Goldilocks and the Three Bears	5
Info Trail	Pearson	Beginner Geography	Which Home?	5
		Beginner History	How to Write a Family Tree	5
		Beginner Science	Day I Felt Ill, The	5
			Don't Bite the Bottom Off Your Ice-cream Cone!	5
			How to Make a Feely Box	5
			Scab on the Knee, A	5
		Emergent History	London's Burning!	5
		Emergent Science	Come and Visit the Moon!	5
Kingscourt Reading, Core	Kingscourt	Level 11 Little Books	Boomerangs	5
		Level 12 Benchmark Bk	Make a Rainbow	5
		Level 12 Collection	Secret Song, The	5
		Level 12 Little Books	Eclipse	5
			How Rabbit Caught the Sun	5
			Summer and Winter	5
		Level 13 Benchmark Bk	Lost	5
		Level 13 Collection	Me, Myself and I	5
		Level 13 Little Books	Grandma's Pie	5

SERIES	PUBLISHER	SET (OR AUTHOR)	TITLE	BAND
Kingscourt Reading, Core	Kingscourt	Level 13 Little Books	Scrapbook of Me	5
		Level 14 Benchmark Bk	Morris Mouse	5
		Level 14 Collection	Surprise!	5
		Level 14 Little Books	Party Animals	5
			Picture-Book People	5
			Snake's Reward	5
		Level 15 Little Books	Town Mouse and Country Mouse	5
Kingscourt Reading, Extension	Kingscourt	Set 5	Bird Song	5
			Boy Who Tried to Hide, The	5
			Celebrations	5
			Daughter of the Sun	5
			Don't Look Down!	5
			Finger Puppets, Finger Plays	5
			Gonna Bird, The	5
			Little Red Hen, The	5
			Malcolm Magpie	5
			My Scrapbook	5
			Whistle Tooth, The	5
			Munching Monster	5
Lighthouse	Ginn	Green: 1	Hats for the Carnival	5
		Green: 2	Whale's Year, The	5
		Green: 3	Jasmine's Duck	5
		Green: 4	Robby in the River	5
		Green: 5	Baked Beans	5
		Green: 6	Goal!	5
		Green: 7	Day the Sky Fell Down, The	5
		Green: 8	Laughing Hyena	5
Literacy Links Plus	Kingscourt	Early A	Sally's Picture	5
		Early B	Grandma's Memories	5
			Grump, The	5
			If You Like Strawberries	5
			My Monster Friends	5
			Odd Socks	5
			Pete's New Shoes	5
			Wide Mouthed Frog, The	5
		Early C	Bossy Bettina	5
			Dad Didn't Mind at All	5
			Dad's Bathtime	5
			Hungry Chickens, The	5
			In the Park	5
			No Extras	5
			What is Bat?	5
			When I'm Older	5
		Early D	Daniel	5
			I Have a Question, Grandma	5
			My House	5
			Papa's Spaghetti	5
			Two Little Mice, The	5
		Fluent D	In the City of Rome	5
National Geographic	Rigby	Green Level	How Does My Bike Work?	5
		Orange Level	Going Fishing	5

SERIES	PUBLISHER	SET (OR AUTHOR)	TITLE	BAND
National Geographic	Rigby	Orange Level	Machines Make Fun Rides	5
		Turquoise Level	Jack's Boat	5
New Way	Nelson Thornes	Green Easy Start Set A	Bad Apple & The Carrot Field, The	5
		Green Easy Start Set B	Cup of Tea, A	5
			It's Not Fair	5
			Secret & The Birthday Surprise, The	5
			Three Kings & Kim's Star, The	5
		Green Platform Books	Big Box & other stories, The	5
			Camping Holiday & other stories, The	5
			Deb's Secret Wish & other stories	5
			Red Doll & other stories, The	5
			Three Billy Goats Gruff, The	5
Oxford Reading Tree	OUP	Fireflies Stage 4	Grandad and Me	5
		Fireflies Stage 5	Magic Tricks	5
		Stage 4 More Stories A	Balloon, The	5
			Camcorder, The	5
			Great Race, The	5
		Stage 5 More Stories A	Underground Adventure	5
			Vanishing Cream	5
			Whatsit, The	5
		Stage 5 More Stories B	Camping Adventure	5
			Mum to the Rescue	5
			New Baby, The	5
			New Classroom, A	5
			Noah's Ark Adventure	5
			Scarecrows	5
		Stage 5 More Stories C	Adventure Park, The	5
			Dad's Run	5
			Drawing Adventure	5
			Kipper and the Trolls	5
			Safari Adventure	5
			Sleeping Beauty	5
		Stage 5 Storybooks	Castle Adventure	5
			Dragon Tree, The	5
			Gran	5
			Pirate Adventure	5
			Village in the Snow	5
		Stage 6 & 7 Stories	In the Garden	5
Pathways	Collins	Year 1	Divali Party, The	5
			Firefighters	5
			Let's Have a Dog	5
			Monster's Baking Day	5
			Our Place	5
			Pack it Up, Ben	5
Pelican Big Bks	Pearson	Body, Wendy	Anna's Amazing Multi-coloured Glasses	5
		Body, Wendy	Whatever the Weather	5
		Cullimore, Stan	Red Riding Hood	5
		McKee, David	Not Now, Bernard	5
		Waddell, Martin	How Billy Duck Learned to Swim	5
PM Gems	Nelson Thornes	Green 12	Little Chimp and the Buffalo	5
			Max Saves a Frog	5

SERIES	PUBLISHER	SET (OR AUTHOR)	TITLE	BAND
PM Gems	Nelson Thornes	Green 12	Prize Day	5
			Woman and the Tiny Bird, The	5
		Green 13	Brad's Birthday Cake	5
			Grandad's Visit	5
			Relay Race, The	5
		Green 14	Clever Jackals, The	5
			Matt's Good Idea	5
			Telling the Truth	5
PM Non-fiction	Nelson Thornes	Blue Level	Dentist, The	5
			Doctor, The	5
			Hairdresser, The	5
			Optometrist, The	5
			Our Parents	5
			Teacher, The	5
PM Photo Stories	Nelson Thornes	Green 12	Anya's Camera	5
			Spinning Tops	5
			Tulips For My Teacher	5
		Green 13	Dancing Gingerbread	5
			Fish Called Goggles, A	5
			Frog Under the Tree, The	5
			Noodle Race, The	5
		Green 14	Late For the Party	5
			Picnic Tree, The	5
			Pony Club, The	5
PM Plus	Nelson Thornes	Green Level	Bears and the Magpie, The	5
			Classroom Caterpillars, The	5
			Coco's Bell	5
			Crow and the Pot, The	5
			Donkey in the Lion's Skin, The	5
			Fawn in the Forest, The	5
			Friend for Max, A	5
			Hospital Party	5
			Jordan's Football	5
			Jungle Frogs, The	5
			Katie's Butterfly	5
			Little Chimp and the Termites	5
			Locked In	5
			Lollipop, the Old Car	5
			Look in the Garden	5
			Lost Keys, The	5
			Max and Jake	5
			Nest on the Beach, The	5
			New Glasses for Max	5
			Picnic Boat, The	5
			Popcorn Fun	5
			Red Squirrel Adventure	5
			Sam's Haircut	5
			Skipping Rope, The	5
			Snowball, the White Mouse	5
			Swimming with a Dragon	5
			Teasing Mum	5

SERIES	PUBLISHER	SET (OR AUTHOR)	TITLE	BAND
PM Plus	Nelson Thornes	Green Level	Three Little Mice in Trouble	5
			Tree Horse, A	5
			Wheelbarrow Garden, The	5
PM Plus Non-fiction	Nelson Thornes	Blue Level	Animal Homes	5
			Building a House	5
			Houses and Homes	5
		Green Level	Families and Feasts	5
			Feeding the Lambs	5
			Healthy Food	5
			Where Does Food Come From?	5
PM Storybooks	Nelson Thornes	Blue Set A	Lion and the Mouse, The	5
			Locked Out	5
		Green Set A	Ben's Tooth	5
			Brave Triceratops	5
			Candlelight	5
			Clever Penguins, The	5
			Cross Country Race	5
			Flood, The	5
			Fox Who Foxed, The	5
			Househunting	5
			Island Picnic, The	5
			Little Red Bus, The	5
			Mrs Spider's Beautiful Web	5
			Naughty Ann, The	5
			Pepper's Adventure	5
			Pete Little	5
			Ten Little Garden Snails	5
			Waving Sheep, The	5
		Green Set B	After the Flood	5
			Babysitter, The	5
			Father Bear's Surprise	5
			Flying Fish, The	5
			Joey	5
			Rescue, The	5
			Snow on the Hill	5
			Try Again, Hannah	5
Rigby Star	Rigby	Green Level	Clever Chick, The	5
			Fantastic Pumpkin, The	5
			Josie Goes on Holiday	5
			Singing Giant, The (play)	5
			Singing Giant, The (story)	5
			Stone Soup	5
			Wind and the Sun, The	5
			Yo-Yo a Go-Go	5
		Orange Level	No Ball Games!	5
Rigby Star Non-fiction	Rigby	Blue Level	Make Your Own Monster!	5
		Green Level	Animal Feet	5
			Camping	5
		Orange Level	Is it a Fruit?	5
Story Chest	Kingscourt	Stage 2	Birthday Cake, The	5
			Help Me	5

SERIES	PUBLISHER	SET (OR AUTHOR)	TITLE	BAND
Story Chest	Kingscourt	Stage 2	Kick-a-Lot Shoes, The	5
		Stage 3	Yum and Yuk	5
		Stage 4	Barrel Of Gold, The	5
Story Street	Pearson	Step 4	Ben and the Pop Star	5
			Moon Adventure	5
			Rope That Cow!	5
			Spock the Donkey	5
			Story Time with Mick	5
		Step 5	Babysitter, The	5
			Day at the Beach, A, Part 1	5
			Day at the Beach, A, Part 2	5
			Looking After Pip	5
Storyworlds	Heinemann	Stage 5 Once Upon a Time	Straw House, The	5
			Wolf and the Kids, The	5
		Stage 5 Our World	Grandma's Surprise	5
		Stage 6 Fantasy World	Slug, the Sea Monster	5
		Stage 6 Once Upon a Time	Cooking Pot, The	5
			Gingerbread Man, The	5
			Old Woman Who Lived in a Vinegar Bottle, The	5
			Princess and the Pea, The	5
		Stage 7 Animal World	Kiboko and the Water Snake	5
			Mamba and the Crocodile Bird	5
			Twiga and the Moon	5
		Stage 7 Fantasy World	Magic Boots, The	5
Sunshine Readers	Gardner	Light Blue Level Supplementary	Rescue!	5
		Orange Level Supplementary	Busking	5
			Graffiti	5
Web Fiction	OUP	Stage 4 (Variety)	Wizard's Hat, The	5
		Stage 5 (Variety)	Forest Giants, The	5
			Genie in the Bottle, The	5
			Sir Ben and the Monster	5
			Sir Ben and the Robbers	5
Web Guided Reading	OUP	Stage 5 (Duck Green)	Dragon Kite	5
			Wiz	5
Web Weavers Non-fiction	OUP	First Non-fiction: Pack A	How Do You Sleep?	5
			Ladybird, Ladybird	5

Band 6   ORANGE

Reading Recovery Levels 15–16

NATIONAL CURRICULUM LEVEL 1

WORKING TOWARDS LEVEL 2: LEARNING OPPORTUNITIES
Aligned with Phases 5/6 Progression in Phonics

- Get started on fiction after briefer introductions and without relying so heavily on illustrations.

- Examine non-fiction layout and use the contents page to select which sections of a book to read.

- Read longer phrases and more complex sentences.

- Blend phonemes in unfamiliar words more fluently, cross-checking with meaning and syntax.

- Attend to a greater range of punctuation and text layout.

- Search for and use familiar syllables within words to read longer words.

- Infer meaning from the text.

- Check information in text with illustrations, particularly in non-fiction, and comment on content.

- Begin to use appropriate terminology when discussing different types of text.

TEXT CHARACTERISTICS

- stories are longer, up to 250–300 words

- increased proportion of space allocated to print rather than pictures

- illustrations support overall meaning of text

- more literary language used

- sentence structures becoming more complex

- range of text provision, e.g. plays, simple poetry, simple non-fiction of different types

- non-fiction texts contain more formal sentences and a widening range of unfamiliar terms

SHIMBIR
Dragonflies

Written by Alan Bagnall
Illustrated by Don DeMacedo

Published by Learning Media (2006)
Distributed by Gardner Education

ISBN 0 790 31720 6

LEARNING OUTCOMES

Most children:
- use titles, cover pages and pictures to predict the content of unfamiliar texts
- give reasons why some things happen in stories
- make imaginative links to their own experiences
- apply phonic knowledge and skills as the prime approach to reading unfamiliar words, and check with the storyline
- retell stories, ordering events using story language.

TEXT SELECTION NOTES

It was Anisha's first day at school in a new country. She could not speak English but she painted a 'shimbir' singing in a tree. Another girl in the class describes how the teacher worked with the class to write a simple report based on Anisha's picture, which her classmates also illustrated. On the way home with Anisha and her mother, they see some birds and can all use Anisha's word 'shimbir' to communicate.

This simple little story provides the basis for discussion about the feeling of isolation created by language barriers. The teacher effectively draws Anisha into the heart of the class activity and enables her to share her knowledge with all of the children. The readers must infer this theme as it is not overtly described, so there is plenty to discuss in a Guided Reading setting.

LINK TO WHOLE-CLASS WORK

Children in Year 2 are becoming aware of themes in stories, and can identify with the way various characters behave based on their own experiences. There is a clear link with the PSHE curriculum. The issue of integration and communication is rarely dealt with in simple reading books, so this story is especially valuable.

There is a wide range of medium frequency words in this story, some two- and three-syllable words and common verb inflections that link appropriately with whole-class work.

TEXT INTRODUCTION

Ask the children to read the title, author and illustrator of the book using their phonic knowledge. Use the pictures on the front and back covers and the blurb as a basis for a brief discussion about the challenge of starting school in a new country unable to speak the language.

Open the book at page 3. Here is Anisha. The girl on the other side of the teacher is the girl who is telling us this story. Look through the book. What do you notice? Yes, in the middle there's the book called Shimbir made by the class.

STRATEGY CHECK

After you've blended the phonemes to read a new word, check whether it makes sense.

INDEPENDENT READING

Observe different children and listen in on individuals, praising and prompting appropriately, for example:

p. 4 (**proudly**) *I like the way you sounded the phonemes right through that word, and then read the sentence again. Does 'proudly' make sense? Yes, it **is** beautiful!*
p. 4 (**beginning**) *How many syllables does this word have? Now read each one and blend them together. Carry on to the end of the sentence. What do we know about Anisha? Yes, she has come from another country.*

RETURN TO THE TEXT

Discuss with the children the theme of the story – namely the integration of a new child into the class by the teacher, and the gesture of her classmate in walking home with her, for example:

Why do you think the teacher decided to make a class book using Anisha's painting on the cover? Who do you think painted the other bird pictures? Why did everyone laugh when Anisha called out 'Shimbir!'

How do you think you'd feel if you couldn't speak to anyone in your class? I want you to work with a partner and take turns in pretending that you are Anisha. You've just come home from school and you're telling your Grandpa what happened and how you felt at school.

INDEPENDENT ACTIVITY

Ask the children to go through the book carefully and write down all the words with **-ed**, **-ing**, **-ly** and **-ful** endings.

SERIES	PUBLISHER	SET (OR AUTHOR)	TITLE	BAND
Alphakids	Gardner	Transitional Level 13	Bakery, The	6
			Lost in the Park	6
			Snails	6
		Transitional Level 14	Big Dog, The	6
			Elves and the Shoemaker, The	6
			Insects	6
		Transitional Level 15	Butterfly, the Bird, the Beetle and Me, The	6
			Looking After Chickens	6
			We Need More Trees!	6
		Transitional Level 16	Animal Diggers	6
			Loudest Sneeze, The	6
			My Shells	6
			My Street	6
			School News, The	6
		Transitional Level 17	Sea Stars	6
		Extending Level 18	Rosie Moon	6
Alphakids Plus	Gardner	Early Level 9	Whales	6
		Early Level 11	Flying Machines	6
			Gorillas	6
			Your Amazing Body	6
		Transitional Level 12	Looking Like Plants	6
		Transitional Level 13	Getting Around	6
			Tigers	6
			Trail Riding	6
		Transitional Level 14	Making Pots with Dad	6
			Seahorses	6
		Transitional Level 15	Hunting in the Dark	6
			Last Word, The	6
			Shut in the Barn	6
			Silva the Seal	6
		Transitional Level 16	Three Wishes, The	6
		Transitional Level 17	Amazing Ants	6
			Dancing Dudley	6
			Princess Jo	6
		Extending Level 18	Cheerful Cricket, The	6
AlphaWorld	Gardner	Band 6: Orange	After the Storm	6
			Present For Our Teacher, A	6
			Saving Up	6
			Storm Is Coming, A	6
		Band 7: Turquoise	Seeds on the Move	6
		Level 14 (trans)	At Lunchtime	6
			Day at the Market, A	6
		Level 15 (trans)	Amazing Sea Lizards	6
			Magnets	6
			Mighty Mountains	6
			Special Places at School	6
		Level 16 (trans)	Coral Reef Diary	6
			In the Treetops	6
			Looking in Mirrors	6
			Shark Attack!	6
		Level 17 (trans)	Silkworms	6

SERIES	PUBLISHER	SET (OR AUTHOR)	TITLE	BAND
Badger NF Guided Reading	Chrysalis	Baby Animals	Chick	6
	Evans Bros	Rainbows	Caterpillar Story, The	6
	Raintree	Read and Learn	Divali	6
	A&C Black	Science Buzzwords	Is it Shiny?	6
Beginner Books	Collins	Seuss, Dr	Green Eggs and Ham	6
			Hop on Pop	6
			I Can Read With My Eyes Shut	6
		Stone, Rosetta	Because a Little Bug Went Ka-choo!	6
Big Cat	Collins	Green	Big Cat Babies	6
			Nick Butterworth: Making Books	6
		Orange	Bounce, Catch, Kick, Throw	6
			Kind Emma	6
			Letter to New Zealand, A	6
		Turquoise	Stone Cutter, The	6
Bright and Early Books	Collins	Seuss, Dr	Great Day for Up!	6
Discovery World Links	Heinemann	Stage D	Animal Rescue	6
Dragonflies	Gardner	Orange	Finding Tibs	6
			Hole in the King's Sock, The	6
			Is That an Earthquake?	6
			My Name is Shoshana	6
			Pop! Pop! Pop!	6
			Shimbir	6
Four Corners	Pearson	Year 1	Eat Your Vegetables!	6
			Eva the Beekeeper	6
			Follow a River	6
			Let's Make Music	6
		Year 2	Fun With Shadows	6
Genre Range	Pearson	Emergent Letters	Ben's Get Well Cards	6
		Emergent Traditional Tales	Blue Jackal, The	6
I Love Reading	Ticktock	Orange Level	Airline Pilot	6
			Animal Hospital	6
			Bug Watch	6
			Orang-utan Baby	6
			Scary Snakes	6
			Tiger Cub	6
Info Trail	Pearson	Beginner Geography	How to Read the Sky	6
		Emergent Geography	Come to My Party!	6
			Is Lightning Most Frightening?	6
		Emergent Science	How to Look After a Rat	6
			Is Simba Happy in the Zoo?	6
Kingscourt Reading, Core	Kingscourt	Level 13 Little Books	Body Talk	6
		Level 15 Benchmark Bk	Shoe Grabber, The	6
		Level 15 Collection	Mice	6
		Level 15 Little Books	Cat-Flap Trap, The	6
			Mice at School	6
		Level 16 Benchmark Bk	Fight on the Hill, The	6
		Level 16 Collection	Something is There	6
		Level 16 Little Books	Brave Little Mouse	6
			Dinosaur Discovery	6
			Horns, Scales, Claws, and Tails	6
		Level 17 Little Books	Dog School	6

SERIES	PUBLISHER	SET (OR AUTHOR)	TITLE	BAND
Kingscourt Reading, Extension	Kingscourt	Set 5	Man in the Moon, The	6
		Set 6	Dear Grandma	6
			Down in the Woods	6
			Families	6
			How Bat Learned to Fly	6
			How the Camel Got His Hump	6
			Lion Talk	6
			Meet Me at the Water Hole	6
			Off to the Shop	6
			Shoo, Fly!	6
			Shopping List, The	6
			Ski Lesson, The	6
			That's the Life!	6
			What Am I Going to Be?	6
			Winter	6
			Year With Mother Bear, A	6
Lighthouse	Ginn	Orange: 1	Try Again, Emma	6
		Orange: 2	Animal Tails	6
		Orange: 3	Greedy King, The	6
		Orange: 4	Jolly Hungry Jack	6
		Orange: 5	Jo the Model Maker	6
		Orange: 6	Dog From Outer Space, The	6
		Orange: 7	Dream Team, The	6
		Orange: 8	Two Baby Elephants	6
Literacy Links Plus	Kingscourt	Early C	Boxes	6
			Crab at the Bottom of the Sea, The	6
			Gregor, The Grumblesome Giant	6
			Hippo's Hiccups	6
			Making Caterpillars and Butterflies	6
			Only an Octopus	6
			Philippa and the Dragon	6
			Pizza For Dinner	6
		Early D	Deer and the Crocodile, The	6
			Dinosaur's Cold, The	6
			Fastest Gazelle, The	6
			Frog Princess, The	6
			Mice	6
			Queen's Parrot, The	6
			Rice Cakes	6
			Too Much Noise	6
			Why Elephants Have Long Noses	6
			Wind and Sun	6
		Fluent A	Knit, Knit, Knit, Knit	6
			Tommy's Treasure	6
		Traditional Tale	Jack and the Beanstalk	6
National Geographic	Rigby	Green Level	Mighty Machines	6
			People Live in the Desert	6
		Orange Level	Wind Power	6
New Way	Nelson Thornes	Blue Core Book	Dressing Up & other stories	6
		Blue Parallel Books	Blue Rabbit & other stories, The	6
		Green Easy Start Set B	Big-head & The Greedy Dog	6

SERIES	PUBLISHER	SET (OR AUTHOR)	TITLE	BAND
New Way	Nelson Thornes	Green Platform Books	Little Red Hen & other stories	6
			Paper Boy & other stories, The	6
			Two Animal Stories	6
Oxford Reading Tree	OUP	Fireflies Stage 4	From Curry to Rice	6
			World Instruments	6
		Fireflies Stage 5	E-mails Home	6
		Fireflies, More – Stage 5	Julia Donaldson, A Biography	6
			Seaside, Then and Now, The	6
			Sharks	6
			Unusual Birds	6
		Stage 5 More Stories A	It's Not Fair	6
		Stage 6 & 7 More Stories B	Dad's Grand Plan	6
			Don't Be Silly	6
			Mirror Island	6
		Stage 6 & 7 Stories	Kipper and the Giant	6
			Land of the Dinosaurs	6
			Robin Hood	6
		Stage 6 More Stories A	Christmas Adventure	6
			Fright in the Night, A	6
			Go-kart Race, The	6
			Laughing Princess, The	6
			Rotten Apples	6
			Shiny Key, The	6
		Stage 7 More Stories C	Australian Adventure	6
			Power Cut, The	6
			Sea Mystery, A	6
		Stage 8 Stories	Kidnappers, The	6
		Traditional Tales 5–7	Donkey That Sneezed, The	6
			Jack and the Beanstalk	6
Pathways	Collins	Year 1	Davina and the Dinosaurs	6
			Hop, Hop, Kangaroo	6
			Owl's Party	6
			Tadpoles	6
			Watch Out!	6
		Year 2	Grabber	6
			Miss Blossom	6
			Red Riding Hood (play)	6
Pelican Big Bks	Pearson	Dupasquier, Philippe	Dear Daddy ...	6
		Palmer, Sue	Simple Rhyming Dictionary, A	6
		Waddell, Martin	Duck In The Hat, The	6
PM Non-fiction	Nelson Thornes	Green Level	In the Afternoon	6
			In the Morning	6
			Walking in the Autumn	6
			Walking in the Spring	6
			Walking in the Summer	6
			Walking in the Winter	6
		Orange Level	Budgies	6
			Cats	6
			Dogs	6
			Goldfish	6
			Guinea Pigs	6

SERIES	PUBLISHER	SET (OR AUTHOR)	TITLE	BAND
PM Non-fiction	Nelson Thornes	Orange Level	Mice	6
PM Plus	Nelson Thornes	Orange Level	Ant and the Dove, The	6
			Big Bad Wolf, The	6
			Bike for Alex, A	6
			Blow-away Kite, The	6
			Chooky	6
			Goats in the Turnip Field, The	6
			Jordan at the Big Game	6
			Lions and the Buffaloes, The	6
			Little Blue Horse, The	6
			Little Work Plane, The	6
			Look Out!	6
			Mice Have a Meeting, The	6
			More Spaghetti!	6
			Rocket Ship, The	6
			Saving Hoppo	6
			Secret Cave, The	6
			Swoop!	6
			Triceratops and the Crocodiles, The	6
			Work Helicopter, The	6
			Youngest Giraffe, The	6
PM Plus Non-fiction	Nelson Thornes	Green Level	Food is Fun	6
			Making Party Food	6
		Orange Level	Games We Play	6
			Living and Growing	6
			Our Bodies	6
			Our Clothes	6
PM Storybooks	Nelson Thornes	Orange Set A	Biggest Tree, The	6
			Dinosaur Chase	6
			Jack and Chug	6
			Toby and BJ	6
			Toby and the Big Tree	6
			Toy Farm, The	6
		Orange Set B	Jessica in the Dark	6
			Just One Guinea Pig	6
			Mitch to the Rescue	6
			Pterosaur's Long Flight	6
			Sarah and the Barking Dog	6
			Toby and the Big Red Van	6
		Orange Set C	Busy Beavers, The	6
			Careful Crocodile, The	6
			Lost in the Forest	6
			Rebecca and the Concert	6
			Roller Blades for Luke	6
			Two Little Goldfish	6
PM Traditional Tales	Nelson Thornes	Orange Level	Chicken-Licken	6
			Gingerbread Man, The	6
			Little Red Hen, The	6
			Tale of the Turnip, The	6
			Three Billy Goats Gruff, The	6
			Three Little Pigs, The	6

SERIES	PUBLISHER	SET (OR AUTHOR)	TITLE	BAND
Rigby Star	Rigby	Orange Level	Chloe the Chameleon	6
			Fizzkid Liz	6
			Giant and the Frippit, The	6
			Hot Surprise, The	6
			How Turtle Got His Shell	6
Rigby Star Non-fiction	Rigby	Green Level	How Does Water Change?	6
		Orange Level	Clay Creatures	6
Spotlight on Fact	Collins	Y1 Toys and Games	Toys of the Past 50 Years	6
Story Chest	Kingscourt	Stage 2	Pirates, The	6
			Roly-Poly	6
			Sun Smile	6
			Wet Grass	6
		Stage 3	Dragon, The	6
			Hungry Monster	6
			Jack-in-the-Box	6
			Let Me in	6
Story Street	Pearson	Step 5	Ben and the Bird	6
			Clang!	6
			Pirates Ahoy!	6
		Step 6	Bad Bert in Trouble	6
			Dog in School	6
			Losing Lucky	6
			Rubbish Monster, The	6
Storyworlds	Heinemann	Stage 6 Animal World	Harry's Elephant	6
			Harry's Monkey	6
			Harry's Seal	6
			Harry's Snake	6
		Stage 6 Fantasy World	Flora to the Rescue	6
			Magic Trident, The	6
			Olly the Octopus	6
		Stage 6 Our World	Big Boots	6
			Castle, The	6
			Lost Costume, The	6
			School Fair, The	6
		Stage 7 Fantasy World	Magic Coat, The	6
			Magic Hat, The	6
			Magic Shoes, The	6
		Stage 7 Once Upon a Time	Elves and the Shoemaker, The	6
			Frog Prince, The	6
			Pied Piper, The	6
			Tug of War, The	6
		Stage 7 Our World	Bouncer Comes to Stay	6
			Cricket Bat Mystery, The	6
			New Boy, The	6
			Next Door Neighbour, The	6
		Stage 8 Animal World	Bear That Wouldn't Growl, The	6
			Elephant That Forgot, The	6
			Shark With No Teeth, The	6
			Snake That Couldn't Hiss, The	6
		Stage 8 Fantasy World	Kim and the Computer Giant	6
Sunshine Readers	Gardner	Light Blue Level	Big Rad	6

SERIES	PUBLISHER	SET (OR AUTHOR)	TITLE	BAND
Sunshine Readers	Gardner	Light Blue Level	Forgetful Giraffe	6
			Skipper McFlea	6
			That's My Boy!	6
		Light Blue Level Supplementary	Day the Gorilla Came to School, The	6
			Rose Rest-home, The	6
			Stuck on an Island	6
		Orange Level	20 Questions	6
			Betcha!	6
			Dolphin in the Net, A	6
			Helping Hand, A	6
			This is a Bad Day!	6
			Too Good to Waste	6
			Trouble at the Supermarket	6
			Vegetables Make Me Laugh	6
		Orange Level Supplementary	Dad and the Mosquito	6
			Rainbow Fish, The	6
Web Guided Reading	OUP	Stage 6 (Duck Green)	Rescue, The	6
		Stage 7 (Duck Green)	Corker, The	6
			Magic Puppet, The	6
			Moon Cheese	6
			Year at Duck Green, A	6
Web Weavers Non-fiction	OUP	Non-fiction – Toys	How to Make Toys from the Past	6
			My Toys, Gran's Toys	6

Band 7 Turquoise

Reading Recovery Levels 17–18
WORKING TOWARDS LEVEL 2

WORKING TOWARDS LEVEL 2: LEARNING OPPORTUNITIES
Aligned with Phases 5/6 Progression in Phonics

- Extract meaning from the text while reading with less dependence on illustrations.

- Approach different genres with increasing flexibility.

- Use punctuation and text layout to read with a greater range of expression and control.

- Sustain reading through longer sentence structures and paragraphs.

- Tackle a higher ratio of more complex words using known vocabulary, phonic knowledge and syllables.

- Find a way around alphabetically ordered texts such as indexes, glossaries and dictionaries.

TEXT CHARACTERISTICS

- elaborated episodes and events

- more extended descriptions

- more use of literary phrasing

- may have more print, more illustrations and more elaborate layout on the page

- more unusual and challenging vocabulary, particularly in non-fiction

- illustrations provide a lower level of support in fictional texts, and include graphs, maps and diagrams in non-fiction

- non-fiction texts contain longer, more formal sentences, though still with some repeated terms and structures

GUIDED READING

TURQUOISE BAND

NON-FICTION

DIARY OF A SUNFLOWER
Kingscourt/McGraw-Hill

**Written by Chelsea Evans
and Britney Jannsen**

Distributed by Kingscourt Publishing Ltd 2000

ISBN 0 7901 2131 X

LEARNING OUTCOMES

Most children:
- use key structural features of non-fiction text
- read and explain a range of headings, labels, diagrams, maps, instructions
- use simple organisational features such as arrows, lines, boxes, keys to indicate sequences and relationships
- know how to tackle unfamiliar words that are not completely decodable
- use syntax and context to build up their store of vocabulary when reading for meaning
- spell new words from reading linked to particular topics
- identify simple questions about a topic and use text to find the answers.

TEXT SELECTION NOTES

A 'handwritten' diary format covering 12 weeks from spring to the end of summer provides an overall structure for this unusually rich, attractive and compact text.

Within a personalised account featuring planting procedures, growth measurement, botanical features and the life cycle of a sunflower, there are mini-sections on the compass, reference to a field of sunflowers matching Van Gogh's famous painting, and the use of sunflower seed as a crop.

LINK TO WHOLE-CLASS WORK

The Shared Reading of non-fiction texts and the language and terminology associated with them is an important feature of the Key Stage 1 curriculum. Using a book such as this in Guided Reading enables individual children to use a wide range of this language and terminology themselves as they read and discuss.

TEXT INTRODUCTION

Let's read the title and the front cover. Look through the book and note how it's set out. What do you notice? What type of book do you think it is?

*p. 2 This page is headed **Week 1**, **Day 1**. Why? Check the title again. Can you find other pages set out like a diary?*
p. 3 There are four photos on this page with arrows joining them. Why? Do you know what this is called? (Procedure)
Arrows are used on another page. Can you find them? (p. 8)
Why are they used here?

STRATEGY CHECK

We don't usually read non-fiction books from cover to cover.
Check the headings carefully and just read the diary sections first.
Then we'll read the special sections separately.
Think about what happens as the sunflowers grow, and get ready to talk about the different diary entries when you have finished reading.
Make sure you check the photos carefully as you read.

INDEPENDENT READING

*p. 6 (**measured**) Read through this word. Does it sound like a word you know? Check the photo to see what the girl is doing.*
p. 7 I like the way you paused after each comma, and made it sound like talking.
Why is it important to save some of the sunflower seeds?

RETURN TO THE TEXT

Why are the leaves called the plant's 'food factory'?
Let's turn to pages 8 and 9 and find out what the different parts of the sunflower are named.
Study the chart on page 15 and find out how long it took the sunflowers to reach full bloom.
See if you can find out what sunflower seeds are used for.

INDEPENDENT ACTIVITY

Plant some sunflower seeds, beans or other types of seed following the instructions. Ask the children to write a diary following their development.

Learn to spell topic words such as: 'soil', 'seedling', 'soak', 'water', 'leaf'/'leaves', 'petals'. Write labels for a display.

SERIES	PUBLISHER	SET (OR AUTHOR)	TITLE	BAND
Alphakids	Gardner	Transitional Level 15	Sebastian's Special Present	7
			Space Travel	7
		Transitional Level 16	Predators	7
		Transitional Level 17	Animal Builders	7
			Dress-up Parade, The	7
			Enjoy! Enjoy!	7
			Lonely Troll, The	7
		Extending Level 18	Betty Boots	7
			If I Were Invisible ...	7
			Sebastian Tidies Up	7
		Extending Level 19	Great Sebastian, The	7
		Extending Level 20	Bird Hide, The	7
Alphakids Plus	Gardner	Transitional Level 15	Crocodile Watching	7
		Transitional Level 16	Crabs	7
			Seashore Plants	7
			Skate Rider	7
		Transitional Level 17	My Grandpa Plants the Rainforest	7
			Sharks	7
		Extending Level 18	City and Country	7
			Farmyard Friends	7
			Veronica Who Lived in a Vinegar Bottle	7
		Extending Level 19	Mice in School	7
		Extending Level 20	Finding Rainbow	7
AlphaWorld	Gardner	Band 7: Turquoise	Classroom Animals	7
			Eyes	7
		Level 14 (trans)	Mushrooms and Toadstools	7
		Level 17 (trans)	Tunnels	7
			We Made a Dragon	7
			What Am I?	7
		Level 18 (ext)	Frog Alert	7
			Let's Party	7
			Star Gazing	7
Badger NF Guided Reading	Aladdin/Watts	Reading About	Dinosaurs	7
			Things on Wheels	7
	Chrysalis	Veronica Watts	My First Cat	7
Beginner Books	Collins	Le Seig, Theo	Ten Apples Up On Top	7
		Seuss, Dr	Cat in the Hat, The	7
Big Cat	Collins	Orange	Fire! Fire!	7
			How to Make Pop-up Cards	7
		Turquoise	Castles	7
			Fly Facts	7
			Good Fun Farm	7
			Harry the Clever Spider	7
			Horses' Holiday	7
			How to Make Storybooks	7
			Visit to the Farm, A	7
Bright and Early Books	Collins	Le Seig, Theo	Tooth Book, The	7
Crunchies	Orchard	Seriously Silly Rhymes	Old King Cole Played in Goal	7
		The One And Only	Bruno the Bravest Man	7
			Micky the Muckiest Boy	7
			Ruby the Rudest Girl	7

SERIES	PUBLISHER	SET (OR AUTHOR)	TITLE	BAND
Crunchies	Orchard	Twice Upon a Time	Runaway Cakes and Skipalong Pots	7
Discovery World	Heinemann	Stage E	Everyday Forces	7
			Maps	7
Discovery World Links	Heinemann	Stage D	Road Safety	7
Dragonflies	Gardner	Turquoise/Purple	All Aboard	7
			King's Birthday, The	7
First Facts	Badger	Level 4	Doctor and Dentist	7
			Polar Bears	7
Four Corners	Pearson	Year 1	Clouds	7
			Great Inventions	7
		Year 2	All About Me	7
			Animal Look-alikes	7
			Balloons	7
			Catching the Wind	7
			Coconut: Seed or Fruit?	7
			Could We Live on the Moon?	7
			Going to School	7
			Meet Erdene	7
Genre Range	Pearson	Emergent Traditional Tales	Sleeping Beauty	7
Info Trail	Pearson	Beginner Geography	Do All Rivers Go to the Sea?	7
		Beginner History	Did a Hamster Go into Space?	7
			Knucklebones	7
		Beginner Science	Feet	7
			Would You Be a Bee?	7
		Emergent Science	Don't Be a Beetroot!	7
Kingscourt Reading, Core	Kingscourt	Gold	Bella's Baby Bird	7
			Rabbit Rescue	7
		Level 17 Benchmark Bk	Fairy-Tale Flowers	7
		Level 17 Collection	My Dog	7
		Level 17 Little Books	Dog Family, The	7
			Laughing Place, The	7
		Level 18 Benchmark Bk	Interesting Insects	7
		Level 18 Collection	Dandelion	7
		Level 18 Little Books	Diary of a Sunflower	7
			Giant Grass	7
			Little Red Riding Hood	7
		Level 20 Little Books	Top Cat	7
Kingscourt Reading, Extension	Kingscourt	Set 6	Please Don't Sneeze!	7
		Set 7	Amazing Tricks	7
			Bun, The	7
			Crocodile's Bag	7
			Fast Food for Butterflies	7
			Fowler's Family Tree	7
			Granny Garcia's Gifts	7
			Hat Chat	7
			It's About Time	7
			Lizzie's Lizard	7
			Parachutes	7
			Please Do Not Drop Your Jelly Beans	7
			Sarah's Pet	7
			Turtle Talk	7

SERIES	PUBLISHER	SET (OR AUTHOR)	TITLE	BAND
Lighthouse	Ginn	Turquoise: 1	Grown-ups Make You Grumpy	7
		Turquoise: 2	Boring Old Bed	7
		Turquoise: 3	From a Bean to a Bar	7
		Turquoise: 4	Cat and Rat Fall Out	7
		Turquoise: 5	Clay Dog, The	7
		Turquoise: 6	How Big is it?	7
		Turquoise: 7	Monster in the Cave, The	7
		Turquoise: 8	What a Load of Rubbish	7
Literacy Links Plus	Kingscourt	Early B	What Tommy Did	7
		Early C	Brand-new Butterfly, A	7
			Emma's Problem	7
			Goodness Gracious!	7
			Just My Luck	7
		Early D	Half for You, Half for Me	7
			How Fire Came to Earth	7
			How Turtle Raced Beaver	7
			Monkey and Fire	7
			Trees	7
			Vagabond Crabs	7
		Fluent A	Don't Worry	7
			Grandpa's Birthday	7
			Souvenirs	7
		Fluent B	Dogstar	7
			Little Girl and Her Beetle, The	7
			Pumpkin House, The	7
		Fluent D	Boy Who Went to the North Wind, The	7
			Smallest Tree, The	7
			White Horse, The	7
		Traditional Tale	Rumpelstiltskin	7
			Three Billy Goats Gruff, The	7
National Geographic	Rigby	Green Level	What Do You Know About Dolphins?	7
		Orange Level	Animal Armour	7
		Purple Level	Tunnels	7
New Way	Nelson Thornes	Blue Parallel Books	Peter and the Wolf & other stories	7
			Pol and Pax	7
		Violet Platform Books	Clarence the Crocodile	7
			Goat Monster & other stories, The	7
		Yellow Core Book	Terrible Tiger & other stories	7
		Yellow Platform Books	Stone Soup & other stories	7
Oxford Reading Tree	OUP	Fireflies Stage 5	Houses Then and Now	7
			Looking After Your Dog	7
			Public Art	7
		Fireflies, More – Stage 5	How to Make a Wormery	7
			Volcanoes	7
		Stage 6 & 7 More Stories B	Joke Machine, The	7
			Submarine Adventure	7
			Willow Pattern Plot, The	7
		Stage 6 & 7 Stories	Broken Roof, The	7
			Lost in the Jungle	7
			Lost Key, The	7
			Outing, The	7

SERIES	PUBLISHER	SET (OR AUTHOR)	TITLE	BAND
Oxford Reading Tree	OUP	Stage 6 & 7 Stories	Red Planet	7
			Treasure Chest	7
		Stage 7 More Stories A	Bully, The	7
			Chinese Adventure	7
			Hunt for Gold, The	7
			Jigsaw Puzzle, The	7
			Motorway, The	7
			Roman Adventure	7
		Stage 7 More Stories C	Big Breakfast, The	7
			Riddle Stone, The; Part 1	7
			Riddle Stone, The; Part 2	7
		Stage 8 More Stories A	Flood!	7
		Stage 8 Stories	Viking Adventure	7
		Stage 8 True Stories	Travels with Magellan	7
		Stage 9 More Stories A	Dutch Adventure	7
			Flying Machine, The	7
			Key Trouble	7
		Stage 9 Stories	Litter Queen, The	7
			Storm Castle	7
			Superdog	7
Pathways	Collins	Year 1	Hide and Seek	7
		Year 2	Hattie Hates Hats	7
			Owl	7
			Rain Arrow, The	7
Pelican Big Bks	Pearson	Body, Wendy	Absolutely Brilliant Crazy Party, The	7
		Cullimore, Stan	Turtle Who Danced with the Crane, The	7
		Purkis, Sallie	Looking at Teddy Bears	7
PM Plus	Nelson Thornes	Turquoise Level	Bird That Could Think, The	7
			Come Back, Pip!	7
			Danger at the Car Park	7
			Ducks on the Run!	7
			First Flight	7
			Fox and the Crow, The	7
			Gibbon Island	7
			Hermie the Crab	7
			Hut in the Old Tree, The	7
			Jets and the Rockets, The	7
			Mouse-deer and the Crocodiles, The	7
			Mouse-deer Escapes, The	7
			Puppy at the Door	7
			School Fair, The	7
			Smallest Horses, The	7
			Surprise for Zac, A	7
			Swimming Across the Pool	7
			That's Not Our Dog	7
			Tricking the Tiger	7
			Wet Weather Camping	7
PM Plus Non-fiction	Nelson Thornes	Orange Level	Living with Others	7
			Taking Care of Ourselves	7
		Turquoise Level	Big Machines at Sea	7
			Big Machines for Fun and Sport	7

SERIES	PUBLISHER	SET (OR AUTHOR)	TITLE	BAND
PM Plus Non-fiction	Nelson Thornes	Turquoise Level	Big Machines in the Air	7
			Big Machines on the Road	7
PM Storybooks	Nelson Thornes	Turquoise Set A	Cabin in the Hills, The	7
			Jonathan Buys a Present	7
			Monkey Tricks	7
			Nelson, the Baby Elephant	7
			Toby and the Accident	7
			When the Volcano Erupted	7
		Turquoise Set B	Bird's Eye View	7
			Hailstorm, The	7
			Little Dinosaur Escapes	7
			Number Plates	7
			Rescuing Nelson	7
			Seat Belt Song, The	7
		Turquoise Set C	Ant City	7
			Grandad's Mask	7
			Jordan's Lucky Day	7
			Nesting Place, The	7
			Race to Green End, The	7
			Riding to Craggy Rock	7
PM Traditional Tales	Nelson Thornes	Turquoise Level	Brave Little Tailor, The	7
			Elves and the Shoemaker, The	7
			Goldilocks and the Three Bears	7
			Little Red Riding Hood	7
			Stone Soup	7
			Ugly Duckling, The	7
Rigby Star	Rigby	Turquoise Level	Flyers	7
			Giant Jumperee, The	7
			Is the Wise Owl Wise?	7
			Korka the Mighty Elf	7
			Perfect Pizza, The	7
			That's Not My Hobby!	7
Rigby Star Non-fiction	Rigby	Orange Level	Ambulance Service, The	7
			Where Do All the Puddles Go?	7
		Purple Level	Grow your Own Bean Plant!	7
			Peanuts	7
		Turquoise Level	Home for Bonnie, A	7
Rockets	A&C Black	Morgan, Michaela	Sausage and the Little Visitor	7
			Sausage and the Spooks	7
			Sausage in Trouble	7
			School for Sausage	7
		Rodgers, Frank	What Mr Croc Forgot	7
Skyrider LM Chapters	Gardner	Set 1	Coyote in Trouble	7
			Horse Power	7
			Pet Vet	7
			Whacky Wheels	7
		Set 2	Dinosaur Detectives	7
Spotlight on Fact	Collins	Y2 The Seaside	Along the Seashore	7
			Packing for a Holiday	7
Stopwatch	A&C Black		Broad Bean	7
			Chicken and Egg	7

SERIES	PUBLISHER	SET (OR AUTHOR)	TITLE	BAND
Stopwatch	A&C Black		Tadpole and Frog	7
Story Chest	Kingscourt	Stage 4	Clever Mr Brown	7
			Just Like Me	7
			Where is My Spider?	7
		Stage 5	Captain Bumble	7
Story Street	Pearson	Step 5	Wind and Fire, Part 1	7
			Wind and Fire, Part 2	7
		Step 6	Present for Jojo, A	7
			Snow Games	7
Storyworlds	Heinemann	Stage 8 Once Upon a Time	Little Red Riding Hood	7
			Three Wishes, The	7
			Tiger and the Jackal, The	7
		Stage 8 Our World	Highland Cattle, The	7
			Highland Games, The	7
			Lost in the Mist	7
			Rescue at Sea	7
		Stage 9 Animal World	Canal Boat Cat	7
Sunshine Readers	Gardner	Light Blue Level	Goodbye, Ebony	7
			Gramps	7
			Lucy's Luck	7
			My Sad Skeleton	7
		Purple Level	Fred's Super Scooter	7
			Mike's Parachute Jump	7
			Yawn, Yawn, Yawn	7
Web Fiction	OUP	Stage 7 (Variety)	Boy Who Talked to the Birds, The	7
			King's Ears, The	7
			Strange Dream, The	7
		Stage 9 (Variety)	Daylight Robbery	7
			Dormouse Pot, The	7
			Miss Ross is Cross	7
Web Guided Reading	OUP	Stage 6 (Duck Green)	Giants, The	7
			Leela and the Lost Shoe	7
			Lucky Ducks	7
			Songbird, The	7
			Sports Day	7
		Stage 7 (Duck Green)	Bird in the Bush, A	7
			Wolf Whistle, The	7
		Stage 8 (Duck Green)	Dinosaur Danger!	7
			Summer Fair, The	7
			Watch the Birdie!	7
Web Weavers Non-fiction	OUP	Non-fiction – Animals	Dinosaur Alphabet	7
			Elephant Diary	7
			Keep Your Hamster Happy	7
		Non-fiction – Toys	All Kinds of Dolls	7
			How My Bike Was Made	7
			Kites	7

Band 8 Purple

Reading Recovery Levels 19–20

NATIONAL CURRICULUM LEVEL 2C

WORKING WITHIN LEVEL 2: LEARNING OPPORTUNITIES
Aligned with Phase 6
Progression in Phonics

- Look through a variety of fiction and non-fiction with growing independence to predict content, layout and story development.

- Read silently or quietly at a more rapid pace, taking note of punctuation and using it to keep track of longer sentences.

- Solve most unfamiliar words on the run by blending long vowel phonemes, recognising and using them in longer and more complex words.

- Adapt to fiction, non-fiction and poetic language with growing flexibility.

- Take more conscious account of literacy effects used by fiction writers, and the formal language of different types of non-fiction.

- Begin to make more conscious use of reading to extend speaking and writing vocabulary and syntax.

TEXT CHARACTERISTICS

- sentence structures becoming longer and more complex

- storyline may be more involved and reflect the feelings of the writer

- wider variety of genre but still illustrated

- some books with short chapters for more sustained reading

- characters are more distinctive and rounded than at earlier levels

- non-fiction texts cover an increasing curriculum range and different text formats

- alphabetically ordered texts such as dictionaries and simple encyclopaedias, glossaries and indexes

GUIDED READING

PURPLE BAND

TRADITIONAL TALE as NARRATIVE and PLAY

PUSS-IN-BOOTS
PM Traditional Tales and Plays

Retold by Annette Smith
Illustrated by Naomi C. Lewis

Published by Nelson Thornes (1999)

ISBN 1 86961 276 0

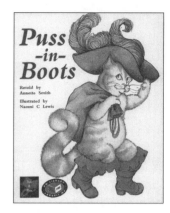

LEARNING OUTCOMES

Most children:
- discuss story setting and compare with similar traditional tales
- draw together ideas and information from across a whole text
- identify and describe characters
- read with intonation and expression appropriate to the grammar, punctuation and character
- know how to tackle unfamiliar words that are not completely decodable
- discuss time and sequential relationships in stories, and use the language of time
- present traditional stories in play form for members of their own class.

TEXT SELECTION NOTES

In this PM series, there are 36 traditional tales and plays in Orange–White Bands. In each book, the story appears first in illustrated narrative form, and then in play format. Line breaks in the text indicate the ends of phrases, clauses or sentences, and are intended to promote fluency and expressive phrasing.

In the play versions, each speech is colour-coded according to narrator and character. This layout is very helpful in supporting children to carry out independent play readings.

LINK TO WHOLE-CLASS WORK

Traditional tales are a major part of Key Stage 1 literature, and provide a strong basis for an early appreciation of plot and character. As they participate in plays, children step into the roles of their favourite characters and enrich their experience as readers and performers.

TEXT INTRODUCTION

Let's read the title and look at the illustrations on the front and back covers. What type of story do you think this is? Can you say something about traditional tales? How do they usually begin? Check the first page and see if you are right.

This old man is a miller. Here's his mill. Do you know what that's for? And this is his youngest son.
p. 4 Why do you think the cat gets dressed up? Have you ever heard of a cat like this one? Do you think it's a true story?
On page 9 the cat pretends that his master is the Marquis of Carabas. (Write name on whiteboard and rehearse if necessary.)
Now look through the book up to page 20 at the illustrations and talk about what you think happens in the rest of the story.

STRATEGY CHECK

Who are the main characters in this story? Yes, there's the miller's son, the cat, the king and the princess, and a lion.
There's a lot of speaking in this story, so remember to make your reading sound as though you are the character talking, even when you're reading silently.

INDEPENDENT READING

While each child reads their own book, the teacher works with one and then another, asking the child to read aloud from where they are up to. Prompting suggestions:

*p. 2 (**youngest**) Sound through this word. Well done for noticing the suffix **est**. Now read from the beginning of the sentence and check that it makes sense.*
*p. 4 (meaning of **fortune**) Think about this word as you read on.*
*p. 12 (**fiercely**) Point out that **fi** is a separate syllable, and then encourage the child to sound the phonemes.*
*p. 12 You said 'belongs' (**belong**). Read the sentence again a bit more quickly, listening to how it sounds, and look more carefully.*

RETURN TO THE TEXT

Let's find words to describe the main characters, for example:
Puss-in Boots: 'clever', 'scheming', 'powerful', 'bold', 'loyal'
Miller's son: 'obedient', 'good-looking', 'dishonest'
Let's find some words or groups of words that tell us about time: 'Once upon a time'; 'He waited until …'; 'soon'; 'In the meantime'; 'Later that evening …'; 'The very next day …'; 'ever after'.

INDEPENDENT ACTIVITY

Group reads through the playscript in the second half of the book, taking different roles in preparation for presentation to the rest of the class, or the school.

SERIES	PUBLISHER	SET (OR AUTHOR)	TITLE	BAND
Alphakids	Gardner	Transitional Level 17	Staying Alive	8
		Extending Level 18	Hot-air Balloons	8
			Looking After Their Young	8
		Extending Level 19	Cat and Dog	8
			Natural Disasters	8
			Real Princess, The	8
			Under the Sea	8
		Extending Level 20	Annie and the Pirates	8
			My Diary by Fairy Godmother	8
			Ugly Duckling	8
			Vote for Me!	8
		Extending Level 21	Sir Andrew the Brave	8
		Extending Level 22	Johann and the Birds	8
Alphakids Plus	Gardner	Transitional Level 15	Coastlines	8
		Transitional Level 16	Animals That Sting	8
		Transitional Level 17	Super Sea Birds	8
		Extending Level 18	Bird Families	8
			X-Rays	8
		Extending Level 19	Dragon's Rescue, The	8
			Gelati	8
			Jellyfish	8
			Our New Year Dragon	8
			Penguins	8
		Extending Level 20	Butterfly Garden	8
			Chocolate Tree, The	8
			I'm in an Ad	8
			Sea Giants	8
			Ungrateful Tiger, The	8
		Extending Level 21	Best of Friends	8
			Jack and the Beanstalk	8
		Extending Level 22	Dragons	8
			Giant's Diary, The	8
			I Want to be an Acrobat	8
AlphaWorld	Gardner	Band 7: Turquoise	Food For Animals	8
		Band 8: Purple	Amazing Plants	8
			Animal Close-ups	8
			Kites	8
			Using Colour	8
		Level 18 (ext)	Killer Plants	8
		Level 19 (ext)	How Do Plants Grow Here?	8
			How Spiders Catch Their Food	8
			Making Work Easy	8
			Now I Am Eight	8
		Level 20 (ext)	Frog Bog	8
			Looking After Eggs	8
			Port, The	8
			Saving The Rainforests	8
Badger NF Guided Reading	Wayland	Changes	Toys and Games	8
	Franklin Watts	Changing Times	Seaside, The	8
	Ticktock	I Love Reading, Purple Level	Animal Hospital	8
	Neate Publishing	Literacy and Science	Body Parts	8

SERIES	PUBLISHER	SET (OR AUTHOR)	TITLE	BAND
Badger NF Guided Reading	Chrysalis	Living Nature	Reptiles	8
		My Healthy Body	Eating	8
	Ticktock	Stepping Stones	Why Does the Moon Change Shape?	8
Big Cat	Collins	Gold	Pirate Party	8
		Purple	Buzz and Bingo in the Monster Maze	8
			Hector and the Cello	8
			How To Draw Cartoons	8
			Let's Go To Mars	8
			Pacific Island Scrapbook	8
			Pet Detectives: Tortoise Trouble	8
			Star Boy's Surprise	8
			Unusual Traditions	8
Crunchies	Orchard	Colour Crackers	Hot Dog Harris	8
			Pipe Down, Prudle!	8
			Precious Potter	8
			Sleepy Sammy	8
			Stella's Staying Put	8
			Too Many Babies	8
			Welcome Home, Barney	8
		Raps	Big Bad Raps	8
		Seriously Silly Rhymes	Ding Dong Bell, What's That Funny Smell?	8
			Ghostyshocks and the Three Scares	8
		The One And Only	Boris the Brainiest Baby	8
			Harold the Hairiest Man	8
			Polly the Most Poetic Person	8
			Tina the Tiniest Girl	8
		Twice Upon a Time	Bad Bears and Good Bears	8
			Greedy Guts and Belly Busters	8
			Knock, Knock! Who's There?	8
			Over the Stile and Into the Sack	8
			Sneaky Deals and Tricky Tricks	8
Discovery World	Heinemann	Stage C	Day in the Life of a Victorian Child, A	8
			Minibeast Encyclopaedia	8
Discovery World Links	Heinemann	Stage C	How to Grow a Nasturtium	8
		Stage F	Animal Life Cycles	8
Dragonflies	Gardner	Turquoise/Purple	Blink-off, The	8
			Clumsy Tiger, The	8
			Competition, The	8
			Magpie Tree, The	8
First Explorers	Kingscourt	Level 1	Food For All	8
			Look Up	8
			Nests and Shelters	8
			On the Move	8
			Plants All Round	8
			Ponds and Rivers	8
			Sense This	8
		Level 2	Handle with Care	8
			People and Places	8
First Facts	Badger	Level 4	How Do Birds Fly?	8
			Life in Space	8
			Lift-off!	8

SERIES	PUBLISHER	SET (OR AUTHOR)	TITLE	BAND
First Facts	Badger	Level 4	Lions and Tigers	8
			Penguin Rescue	8
			People Who Help Us	8
			Planets, The	8
Four Corners	Pearson	Year 1	Inventing the Telephone	8
		Year 2	Changing Shores	8
			Crossing the Atlantic	8
			On the Farm	8
			We Need Insects!	8
Go Facts	A&C Black	Animals	Birds	8
			Insects	8
I Love Reading	Ticktock	Purple Level	Airline Pilot	8
			Animal Hospital	8
			Bug Watch	8
			Orang-utan Baby	8
			Scary Snakes	8
			Tiger Cub	8
Info Trail	Pearson	Beginner Science	Does Cheese Come From Cows?	8
		Emergent Geography	Alien Landing	8
			Birthday Treasure Hunt, The	8
		Emergent History	History of Football, The	8
		Emergent Science	Tongues	8
			Training with Ali and Emma	8
Kingscourt Reading, Core	Kingscourt	Level 19 Benchmark Bk	Elephant in the House, An	8
		Level 19 Collection	Dragonfly Dreams	8
		Level 19 Little Books	Ant and the Grasshopper, The	8
			Just the Bee's Knees	8
			Spider Bank, The	8
		Level 20 Benchmark Bk	Animal Biscuits	8
		Level 20 Collection	Cats	8
		Level 20 Little Books	Bird Lady, The	8
		White	Special Table, The	8
Kingscourt Reading, Extension	Kingscourt	Set 7	Knitting for Penguins	8
		Set 8	Adventures of the Robber Pig, The	8
			Camels and Their Cousins	8
			Coyote, Fox, and Wolf Tales	8
			Dream Catchers	8
			Elephant Walk	8
			Feathers	8
			Fire! Fire!	8
			Frog Day	8
			Happily Ever After	8
			Look Inside	8
			Pandora's Box	8
			Rhyming Princess, The	8
			School Days, Cool Days	8
			Solve This!	8
			Wild Easts and the Wild West, The	8
			Winter Woollies	8
Lighthouse	Ginn	Purple: 1	Ozlo's Beard	8
		Purple: 2	Make a Bottle Garden	8

SERIES	PUBLISHER	SET (OR AUTHOR)	TITLE	BAND
Lighthouse	Ginn	Purple: 3	Best Pet, The	8
		Purple: 4	Jade Emperor and the Four Dragons, The	8
		Purple: 5	Mouse Stone, The	8
		Purple: 6	Rescue!	8
		Purple: 7	Stop Thief!	8
		Purple: 8	Wild Cat Guide, The	8
Literacy and Science	Neate Publishing		Animal Sets	8
			Body Parts	8
			Colours Around Us	8
Literacy Links Plus	Kingscourt	Early D	Gallo and Zorro	8
		Fluent A	Awumpalema	8
			Cat Concert	8
			He Who Listens	8
			Turtle Flies South	8
		Fluent B	Hare and the Tortoise, The	8
			Lonely Giant, The	8
			Mrs Pepperpot's Pet	8
			Oh, Columbus!	8
			Skeleton on the Bus, The	8
			T-shirt Triplets, The	8
		Fluent C	Look Out for Your Tail	8
			Trojan Horse, The	8
			Why the Sea is Salty	8
			Yellow Overalls	8
		Fluent D	Cabbage Princess, The	8
			Crosby Crocodile's Disguise	8
			Misha Disappears	8
			Rapunzel	8
			Tony and the Butterfly	8
		Traditional Tale	Fisherman and His Wife, The	8
			Puss-in-Boots	8
			Why Frog and Snake Can't Be Friends	8
National Geographic	Rigby	Turquoise Level	Corn	8
New Way	Nelson Thornes	Blue Parallel Books	King of the Ostriches & other stories	8
		Orange Platform Books	Cat Called Tim, A	8
		Violet Core Book	Kind Prince & other stories, The	8
		Violet Parallel Books	Great-aunt Gertrude Comes to Stay	8
		Violet Platform Books	Water Lilies & other stories	8
		Yellow Platform Books	Four Friends & other stories, The	8
			Hansel and Gretel	8
			King's Race & other stories, The	8
			Not Too Young & other stories	8
			Pol and Pax on the Third Moon	8
Oxford Reading Tree	OUP	All Stars Pack 1	Cosmo for Captain	8
			Farmer Skiboo	8
			Magic Porridge Pot, The	8
			Two Brown Bears	8
		Fireflies Stage 6	Food as Art	8
			Tour de France	8
			Unusual Buildings	8
			Wild Weather	8

SERIES	PUBLISHER	SET (OR AUTHOR)	TITLE	BAND
Oxford Reading Tree	OUP	Fireflies Stage 7	Making a Space Shuttle	8
			What Do You Want to Be?	8
		Fireflies Stage 8	Freaky Fish	8
		Robins Pack 1	Kate and the Sheep	8
			Old Vase, The	8
			Proper Bike, A	8
		Robins Pack 2	Holiday, The	8
			Secret Plans, The	8
		Stage 8 More Stories A	Egyptian Adventure	8
			Evil Genie, The	8
			Pocket Money	8
			Save Floppy!	8
			What Was it Like?	8
		Stage 8 Stories	Day in London, A	8
			Flying Carpet, The	8
			Rainbow Adventure, The	8
			Victorian Adventure	8
		Stage 8 True Stories	Alex Brychta	8
		Stage 9 More Stories A	Blue Eye, The	8
			Finest in the Land, The	8
			Rescue!	8
		Stage 9 Stories	Green Island	8
			Survival Adventure	8
		Traditional Tales 5-7	Magic Doctor, The	8
			Pied Piper of Hamelin, The	8
Pathways	Collins	Year 1	Look Closer	8
			Weather	8
		Year 2	All Aboard	8
			Bronwen The Brave	8
			Ginger, Where Are You?	8
			Letters From Lucy	8
			You Can't Park an Elephant	8
Pelican Big Bks	Pearson	Cullimore, Stan	Cinderella	8
		Witherington, Anne	Food For Festivals	8
			What Babies Used To Wear	8
PM Non-fiction	Nelson Thornes	Turquoise Level	Brown Bears	8
			Elephants	8
			Hippos	8
			Kangaroos	8
			Lions and Tigers	8
			Monkeys and Apes	8
PM Plus	Nelson Thornes	Purple Level	Anyone Can Have a Pet	8
			Bear and the Bees, The	8
			Bend, Stretch and Leap	8
			Bird Watching	8
			Carnival Horse, The	8
			Chocolate Cake, The	8
			Diving at the Pool	8
			Giant Seeds, The	8
			Kindest Family, The	8
			Mack's Big Day	BAND

SERIES	PUBLISHER	SET (OR AUTHOR)	TITLE	BAND
PM Plus	Nelson Thornes	Purple Level	Prickles the Porcupine	8
			Rally Car Race	8
			Rex Plays Fetch	8
			Roller-Coaster Ride	8
			Running Shoes, The	8
			Sea Otter Goes Hunting	8
			Spider in My Bedroom, A	8
			Star and Patches	8
			Truck Parade, The	8
			Winter on the Ice	8
PM Plus Non-fiction	Nelson Thornes	Purple Level	How Animals Move Around	8
			How News Travels	8
			How People Move Around	8
			Seasons and Weather	8
			Sky Changes	8
			Electricity Makes Things Work	8
		Turquoise Level	Big Machines in Emergencies	8
			Big Machines on Rails	8
PM Storybooks	Nelson Thornes	Purple Set A	Dog Called Bear, A	8
		Purple Set A	Moppet on the Run	8
			Nelson Gets a Fright	8
			Pedlar's Caps, The	8
			Roller Blade Run, The	8
			Zala Runs for Her Life	8
		Purple Set B	Bike for Brad, A	8
			Green Dragons, The	8
			Muffin is Trapped	8
			New School for Megan, A	8
			Surf Carnival, The	8
			Troop of Little Dinosaurs, A	8
		Purple Set C	Gorgo Meets Her Match	8
			Jordan's Catch	8
			Marble Patch, The	8
			Riding High	8
			Toby at Sandy Bay	8
			Two Red Tugs	8
PM Traditional Tales	Nelson Thornes	Purple Level	Animal Band, The	8
			Boy Who Cried Wolf, The	8
			Hare and the Tortoise, The	8
			Puss-in-Boots	8
			Sly Fox and Little Red Hen	8
			Town Mouse and Country Mouse	8
Rigby Star	Rigby	Purple Level	Cherokee Little People, The	8
			Elves and the Shoemaker, The	8
			Jumping Jack	8
			King of the Birds, The	8
			Poles Apart	8
			Rabbit's Surprise Birthday	8
		Star Plus	Woodcutter and the Bear, The	8
Rigby Star Non-fiction	Rigby	Gold Level	Art in the Past	8
			Magnets	8

SERIES	PUBLISHER	SET (OR AUTHOR)	TITLE	BAND
Rigby Star Non-fiction	Rigby	Purple Level	Pedal Power	8
		Turquoise Level	How Music is Made	8
			World of Sport, A	8
		White Level	Our Feelings	8
Rockets	A&C Black	Anderson, Scoular	Muddled Monsters, The	8
			Perfect Pizza, The	8
		Rodgers, Frank	Mr Croc's Clock	8
			Mr Croc's Silly Sock	8
Skyrider LM Chapters	Gardner	Set 1	Billie the Hippo	8
			Divers' Dream	8
			Flicking the Switch	8
			Home for Diggory, A	8
			Painting Lesson, The	8
			Ready, Set, Go!	8
			Rhythm and Shoes	8
			Sam and Kim	8
			Strike	8
		Set 2	Cephalopods	8
			Concrete Jungle	8
			Going on Safari	8
			Going Up the Wall	8
			Guard Dog Diggory	8
			Marty's Birthday	8
			Maze Craze, The	8
			Pot of Gold, A	8
			Two Tricky Tales	8
			Where is White Rabbit?	8
Stopwatch	A&C Black		Ladybird	8
Story Chest	Kingscourt	Stage 5	Cat on the Roof	8
			Day in Town, A	8
			Sunflower That Went Flop, The	8
			Well I Never	8
Story Street	Pearson	Step 6	Carnival, The	8
			Christmas Disco, The	8
			Stop Thief!	8
		Step 7	Jojo Makes the Team	8
			Rat for Mouse, A	8
Storyworlds	Heinemann	Stage 8 Fantasy World	Kim and the Computer Mouse	8
			Kim and the Missing Paint Pot	8
			Kim and the Shape Dragon	8
		Stage 8 Once Upon a Time	Ali, Hassan and the Donkey	8
Sunshine Readers	Gardner	Purple Level	Mother's Day Harmony	8
			Watch Dog Who Wouldn't, The	8
Walker Starters	Walker	Crebbin, June	Dragon Test, The	8
			Hal the Highwayman	8
		West, Colin	Percy the Pink	8
Web Fiction	OUP	Stage 6 (Variety)	Fantastic Four and the Winter Games, The	8
			Fantastic Four at Frog Farm, The	8
			Fantastic Four at the Seaside, The	8
			Hay Cart, The	8
			Sheepless Night, A	8

SERIES	PUBLISHER	SET (OR AUTHOR)	TITLE	BAND
Web Fiction	OUP	Stage 6 (Variety)	What Am I For?	8
		Stage 7 (Variety)	Costume Parade, The	8
			Rohan Goes to Big School	8
		Stage 8 (Variety)	Moneypenny and the Pond	8
			Moneypenny Goes Camping	8
			Moneypenny's Big Walk	8
		Stage 9 (Variety)	Josh and the Magic Beanstalk	8
			Magic Number, The	8
Web Guided Reading	OUP	Stage 8 (Duck Green)	Spooky Eyes, The	8
			Troll's Hat, The	8
Web Weavers Non-fiction	OUP	Non-fiction – Animals	Salmon's Journey, The	8
			Spiders Are Amazing	8
			Tigers	8

Band 9 Gold

Reading Recovery Levels 21–22
NATIONAL CURRICULUM LEVEL 2B

WORKING WITHIN LEVEL 2:
LEARNING OPPORTUNITIES
Aligned with Phase 6
Progression in Phonics

- Look through a variety of books with growing independence to predict content and story development, and make full use of non-fiction layout.

- Read silently or quietly at a more rapid pace, taking note of punctuation and using it to keep track of longer sentences.

- Solve most unfamiliar words on the run by blending long vowel phonemes, recognising and using them in longer and more complex words.

- Adapt to fiction, non-fiction and poetic language with growing flexibility.

- Take more conscious account of literacy effects used by writers.

- Make more conscious use of reading to extend speaking and writing vocabulary and syntax.

- Locate and interpret information in non-fiction.

TEXT CHARACTERISTICS

- somewhat more challenging than in Band 8

- sentence structures becoming longer and more complex

- storyline may be more involved and reflect the feelings of the writer

- wider variety of text genre but still illustrated

- some books with chapters for more sustained reading

- characters are more distinctive and rounded than at earlier levels

- widening vocabulary and range of terminology, but still a controlled proportion of unknown words used per paragraph/page

- non-fiction texts cover an increasing curriculum range, and involved a range of text type and formats

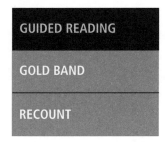

WHALES ON THE WORLD WIDE WEB
Alphakids

Written by Sarah Prince

Published by Gardner Education (2000)

ISBN 0 7253 1862 7

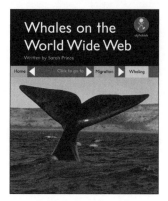

GUIDED READING

GOLD BAND

RECOUNT

LEARNING OUTCOMES

Most children:

- skim-read title, illustrations and sub-headings to speculate what the book might be about
- pose questions, and record these in writing, prior to reading non-fiction, to find answers
- scan the text to find specific sections
- locate parts of the text that give particular information
- evaluate the usefulness of a text for its purpose
- understand and use new words from reading.

TEXT SELECTION NOTES

A variety of text types and non-fiction language registers are represented in this compact book illustrated with photos, diagrams, a map, labels and captions. The text describes how a class of children sets out to deepen their knowledge about whales by obtaining information from the web. They then construct their own web pages in order to share this information with other children. A boy recounts how he and his classmates carry out the project, and in doing so uses key word processing vocabulary. Technical terms associated with whales, and basic historical information are introduced through the depiction of web pages.

LINK TO WHOLE-CLASS WORK

There are links with a number of curriculum areas apart from English, including information technology, biology, ecology and geography. The book provides a simple, practical teaching model for project work in a modern school.

TEXT INTRODUCTION

Read the title and take a good look at the cover. What type of text do you think this is?
Let's write some questions we'd each like the answers to about whales or about the World Wide Web.
Now look through the book and see if you can spot the difference between the pages on the left-hand side, and those on the right.
How could you describe the type of texts that you noticed? (Paragraphs, diagrams, maps websites, email.)

STRATEGY CHECK

Read pages 2 to 5 and find out what the class decided to do. (Each child reads) *Describe their plans in your own words.*
Now I want you to read in pairs pages 6/7, 8/9, 10/11, talk about what you read and prepare to tell the others about it.
Read slowly and think about the terms we've just used so that you can explain clearly, or prepare questions about those things you don't understand.

INDEPENDENT READING

Prompts for unfamiliar vocabulary:
Compound words such as 'coastline', 'whalebone', 'Humpback'. *Split them into two parts and read each part separately* (link back to Phonic Phase 5).
Multi-syllabic words such as 'designed', 'suggested', 'migrate', 'information'.
Find parts of the word you know. Try clapping and counting the separate syllables. Now read right through the word. (Phonic Phase 6)
Re-read the sentence and check that it makes sense.

Now read page 12 to the end to find out what happened.
Were other children able to find out about whales from their website?

RETURN TO THE TEXT

Now you can report back to the group on the section you read. Can you show us where you found that information?

Let's return to our questions. Did we find the answers?
Where could we go to find out more?
There were some words I'd like you to discuss: e.g. 'linked', 'scanned', 'migration', 'baleen', 'polluted'.

INDEPENDENT ACTIVITY

Suggest that the children check other sources including the World Wide Web to satisfy unanswered questions, and record the answers in diagrammatic form.
Use this book as a model to create a group or class topic.

SERIES	PUBLISHER	SET (OR AUTHOR)	TITLE	BAND
Alphakids	Gardner	Extending Level 19	Animal Communications	9
		Extending Level 20	Whales on the World Wide Web	9
		Extending Level 21	Great Tin-rolling Race, The	9
			Pollution	9
			Sour Grapes	9
			Worms at Work	9
		Extending Level 22	Amazing Journeys	9
			Pig's Skin	9
			Present for Dad, A	9
			Under Sail	9
Alphakids Plus	Gardner	Extending Level 21	Amazing Living Things	9
			Making Dips	9
			Rock Climbing	9
			Trains	9
		Extending Level 22	Boy Who Wanted to be Famous, The	9
			Moving Big Trees	9
			Social Insects	9
		Extending Level 23	Good to Eat	9
			Great Big Elephants	9
			Making an Animated Cartoon	9
			Rare Bird, The	9
			Runaway Nose, The	9
			Turtles in Trouble	9
		Extending Level 24	Rainforest Birds	9
			Snakes	9
			Story of Zadig, The	9
AlphaWorld	Gardner	Level 21 (ext)	Amazing Lifetimes	9
			Bridges	9
			Moving Home	9
		Level 22 (ext)	Animal Champions	9
			Fixing Things	9
Badger NF Guided Reading	Chrysalis	Bug Zone	Bug Athletes	9
	Wayland	Changes	Dressing Up	9
	OUP	Graham Peacock	Oxford First Science Dictionary	9
	Heinemann Library	How Do We Know About ...?	Great Fire of London, The	9
	Chrysalis	Science Around Us	Energy	9
		Start Science	Earth and Space	9
	Franklin Watts	Wonderwise	Let's Build a House	9
	Chrysalis	World Of Festivals	Family Festivals	9
Big Cat	Collins	Gold	Buzz and Bingo in the Fairytale Forest	9
			How Does it Work?	9
			How to Be a Pirate in 10 Easy Stages	9
			Ice Cream	9
			Pet Detectives: The Ball Burglary	9
			Swimming With Dolphins	9
			Woman Who Fooled the Fairies, The	9
		Purple	Were They Real?	9
Crunchies	Orchard	Colour Crackers	Birthday For Bluebell, A	9
			Fortune for Yo-Yo, A	9
			Long Live Roberto	9
			Medal for Poppy, A	9

SERIES	PUBLISHER	SET (OR AUTHOR)	TITLE	BAND
Crunchies	Orchard	Colour Crackers	Open Wide, Wilbur!	9
			Phew, Sidney!	9
			Rhode Island Roy	9
			Tiny Tim	9
			We Want William!	9
		Raps	Fangtastic Raps	9
			Royal Raps	9
		Seriously Silly Rhymes	Mary, Mary, Fried Canary	9
		Tall Tales	And Pigs Might Fly	9
			King of the Birds, The	9
		Twice Upon a Time	Bad Boys and Naughty Girls	9
			Hairy Toes and Scary Bones	9
			I Spy Pancakes and Pies	9
			If Wishes Were Fishes	9
			Silly Sons and Dozy Daughters	9
			Ugly Dogs and Slimy Frogs	9
Discovery World	Heinemann	Stage E	How to Choose a Pet	9
		Stage F	Science Dictionary	9
Discovery World Links	Heinemann	Stage D	Then and Now	9
			World's Largest Animals	9
		Stage E	Festival Food	9
			Story of Jeans, The	9
		Stage F	Great Fire of London, The	9
Dragonflies	Gardner	Gold	Any Excuse	9
			Cat and the Stars, The	9
			Dragon's Egg, The	9
			There's A Boy Under the Bed	9
First Explorers	Kingscourt	Level 1	Animal Babies	9
			Going Places	9
			Under Attack	9
			You Are Special	9
		Level 2	Buildings for a Purpose	9
			I Dig Dinosaurs	9
			Rainforest Life	9
First Facts	Badger	Level 4	Sun's Energy, The	9
			Why Recycle?	9
Four Corners	Pearson	Year 2	Book of Space	9
		Year 3	Let's Play	9
		Year 4	They Worked Together	9
		Year 5	Time to Celebrate!	9
Genre Range	Pearson	Beginner Poetry	Rhyming Poems	9
		Emergent Poetry	Songs, Alphabet & Playground Rhymes	9
			Story Poems	9
			Tongue Twisters, Limericks …	9
Go Facts	A&C Black	Animals	Mammals	9
			Reptiles	9
Info Trail	Pearson	Emergent Geography	Are Mountains Like Children?	9
		Emergent History	Did Vikings Eat Chips?	9
			Toilets Through Time	9
			Who Goes on the Bonfire?	9
		Emergent Science	Does Chocolate Grow on Trees?	9

SERIES	PUBLISHER	SET (OR AUTHOR)	TITLE	BAND
Kingscourt Reading, Core	Kingscourt	Gold	Basil's Night Out	9
			Helping Hands	9
			Rabbit Dance, The	9
			While We Sleep	9
		Level 20 Little Books	Meerkat Chat	9
		White	Camping At School	9
			Golden Touch, The	9
Kingscourt Reading, Extension	Kingscourt	Set 9	3,2,1...Lift Off!	9
			Bird Watchers	9
			Birds of Prey	9
			Caves	9
			Clever Coyote and Other Wild Dogs	9
			Flutey Family Fruit Cake, The	9
			Hiding Places	9
			Just Hanging Around	9
			Lunch Bunch, The	9
			News on Shoes	9
			No Space to Waste	9
			Pet Tarantula, The	9
			Rupert Goes to School	9
			Sam's Dad	9
			Sculpture	9
			Squirrels	9
			Those Birds!	9
			Trees, Please!	9
Lighthouse	Ginn	Gold: 1	Amy's Armbands	9
		Gold: 2	Sounds	9
		Gold: 3	Grandpa's Bright Ideas	9
		Gold: 4	Big Bo Peep	9
		Gold: 5	Beanpole Billy	9
		Gold: 6	What Dinah Saw	9
		Gold: 7	Finn MacCool & Big Head MacTavish	9
Literacy Links Plus	Kingscourt	Fluent A	Scare-kid	9
		Fluent B	Bull in a China Shop, A	9
			Oogly Gum Chasing Gum, The	9
		Fluent C	Spider	9
			Vicky the High Jumper	9
		Fluent D	Three Magicians, The	9
			Why Rabbits Have Long Ears	9
National Geographic	Rigby	Gold Level	Rice	9
		Purple Level	Fossils	9
			Rain Forest, The	9
		Turquoise Level	Spiders Spin Silk	9
			Water Can Change	9
New Way	Nelson Thornes	Orange Core Book	Bank Robbery & other stories, The	9
		Orange Parallel Books	Great-aunt Gertrude & the Handbag Thief	9
		Orange Platform Books	Trapped!	9
		Violet Parallel Books	Pol and Pax on Earth	9
			Ugly Duckling, The	9
			Why Flamingoes Have Red Legs	9
		Violet Platform Books	Helpful Harry & other stories	9

SERIES	PUBLISHER	SET (OR AUTHOR)	TITLE	BAND
New Way	Nelson Thornes	Yellow Platform Books	Pumpkin Mountain & The Nightingale	9
			Sandy	9
Oxford Reading Tree	OUP	All Stars Pack 1	Adventure for Robo-dog, An	9
			Sand Witch, The	9
		All Stars Pack 2	Disgusting Denzil	9
			Eric's Talking Ears	9
		All Stars Pack 3	Ronald the Tough Sheep	9
		Citizenship Stories Stage 9/10	Christmas Fair, The	9
			Clever Invention, A	9
			Quarrel, The	9
			Winning	9
		Cross-curricular Jackdaws	Fruits and Seeds	9
			Seaside, The	9
		Fireflies Stage 5	Wonders of the World	9
		Fireflies Stage 6	Dinosaurs	9
			Skateboarding	9
		Fireflies Stage 7	Fire	9
			Glorious Mud	9
			Things That Sting	9
		Fireflies Stage 8	Ice-Maker Ice-Breaker	9
		Fireflies Stage 9	Comic Illustrators	9
			Diamonds	9
			How to Use a Computer	9
			Robots	9
			Training Like an Athlete	9
		More Allstars Pack 1a	Charlie Stories	9
			Lazy Giant, The	9
			Robot's Special Day	9
			Snow Troll	9
			Squirrel	9
			Terry Takes Off	9
		More Allstars Pack 2a	Cleaner Genie	9
			Tom Thumb and the Football Team	9
			Town Dog	9
		Robins Pack 1	Emergency, The	9
			Long Journey, The	9
			Mum's New Car	9
		Robins Pack 2	Photograph, The	9
			Surprise, The	9
			William and the Dog	9
			William's Mistake	9
		Robins Pack 3	Hamid Does His Best	9
			Treasure Hunt, The	9
			Village Show, The	9
			William and the Pied Piper	9
		Stage 9 Stories	Quest, The	9
		Stage 9 True Stories	High Flier	9
			Underground Railroad, The	9
Pathways	Collins	Year 2	I Want a Party	9
PM Non-fiction	Nelson Thornes	Gold Level	Bats	9
			Foxes	9

SERIES	PUBLISHER	SET (OR AUTHOR)	TITLE	BAND
PM Non-fiction	Nelson Thornes	Gold Level	Owls	9
			Racoons	9
			Skunks	9
			Tasmanian Devils	9
		Purple Level	Cattle	9
			Chickens	9
			Goats	9
			Horses	9
			Pigs	9
			Sheep	9
PM Plus	Nelson Thornes	Gold Level	Ant and the Grasshopper, The	9
			Arky, the Dinosaur With Feathers	9
			Bushfire in the Koala Reserve	9
			Carl's High Jump	9
			Dash, the Young Meercat	9
			Family Tree, The	9
			Fishing Trip, The	9
			Freeway Turtles, The	9
			Gigantic Bell, The	9
			Home for Star and Patches, A	9
			Horse and the Bell, The	9
			Japanese Garden, The	9
			Kayaking at the Blue Lake	9
			Motorbike Photo, The	9
			Perfect Paper Planes	9
			Peter and the Wolf	9
			River Rafting Fun	9
			Sailing to a New Land	9
			Surprise Photo, The	9
			Trixie's Holiday	9
PM Plus Non-fiction	Nelson Thornes	Gold Level	Deserts	9
			Forests	9
			Mountains, Hills and Cliffs	9
			Oceans, Seas and Coasts	9
			Rivers, Streams and Lakes	9
			Waterfalls, Glaciers and Avalanches	9
PM Storybooks	Nelson Thornes	Gold Set A	Bear's Diet	9
			Clubhouse, The	9
			Luke's Go-Kart	9
			Owls in the Garden	9
			Secret Hideaway, The	9
			Solo Flyer	9
		Gold Set B	Big Balloon Festival, The	9
			Car Trouble	9
			King Midas and the Golden Touch	9
			Patrick and the Leprechaun	9
			Special Ride, The	9
			Surprise Dinner, The	9
		Gold Set C	Asteroid, The	9
			Dolphins, The	9
			Night Walk, The	9

SERIES	PUBLISHER	SET (OR AUTHOR)	TITLE	BAND
PM Storybooks	Nelson Thornes	Gold Set C	Pandas in the Mountains	9
			Picked for the Team	9
			Shooting Star, The	9
PM Traditional Tales	Nelson Thornes	Gold Level	Beauty and the Beast	9
			Cinderella	9
			Jack and the Magic Harp	9
			Rumpelstiltskin	9
			Seven Foolish Fishermen	9
			Snow White and the Seven Dwarfs	9
Rigby Star	Rigby	Gold Level	Emperor's New Clothes, The	9
			Mantu the Elephant	9
			Monster is Coming! The	9
			Rollercoaster	9
			Tiger Hunt	9
Rigby Star Non-fiction	Rigby	Gold Level	Caring For Our World	9
			Ice-Cream Factory, The	9
		Purple Level	Inventions of Thomas Edison, The	9
		Turquoise Level	Changing Shape	9
		White Level	Great Fire of London, The	9
Rockets	A&C Black	Anderson, Scoular	Posh Party, The	9
			Potty Panto, The	9
		Powling, Chris	Rover Goes to School	9
			Rover Shows Off	9
			Rover the Champion	9
			Rover's Birthday	9
		Rodgers, Frank	Crown Jewels, The	9
			Dragon's Tooth, The	9
			Lizard the Wizard	9
			Mr Croc's Walk	9
			Royal Roar, The	9
		Shulman, Dee	Magenta and the Ghost Babies	9
			Magenta and the Ghost Bride	9
			Magenta and the Ghost School	9
			Magenta and the Scary Ghosts	9
		Smith, Wendy	Circle Magic	9
			Magic Hotel	9
			Star is Born, A	9
			Sun, Sand and Space	9
		Wallace, Karen	Sandwich Scam, The	9
			Stuff-it-in Specials, The	9
		West, Colin	Grandad's Boneshaker Bicycle	9
			Granny's Jungle Garden	9
			Jenny the Joker	9
			Uncle-and-Auntie Pat	9
Skyrider LM Chapters	Gardner	Set 1	Bagels for Kids	9
			Best Birthday, The	9
			Brother Trouble	9
			Cooped Up	9
			Freeze, Goldilocks!	9
			Go, Annie, Go!	9
			Lost in Space	9

SERIES	PUBLISHER	SET (OR AUTHOR)	TITLE	BAND
Skyrider LM Chapters	Gardner	Set 1	Once Upon a Rhyme	9
			Quilt With a Difference, A	9
			Walter's Worries	9
		Set 2	Chameleons of the Rain Forest	9
			Glide, Wriggle, Zoom	9
			Hands Up Wolf!	9
			Know Where to Go	9
			Making Yoghurt	9
			New Girl, The	9
			On the Ball	9
			Scarecrow, The	9
			Tracks on the Ground	9
			Walk Tall	9
			World of Dummies, The	9
			Zoo Overnight	9
Spotlight on Fact	Collins	Y2 The Seaside	Places to Visit	9
			Taking Good Holiday Photos	9
Stopwatch	A&C Black		Butterfly and Caterpillar	9
			Snail	9
Story Chest	Kingscourt	Stage 6	Cooking Pot	9
			Fiddle-dee-dee	9
			Ghost and the Sausage, The	9
			Grandma's Stick	9
			Pie Thief, The	9
			Tell-tale	9
Story Street	Pearson	Step 7	Ben and the Ghost	9
			Monster on the Street, A – Part 1	9
			Monster on the Street, A – Part 2	9
		Step 8	All in a Flap	9
			Man-Eating Snails	9
			New School, A	9
			Sam Runs Away	9
Storyworld Bridges	Heinemann	Stage 10	Monster in the Cupboard, The	9
Storyworlds	Heinemann	Stage 9 Fantasy World	Journey Into the Earth, The	9
			Magic Carpet, The	9
			Voyage into Space	9
		Stage 9 Once Upon a Time	Hansel and Gretel	9
			Jack and the Beanstalk	9
		Stage 9 Our World	Big Barry Baker in Big Trouble	9
			Big Barry Baker on the Stage	9
			Big Barry Baker's Parcel	9
Sunshine Readers	Gardner	Purple Level	Becky's Big Race	9
			Grandad's Star	9
			Latest Dance Craze, The	9
		Purple Level Supplementary	Coconut Lunches	9
			Nothing to be Scared About	9
			Shingo's Grandfather	9
Walker Starters	Walker	Waddell, Martin	Cup Run	9
			Going Up!	9
		West, Colin	Big Wig	9
Web Fiction	OUP	Stage 7 (Variety)	Tale of a Turban, The	9

SERIES	PUBLISHER	SET (OR AUTHOR)	TITLE	BAND
Web Fiction	OUP	Stage 9 (Variety)	Great Stew Disaster, The	9
			Tessa on TV	9
Web Guided Reading	OUP	Stage 8 (Duck Green)	Flying Tea Tray, The	9
Web Weavers Non-fiction	OUP	Non-fiction – Toys	My Journey Around the World	9

Band 10 White

Reading Recovery Levels 23–24

**NATIONAL CURRICULUM LEVEL 2A/
WORKING TOWARDS LEVEL 3**

WORKING AT LEVEL 2A OR TOWARDS LEVEL 3: LEARNING OPPORTUNITIES Progression in Phonics phases cease to be relevant

- Read silently most of the time.

- Sustain interest in longer text, returning to it easily after a break.

- Use text more fully as a reference and as a model.

- Search for and find information in texts more flexibly.

- Notice the spelling of unfamiliar words and relate to known words.

- Show increased awareness of vocabulary and precise meaning.

- Express reasoned opinions about what is read, and compare texts.

- Offer and discuss interpretations of text.

TEXT CHARACTERISTICS

- widening range of genre and writing style

- storyline or theme may be sustained over a longer period of time with chapters or sub-sections of text

- sentence structures may be longer with more subordinate phrases or clauses

- characters may be more fully developed

- more than one point of view may be expressed within the text

- information or action may be implied rather than spelled out

- texts may contain more metaphorical or technical language

- non-fiction texts placed in a broader context and include more detailed information

GUIDED READING

WHITE BAND

FICTION IN FAMILIAR SETTING

THE PERFECT PRESENT
Lighthouse

Written by Marcia Vaughan
Illustrated by Kim Harley

Published by Ginn (2004)

ISBN 0 602 31272 8

LEARNING OUTCOMES

Most children:
- draw together ideas and information across a whole text
- explain organisational features of texts
- use syntax and context to build their store of vocabulary
- explore how particular words are used
- know how to tackle unfamiliar words, and check their meaning in text.

TEXT SELECTION NOTES

This is a family story in three short chapters. It centres on 7-year-old Sam, a gifted young painter, who always paints his father's portrait as a birthday present. This year his older sister, Molly, mocks his lack of imagination and suggests he gets a 'real' present.

Sam's friends offer suggestions which invariably reflect their own passions, and he returns home to Mum's good advice. But he still hands over his latest effort with embarrassment. To his surprise, Molly admires the likeness and asks Sam to paint her portrait; and Dad takes Sam to his office, which is a gallery for all Sam's previous creations.

Terms related to art, imaginative verbs and challenging phrases are designed to extend able readers. The story's emotional message and social interaction between characters offers an excellent basis for discussion.

LINK TO WHOLE-CLASS WORK

There is a particularly strong link with Year 2 work on the use of well-written text as a model for narrative writing. The plot here is simple and time-limited; there is a problem, development and build-up of tension, and satisfactory resolution; the characterisation is simple and effective; and the language is varied and imaginative.

TEXT INTRODUCTION Ask the group to read the blurb, think about it carefully and predict the story line without opening the book.

What do you think Sam usually gives his dad? Why do you think he might have a problem this year? Now look through the book quickly to check your predictions from the illustrations. How well did you do?

STRATEGY CHECK *This story's about a painter, and the writer uses unusual words that help us to picture what is happening in the story.*
If you don't understand a word, use what you know from the story and the character to help you.

INDEPENDENT READING *Read up to the end of page 5 and think about the mood of the story. How is Sam feeling?*

Work with individuals in the group, praising word-solving efforts and attention to punctuation, and discussing any difficult words.

Establish that the mood at the beginning is positive.
Now read to the end of chapter 1, and then discuss with a partner how the mood has changed. Find some words or phrases that illustrate how Sam feels now.

Now read chapter 2. Why does Sam decide to work on the painting after all? How do you think he feels? Finish reading the story and write down some really effective words that help you to see images in your mind. ('crinkled'; 'smiley'; 'craned'; 'stunned'; 'scribbly'; 'splodgy')

RETURN TO THE TEXT *Did you think this story worked well? Why? It was divided into three chapters. Why do you think the author did this?*

Discuss some of the metaphorical words and phrases in the story, e.g. 'absorbed'; 'crushed'; 'stomach tied itself in knots'; 'fished the portrait out of the bin'; 'wrestling with her kite'; 'got a real blast out of it'; 'fighting off tears'; 'brick-heavy feet'; 'Mum craned over'.

INDEPENDENT ACTIVITY Draw cartoons to illustrate one or two of the words and phrases above, and add a caption in the form of a whole sentence using the word or phrase.

SERIES	PUBLISHER	SET (OR AUTHOR)	TITLE	BAND
Alphakids	Gardner	Extending Level 21	Drag Racing	10
		Extending Level 22	Volcanoes	10
		Extending Level 23	Big Pig's Wig	10
			Graeme Base, Writer and Illustrator	10
			Living Together	10
			Making a Torch	10
			Sending Messages	10
			Shooter Shrinker, The	10
Alphakids Plus	Gardner	Extending Level 24	Alpine Search Dogs	10
			Firefighters	10
			When the Bus Was Late	10
AlphaWorld	Gardner	Level 21 (ext)	Saving the Oceans	10
		Level 22 (ext)	Robots	10
			Weather	10
		Level 23 (ext)	Erosion	10
			Monster Machines	10
			Summer in Antarctica	10
			Things People Make	10
		Level 24 (ext)	Animals of the African Grasslands	10
			By Land, Sea and Air	10
			Side By Side	10
			Some Things Keep Changing	10
Badger NF Guided Reading	QED	Animal Lives	Elephants	10
	Heinemann Library	How Do We Know About ...?	Florence Nightingale and the Crimean War	10
Crunchies	Orchard	Raps	Robin Hood Raps	10
		Seriously Silly Rhymes	Little Bo Peep Has Knickers That Bleep	10
		Seriously Silly Stories	Fried Piper of Hamstring, The	10
			Little Red Riding Wolf	10
			Rather Small Turnip, The	10
			Shampoozal	10
Discovery World Links	Heinemann	Stage E	Changing Materials	10
			I Love the UK	10
			Jamie's Food Guide	10
		Stage F	Interview with Florence Nightingale, An	10
First Explorers	Kingscourt	Level 1	Earth Materials	10
		Level 2	Forces of Nature	10
			Lights On	10
			Sounds All Round	10
			Spy on Spiders	10
Four Corners	Pearson	Year 2	Changing Earth, The	10
			Journey to the Undersea Gardens	10
			World Atlas	10
Go Facts	A&C Black	Plants	Plants	10
			Plants as Food	10
Info Trail	Pearson	Emergent Geography	Millennium Scrapbook, A	10
Kingscourt Reading, Core	Kingscourt	White	Earth's Riches	10
			Good Old Wood	10
			Wild Nature	10
Kingscourt Reading, Extension	Kingscourt	Set 10	Crazy Miss Maisey's Alphabet Pets	10
			Masterpiece, The	10
			Monkey Business	10

SERIES	PUBLISHER	SET (OR AUTHOR)	TITLE	BAND
Kingscourt Reading, Extension	Kingscourt	Set 10	Sea Otters	10
			Storytellers	10
			Sugar and Spice and All Things Nice	10
			Things with Wings	10
			Zoom In!	10
Lighthouse	Ginn	Gold: 8	Natalie Du Toit	10
		White 1	Gordon Gets Even	10
		White 2	Perfect Present, The	10
		White 3	Teeth	10
		White 4	My Brother, the Bridesmaid	10
		White 5	Tracking the Caribou	10
		White 6	Horses of the Sea	10
		White 7	Little Match Girl, The	10
		White 8	Great Pyramid, The	10
Literacy Links Plus	Kingscourt	Fluent A	Morning Star	10
			Tongues	10
		Fluent B	Lucy Meets a Dragon	10
			Tom's Handplant	10
		Fluent C	Bringing the Sea Back Home	10
			Three Sillies, The	10
		Fluent D	Charlie	10
			Grandad	10
			I'm a Chef	10
National Geographic	Rigby	Gold Level	Olympics, The	10
			On Safari	10
			Strange Plants	10
		Purple Level	Magnets	10
		White Level	Divers of the Deep Sea	10
			Race to the Pole	10
			Up the Amazon	10
New Way	Nelson Thornes	Orange Parallel Books	Pol and Pax in the Salty Red Sea	10
			Snow Queen, The	10
			Swan Lake	10
		Orange Platform Books	Happy Prince & The Selfish Giant, The	10
			Hound Gelert & Wookey Witch	10
Oxford Reading Tree	OUP	All Stars Pack 2	Doris Bean and the Queen	10
			High Five Henry	10
			Sausage	10
			Yummy Scrummy	10
		All Stars Pack 3	Brer Rabbit's Trickbag	10
			Clever Monkey	10
			Psid and Bolter	10
			Toffee and Marmalade	10
Oxford Reading Tree	OUP	Citizenship Stories Stage 9/10	Concert, The	10
			May-Ling's Party	10
		Cross-curricular Jackdaws	Bang the Drum	10
			Emergencies	10
		Fireflies Stage 7	Sport Then and Now	10
		Fireflies Stage 8	Modern Day Explorer: Steve Fossett	10
			Musician: Vanessa Mae	10
			What's Inside Me?	10

SERIES	PUBLISHER	SET (OR AUTHOR)	TITLE	BAND
Oxford Reading Tree	OUP	Fireflies Stage 9	Environmental Disasters	10
		Fireflies Stage 10	Making a Book	10
			Odd Eggs	10
			Romans	10
			Skeletons	10
			Survival	10
			Working in the Film Industry	10
		More Allstars Pack 2a	Badcats	10
			Beastly Basil	10
			Nelly the Monster-sitter	10
		More Allstars Pack 3a	Arabian Nights	10
			Dick Whittington	10
			Huge and Horrible Beast, The	10
			Mary-Anne and the Cat Baby	10
		Robins Pack 3	Discovery, The	10
			Ghost Tricks	10
		Stage 8 True Stories	At the Top of the World	10
		Stage 9 True Stories	Ocean Adventure!	10
		Stage 10 True Stories	Arctic Hero	10
			Pioneer Girl	10
Pathways	Collins	Year 2	Monkeys	10
			Then and Now	10
PM Non-fiction	Nelson Thornes	Silver Level	Antarctic Penguins	10
			Antarctic Seals	10
			Caribou (Reindeer)	10
			Polar Bears	10
			Whales	10
			Wolves	10
PM Plus	Nelson Thornes	Silver Level	Adventure in the Hills	10
			Bully, The	10
			Charlie's Great Race	10
			Choice for Sarah, A	10
			Contest, The	10
			Grandpa Jones & the No-company Cat	10
			Holiday at Lighthouse Rock	10
			In Search of Treasure	10
			Man Who Rode the Tiger, The	10
			Minh's New Life	10
			Penguin Rescue	10
			Riding the Skateboard Ramps	10
			Robin Hood Meets Little John	10
			Rory's Big Chance	10
			Runaround Rowdy	10
			Separate Ways	10
			Survivors in the Frozen North	10
			Teamwork	10
			Tiny Dinosaurs	10
			Tornado, The	10
PM Plus Non-fiction	Nelson Thornes	Silver Level	Gravity and the Solar System	10
			Storms	10
			Sun, The	10

SERIES	PUBLISHER	SET (OR AUTHOR)	TITLE	BAND
PM Plus Non-fiction	Nelson Thornes	Silver Level	Volcanoes and Geysers	10
			Water and Wind	10
PM Storybooks	Nelson Thornes	Silver Set A	Fair Swap, A	10
			Kerry	10
			Kerry's Double	10
			Little Adventure, A	10
			My Two Families	10
			Nelson is Kidnapped	10
		Silver Set B	Best Part, The	10
			Dolphin on the Wall, The	10
			Fire and Wind	10
			Skating at Rainbow Lake	10
			Talent Quest, The	10
			Walkathon, The	10
		Silver Set C	Jordan and the Northside Reps	10
			Our Old Friend Bear	10
			Right Place for Jupiter, The	10
			Silver and Prince	10
			Spanish Omelet	10
			Story of William Tell, The	10
PM Traditional Tales	Nelson Thornes	Silver Level	Androcles and the Lion	10
			Bear and the Trolls, The	10
			Dick Whittington	10
			Robin Hood and the Silver Trophy	10
			Sleeping Beauty, The	10
			Strange Shoe, The	10
Rigby Star	Rigby	Gold Level	Magic Jigsaw, The	10
		Star Plus	Always Elephant	10
			Headfirst into the Porridge	10
			Middle of Nowhere, The	10
			Mystery Man, The	10
			Mystery of Mrs Kim, The	10
			School Concert, The	10
			Secret, The	10
		White Level	Charlie the Bridesmaid	10
			Gizmos' Party, The	10
			Gizmos' Trip, The	10
			Little Blue, Big Blue	10
			Picky Prince, The	10
			Singing Princess, The	10
Rigby Star Non-fiction	Rigby	Star Plus Level	Jane Goodall	10
			Living in Space	10
			Seven Continents, The	10
		White Level	Count on Your Body	10
			Encyclopaedia of Fantastic Fish	10
			Fish	10
Rockets	A&C Black	Ryan, Margaret	Captain Motley and the Pirate's Gold	10
			Doris's Brilliant Birthday	10
			Kevin and the Pirate Test	10
			Smudger and the Smelly Fish	10
		Smith, Wendy	Space Football	10

SERIES	PUBLISHER	SET (OR AUTHOR)	TITLE	BAND
Rockets	A&C Black	Smith, Wendy	Time Travellers	10
		Wallace, Karen	Minestrone Mob, The	10
			Peanut Prankster, The	10
Spotlight on Fact	Collins	Y2 The Seaside	Holidays Then and Now	10
Spotlight on Plays	Collins	Age 7+	Bendemolena	10
			Brementown Musicians, The	10
			Hairy Toe, The	10
Story Chest	Kingscourt	Stage 7	Big Tease, The	10
			Countdown	10
			Hatupatu and the Birdwoman	10
			Little Brother's Haircut	10
			More! More! More!	10
			Tiddalik	10
Story Street	Pearson	Step 7	Beyond Strange Street	10
		Step 8	More Macdonalds	10
		Step 9	Book Week Goes With a Bang - Part 1	10
			Book Week Goes With a Bang - Part 2	10
Storyworld Bridges	Heinemann	Stage 10	Tom's Birthday Treat	10
			Why Tortoise Has a Cracked Shell	10
		Stage 11	Akbar's Dream	10
		Stage 12	Jumble the Puppy	10
Storyworlds	Heinemann	Stage 9 Animal World	Cherry Blossom Cat	10
			City Cat	10
			Cobra Cat	10
		Stage 9 Fantasy World	Adventure at Sea	10
		Stage 9 Once Upon a Time	Little Girl and the Bear, The	10
			Two Giants, The	10
		Stage 9 Our World	Big Barry Baker and the Bullies	10
Sunshine Readers	Gardner	Purple Level Supplementary	Secret Lives of Mr & Mrs Smith, The	10
Web Fiction	OUP	Stage 9 (Variety)	Helena and the Wild Man	10
			Pirate Gold	10
			Serve Me, Stefan	10
			Tommy in Trouble	10

PART 6

Titles in alphabetical order

TITLE	SERIES	PUBLISHER	SET (OR AUTHOR)	BAND
20 Questions	Sunshine Readers	Gardner	Orange Level	6
3,2,1...Lift Off!	Kingscourt Reading, Extension	Kingscourt	Set 9	9

A

TITLE	SERIES	PUBLISHER	SET (OR AUTHOR)	BAND
Absolutely Brilliant Crazy Party, The	Pelican Big Bks	Pearson	Body, Wendy	7
Absolutely Not!	Kingscourt Reading, Core	Kingscourt	Level 8 Little Books	3
Adam Goes Shopping	Oxford Reading Tree	OUP	Stage 4 Sparrows	3
Adam's Car	Oxford Reading Tree	OUP	Stage 4 Sparrows	3
Addressing a Letter	Info Trail	Pearson	Beginner Geography	3
Adventure at Sea	Storyworlds	Heinemann	Stage 9 Fantasy World	10
Adventure for Robo-dog, An	Oxford Reading Tree	OUP	All Stars Pack 1	9
Adventure in the Hills	PM Plus	Nelson Thornes	Silver Level	10
Adventure Park, The	Oxford Reading Tree	OUP	Stage 5 More Stories C	5
Adventures of the Robber Pig, The	Kingscourt Reading, Extension	Kingscourt	Set 8	8
After School	AlphaWorld	Gardner	Band 4: Blue	4
After the Flood	PM Storybooks	Nelson Thornes	Green Set B	5
After the Storm	AlphaWorld	Gardner	Band 6: Orange	6
Aha!	Story Street	Pearson	Step 3	3
Airline Pilot	I Love Reading	Ticktock	Blue Level	4
Airline Pilot	I Love Reading	Ticktock	Orange Level	6
Airline Pilot	I Love Reading	Ticktock	Purple Level	8
Akbar's Dream	Storyworld Bridges	Heinemann	Stage 11	10
Alex Brychta	Oxford Reading Tree	OUP	Stage 8 True Stories	8
Alex the Ant	Web Fiction	OUP	Stage 4 (Variety)	4
Ali, Hassan and the Donkey	Storyworlds	Heinemann	Stage 8 Once Upon a Time	8
Alien Landing	Info Trail	Pearson	Emergent Geography	8
All Aboard	Dragonflies	Gardner	Turquoise/Purple	7
All Aboard	Pathways	Collins	Year 2	8
All About Me	Four Corners	Pearson	Year 2	7
All in a Flap	Story Street	Pearson	Step 8	9
All Kinds of Dolls	Web Weavers Non-fiction	OUP	Non-fiction – Toys	7
Along the Seashore	Spotlight on Fact	Collins	Y2 The Seaside	7
Alphabet Party	Alphakids Plus	Gardner	Early Level 7	3
Alpine Search Dogs	Alphakids Plus	Gardner	Extending Level 24	10
Always Elephant	Rigby Star	Rigby	Star Plus	10
Ama's Blanket	Spotty Zebra	Nelson Thornes	Pink A – Change	1A
Amazing Ants	Alphakids Plus	Gardner	Transitional Level 17	6
Amazing Journeys	Alphakids	Gardner	Extending Level 22	9
Amazing Lifetimes	AlphaWorld	Gardner	Level 21 (ext)	9
Amazing Living Things	Alphakids Plus	Gardner	Extending Level 21	9
Amazing Plants	AlphaWorld	Gardner	Band 8: Purple	8
Amazing Sea Lizards	AlphaWorld	Gardner	Level 15 (trans)	6
Amazing Tricks	Kingscourt Reading, Extension	Kingscourt	Set 7	7
Ambulance Service, The	Rigby Star Non-fiction	Rigby	Orange Level	7
Amy's Armbands	Lighthouse	Ginn	Gold: 1	9
Anansi Traps a Snake	Web Fiction	OUP	Stage 1 (Variety)	3
And Pigs Might Fly	Crunchies	Orchard	Tall Tales	9
Androcles and the Lion	PM Traditional Tales	Nelson Thornes	Silver Level	10
Animal Armour	National Geographic	Rigby	Orange Level	7

TITLE	SERIES	PUBLISHER	SET (OR AUTHOR)	BAND
Animal Babies	First Explorers	Kingscourt	Level 1	9
Animal Band, The	PM Traditional Tales	Nelson Thornes	Purple Level	8
Animal Biscuits	Kingscourt Reading, Core	Kingscourt	Level 20 Benchmark Bk	8
Animal Builders	Alphakids	Gardner	Transitional Level 17	7
Animal Champions	AlphaWorld	Gardner	Level 22 (ext)	9
Animal Close-ups	AlphaWorld	Gardner	Band 8: Purple	8
Animal Communications	Alphakids	Gardner	Extending Level 19	9
Animal Diggers	Alphakids	Gardner	Transitional Level 16	6
Animal Faces	Oxford Reading Tree	OUP	Fireflies, More – Stage 1+	1A
Animal Feet	Oxford Reading Tree	OUP	Fireflies, More – Stage 4	3
Animal Feet	Rigby Star Non-fiction	Rigby	Green Level	5
Animal Graphs	PM Maths	Nelson Thornes	Stage B	4
Animal Homes	PM Plus Non-fiction	Nelson Thornes	Blue Level	5
Animal Homes	Web Weavers Non-fiction	OUP	Stage 1 First Words NF	1B
Animal Hospital	Badger NF Guided Reading	Ticktock	I Love Reading, Purple Level	8
Animal Hospital	I Love Reading	Ticktock	Blue Level	4
Animal Hospital	I Love Reading	Ticktock	Orange Level	6
Animal Hospital	I Love Reading	Ticktock	Purple Level	8
Animal Hospital, The	National Geographic	Rigby	Pink Level	1A
Animal House	Pathways	Collins	Year 1	4
Animal Life Cycles	Discovery World Links	Heinemann	Stage F	8
Animal Look-alikes	Four Corners	Pearson	Year 2	7
Animal Presents	Rigby Star	Rigby	Red Level	1A
Animal Rescue	Discovery World Links	Heinemann	Stage D	6
Animal Sets	Literacy and Science	Neate Publishing		8
Animal Skeletons	Alphakids	Gardner	Early Level 8	3
Animal Skeletons	Discovery World Links	Heinemann	Stage C	5
Animal Tails	Lighthouse	Ginn	Orange: 2	6
Animals at the Zoo	Web Fiction	OUP	Stage 1 (Variety)	2
Animals of the African Grasslands	AlphaWorld	Gardner	Level 24 (ext)	10
Animals That Sting	Alphakids Plus	Gardner	Transitional Level 16	8
Animals, The	Sails Foundation	Heinemann	Pink A – Can	1A
Anna's Amazing Multi-coloured Glasses	Pelican Big Bks	Pearson	Body, Wendy	5
Annie and the Pirates	Alphakids	Gardner	Extending Level 20	8
Answer the Phone, Fiona!	Lighthouse	Ginn	Blue: 1	4
Ant and the Dove, The	PM Plus	Nelson Thornes	Orange Level	6
Ant and the Dove, The	Storyworlds	Heinemann	Stage 4 Once Upon a Time	3
Ant and the Grasshopper, The	Kingscourt Reading, Core	Kingscourt	Level 19 Little Books	8
Ant and the Grasshopper, The	PM Plus	Nelson Thornes	Gold Level	9
Ant City	PM Storybooks	Nelson Thornes	Turquoise Set C	7
Antarctic Penguins	PM Non-fiction	Nelson Thornes	Silver Level	10
Antarctic Seals	PM Non-fiction	Nelson Thornes	Silver Level	10
Ants, The	Sails Foundation	Heinemann	Pink C – Go	1A
Any Excuse	Dragonflies	Gardner	Gold	9
Anya's Camera	PM Photo Stories	Nelson Thornes	Green 12	5
Anyone Can Have a Pet	PM Plus	Nelson Thornes	Purple Level	8
Apple Star, The	First Stories	Gardner	Emergent B	1B
Apples for Tiffy	PM Photo Stories	Nelson Thornes	Blue 11	4
Arabian Nights	Oxford Reading Tree	OUP	More Allstars Pack 3a	10
Arctic Hero	Oxford Reading Tree	OUP	Stage 10 True Stories	10
Are Mountains Like Children?	Info Trail	Pearson	Emergent Geography	9

TITLE	SERIES	PUBLISHER	SET (OR AUTHOR)	BAND
Arky, the Dinosaur With Feathers	PM Plus	Nelson Thornes	Gold Level	9
Art in the Past	Rigby Star Non-fiction	Rigby	Gold Level	8
Arthur's Fantastic Party	Big Cat	Collins	Orange	5
Artist, The	Spotty Zebra	Nelson Thornes	Red – Ourselves	2
As Heavy As	PM Maths	Nelson Thornes	Stage B	3
Asteroid, The	PM Storybooks	Nelson Thornes	Gold Set C	9
At Last!	Rigby Star	Rigby	Yellow Level	3
At Lunchtime	AlphaWorld	Gardner	Level 14 (trans)	6
At the Aquarium	AlphaWorld	Gardner	Band 1B: Pink	1B
At the Dump	Big Cat	Collins	Red B	2
At the Fair	Web Fiction	OUP	Stage 3 (Variety)	3
At The Library	PM Storybook Starters	Nelson Thornes	Set 2	1B
At the Market	Spotty Zebra	Nelson Thornes	Pink A – Ourselves	1A
At the Park	Oxford Reading Tree	OUP	Stage 1+ Patterned Stories	2
At the Pool	Oxford Reading Tree	OUP	Stage 3 More Stories B	3
At the Seaside	Oxford Reading Tree	OUP	Stage 3 More Stories A	3
At the Top of the World	Oxford Reading Tree	OUP	Stage 8 True Stories	10
At the Toyshop	PM Plus Non-fiction	Nelson Thornes	Red Level	2
At the Weekend	AlphaWorld	Gardner	Level 12 (trans)	5
At the Zoo	Alphakids Plus	Gardner	Emergent Level 1	1A
At the Zoo	PM Storybook Starters	Nelson Thornes	Set 1	1A
Australian Adventure	Oxford Reading Tree	OUP	Stage 7 More Stories C	6
Awumpalema	Literacy Links Plus	Kingscourt	Fluent A	8

B

Babies	Spotty Zebra	Nelson Thornes	Pink B – Ourselves	2
Baby	PM Plus	Nelson Thornes	Starters One	1A
Baby Animals	Rigby Star Non-fiction	Rigby	Yellow Level	2
Baby Bear Climbs a Tree	PM Plus	Nelson Thornes	Blue Level	4
Baby Bear Goes Fishing	PM Storybooks	Nelson Thornes	Yellow Set A	3
Baby Bear Goes Visiting	Alphakids Plus	Gardner	Early Level 10	4
Baby Bear's Hiding Place	PM Plus	Nelson Thornes	Blue Level	4
Baby Bear's Present	PM Storybooks	Nelson Thornes	Blue Set A	4
Baby Bird, The	Web Guided Reading	OUP	Stage 2 (Duck Green)	3
Baby Hippo	PM Storybooks	Nelson Thornes	Yellow Set B	3
Baby Lamb's First Drink	PM Storybooks	Nelson Thornes	Red Set A	2
Baby Owls, The	PM Storybooks	Nelson Thornes	Red Set B	2
Baby Panda	PM Plus	Nelson Thornes	Red Level	2
Baby Shark, The	National Geographic	Rigby	Yellow Level	3
Baby Wakes Up	PM Plus	Nelson Thornes	Red Level	2
Babysitter, The	PM Storybooks	Nelson Thornes	Green Set B	5
Babysitter, The	Story Street	Pearson	Step 5	5
Baby-sitter, The	Oxford Reading Tree	OUP	Stage 2 More Stories A	3
Bad Apple & The Carrot Field, The	New Way	Nelson Thornes	Green Easy Start Set A	5
Bad Bears and Good Bears	Crunchies	Orchard	Twice Upon a Time	8
Bad Bert and the Bully	Genre Range	Pearson	Emergent Comics	5
Bad Bert in Trouble	Story Street	Pearson	Step 6	6
Bad Boys and Naughty Girls	Crunchies	Orchard	Twice Upon a Time	9
Bad Cow & other stories	New Way	Nelson Thornes	Green Core Book	4

TITLE	SERIES	PUBLISHER	SET (OR AUTHOR)	BAND
Bad Day For Little Dinosaur, A	PM Gems	Nelson Thornes	Yellow 8	3
Badcats	Oxford Reading Tree	OUP	More Allstars Pack 2a	10
Bag of Coal, The	Storyworlds	Heinemann	Stage 5 Fantasy World	4
Bagels for Kids	Skyrider LM Chapters	Gardner	Set 1	9
Bake a Cake	Kingscourt Reading, Core	Kingscourt	Level 2 Collection	2
Baked Beans	Lighthouse	Ginn	Green: 5	5
Bakery, The	Alphakids	Gardner	Transitional Level 13	6
Balcony Garden	Kingscourt Reading, Extension	Kingscourt	Set 4	4
Ball Called Sam, A	Rigby Star	Rigby	Blue Level	4
Ball Games	PM Storybook Starters	Nelson Thornes	Set 2	1B
Ballet	Oxford Reading Tree	OUP	Fireflies, More – Stage 4	4
Balloon Ride, The	Sails Foundation	Heinemann	Pink B – See	1A
Balloon, The	Oxford Reading Tree	OUP	Stage 4 More Stories A	5
Balloons	Four Corners	Pearson	Year 2	7
Balloons	PM Plus	Nelson Thornes	Starters One	1A
Balloons Go Pop!	PM Gems	Nelson Thornes	Red 4	2
Balloons!	Kingscourt Reading, Extension	Kingscourt	Set 2	2
Balloons, The	Sails Foundation	Heinemann	Pink C – Going	1A
Balls	Alphakids Plus	Gardner	Emergent Level 2	1B
Band, The	Oxford Reading Tree	OUP	Stage 2 More Patterned Stories	2
Bang the Drum	Oxford Reading Tree	OUP	Cross-curricular Jackdaws	10
Bank Robbery & other stories, The	New Way	Nelson Thornes	Orange Core Book	9
Barbecue, The	Oxford Reading Tree	OUP	Stage 3 More Stories B	4
Barn Dance	Story Chest	Kingscourt	Ready-set-go Set BB	2
Barnaby's New House, The	Literacy Links Plus	Kingscourt	Early D	4
Barrel Of Gold, The	Story Chest	Kingscourt	Stage 4	5
Basil's Night Out	Kingscourt Reading, Core	Kingscourt	Gold	9
Bath-time Goggles	PM Photo Stories	Nelson Thornes	Blue 9	4
Bats	PM Non-fiction	Nelson Thornes	Gold Level	9
Be Quiet!	Rigby Star	Rigby	Yellow Level	3
Beach Boat, The	PM Gems	Nelson Thornes	Blue 9	4
Beach House, The	PM Plus	Nelson Thornes	Blue Level	4
Beach, The	Big Cat	Collins	Red A	1A
Beaks and Feet	Alphakids	Gardner	Early Level 11	5
Beanpole Billy	Lighthouse	Ginn	Gold: 5	9
Bear and the Bees, The	PM Plus	Nelson Thornes	Purple Level	8
Bear and the Trolls, The	PM Traditional Tales	Nelson Thornes	Silver Level	10
Bear Hunt	Lighthouse	Ginn	Yellow: 6	3
Bear That Wouldn't Growl, The	Storyworlds	Heinemann	Stage 8 Animal World	6
Bear Wakes Up	First Stories	Gardner	Emergent E	1B
Bears and the Honey, The	Storyworlds	Heinemann	Stage 2 Once Upon a Time	2
Bears and the Magpie, The	PM Plus	Nelson Thornes	Green Level	5
Bear's Diet	PM Storybooks	Nelson Thornes	Gold Set A	9
Bears' Picnic, The	Story Chest	Kingscourt	Ready-set-go Set AA	2
Bears, Bears, Bears	Kingscourt Reading, Core	Kingscourt	Level 7 Benchmark Bk	3
Bears, The	Sails Foundation	Heinemann	Pink B – Went	1A
Beastly Basil	Oxford Reading Tree	OUP	More Allstars Pack 2a	10
Beatrix Potter	Four Corners	Pearson	Year 1	5
Beauty and the Beast	PM Traditional Tales	Nelson Thornes	Gold Level	9
Because a Little Bug Went Ka-choo!	Beginner Books	Collins	Stone, Rosetta	6
Becky's Big Race	Sunshine Readers	Gardner	Purple Level	9

TITLE	SERIES	PUBLISHER	SET (OR AUTHOR)	BAND
Bed For David, A	Spotty Zebra	Nelson Thornes	Pink B – Change	1A
Bedtime	PM Plus	Nelson Thornes	Red Level	2
Bee, The	Story Chest	Kingscourt	Ready-set-go Set B	1B
Bees and the Bear, The	Kingscourt Reading, Core	Kingscourt	Level 11 Little Books	4
Before I Go to School	Kingscourt Reading, Extension	Kingscourt	Set 2	2
Bella's Baby Bird	Kingscourt Reading, Core	Kingscourt	Gold	7
Ben and the Bird	Story Street	Pearson	Step 5	6
Ben and the Boxes	Story Street	Pearson	Step 3	3
Ben and the Ghost	Story Street	Pearson	Step 7	9
Ben and the Pop Star	Story Street	Pearson	Step 4	5
Ben Gets a Hat	Story Street	Pearson	Step 2	2
Ben Gets Cross	Story Street	Pearson	Step 4	4
Ben the Bold	Literacy Links Plus	Kingscourt	Emergent C	3
Bend, Stretch and Leap	PM Plus	Nelson Thornes	Purple Level	8
Bendemolena	Spotlight on Plays	Collins	Age 7+	10
Ben's Dad	PM Storybooks	Nelson Thornes	Yellow Set A	3
Ben's Get Well Cards	Genre Range	Pearson	Emergent Letters	6
Ben's Jigsaw Puzzle	PM Gems	Nelson Thornes	Red 5	2
Ben's Red Car	PM Storybook Starters	Nelson Thornes	Set 2	1B
Ben's Teddy Bear	PM Storybooks	Nelson Thornes	Red Set A	2
Ben's Tooth	PM Storybooks	Nelson Thornes	Green Set A	5
Ben's Treasure Hunt	PM Storybooks	Nelson Thornes	Red Set A	2
Berry Cake, The	PM Photo Stories	Nelson Thornes	Blue 11	4
Bert's Band	Big Cat	Collins	Blue	4
Best Birthday, The	Skyrider LM Chapters	Gardner	Set 1	9
Best Cake, The	PM Storybooks	Nelson Thornes	Blue Set A	4
Best Children in the World, The	Story Chest	Kingscourt	Ready-set-go Set DD	3
Best Dancer, The	PM Photo Stories	Nelson Thornes	Blue 9	4
Best Fish, The	Web Guided Reading	OUP	Stage 3 (Duck Green)	3
Best Hats, The	PM Plus	Nelson Thornes	Blue Level	4
Best of Friends	Alphakids Plus	Gardner	Extending Level 21	8
Best Part, The	PM Storybooks	Nelson Thornes	Silver Set B	10
Best Pet, The	Lighthouse	Ginn	Purple: 3	8
Best Pizza in the World, The	Alphakids Plus	Gardner	Emergent Level 5	3
Betcha!	Sunshine Readers	Gardner	Orange Level	6
Better Letter, A	Genre Range	Pearson	Beginner Letters	2
Betty Boots	Alphakids	Gardner	Extending Level 18	7
Beyond Strange Street	Story Street	Pearson	Step 7	10
Bicycle, The	Story Chest	Kingscourt	Get-ready Set B	1B
Biff's Aeroplane	Oxford Reading Tree	OUP	Stage 2 More Stories B	3
Big and Little	Kingscourt Reading, Extension	Kingscourt	Set 1	1A
Big and Little	Oxford Reading Tree	OUP	Fireflies Stage 1+	2
Big and Little	PM Plus	Nelson Thornes	Starters Two	1B
Big and Small	Alphakids Plus	Gardner	Emergent Level 1	1B
Big Bad Raps	Crunchies	Orchard	Raps	8
Big Bad Wolf, The	PM Plus	Nelson Thornes	Orange Level	6
Big Balloon Festival, The	PM Storybooks	Nelson Thornes	Gold Set B	9
Big Barry Baker and the Bullies	Storyworlds	Heinemann	Stage 9 Our World	10
Big Barry Baker in Big Trouble	Storyworlds	Heinemann	Stage 9 Our World	9
Big Barry Baker on the Stage	Storyworlds	Heinemann	Stage 9 Our World	9
Big Barry Baker's Parcel	Storyworlds	Heinemann	Stage 9 Our World	9

TITLE	SERIES	PUBLISHER	SET (OR AUTHOR)	BAND
Big Bear's Bad Day	Web Fiction	OUP	Stage 2 (Variety)	2
Big Bear's Party	Web Fiction	OUP	Stage 2 (Variety)	2
Big Bear's Socks	Kingscourt Reading, Extension	Kingscourt	Set 3	4
Big Bo Peep	Lighthouse	Ginn	Gold: 4	9
Big Books and Little Books	Web Guided Reading	OUP	Stage 2 (Duck Green)	3
Big Boots	Storyworlds	Heinemann	Stage 6 Our World	6
Big Box & other stories, The	New Way	Nelson Thornes	Green Platform Books	5
Big Breakfast, The	Oxford Reading Tree	OUP	Stage 7 More Stories C	7
Big Brother	AlphaWorld	Gardner	Band 2: Red	2
Big Cat Babies	Big Cat	Collins	Green	6
Big Cats	Oxford Reading Tree	OUP	Fireflies, More – Stage 4	4
Big Dog, The	Alphakids	Gardner	Transitional Level 14	6
Big Helicopter, The	PM Gems	Nelson Thornes	Yellow 6	3
Big Hill, The	PM Plus	Nelson Thornes	Red Level	2
Big Hit, The	PM Plus	Nelson Thornes	Yellow Level	3
Big Hole, The	PM Gems	Nelson Thornes	Magenta 2/3	1B
Big Kick, The	PM Storybooks	Nelson Thornes	Red Set A	2
Big Machines at Sea	PM Plus Non-fiction	Nelson Thornes	Turquoise Level	7
Big Machines for Fun and Sport	PM Plus Non-fiction	Nelson Thornes	Turquoise Level	7
Big Machines in Emergencies	PM Plus Non-fiction	Nelson Thornes	Turquoise Level	8
Big Machines in the Air	PM Plus Non-fiction	Nelson Thornes	Turquoise Level	7
Big Machines on Rails	PM Plus Non-fiction	Nelson Thornes	Turquoise Level	8
Big Machines on the Road	PM Plus Non-fiction	Nelson Thornes	Turquoise Level	7
Big Pig's Wig	Alphakids	Gardner	Extending Level 23	10
Big Puddle, The	Web Guided Reading	OUP	Stage 3 (Duck Green)	2
Big Rad	Sunshine Readers	Gardner	Light Blue Level	6
Big Sea Animals	PM Plus	Nelson Thornes	Starters Two	1B
Big Shapes and Little Shapes	PM Maths	Nelson Thornes	Stage A	1B
Big Snowball, The	Storyworlds	Heinemann	Stage 5 Fantasy World	4
Big Surprise, The	Storyworlds	Heinemann	Stage 2 Animal World	1B
Big Tease, The	Story Chest	Kingscourt	Stage 7	10
Big Things	PM Storybook Starters	Nelson Thornes	Set 1	1A
Big Wig	Walker Starters	Walker	West, Colin	9
Big Yellow Castle, The	PM Plus	Nelson Thornes	Yellow Level	3
Big, Bigger, Biggest	Rigby Star Non-fiction	Rigby	Pink Level	2
Biggest Tree, The	PM Storybooks	Nelson Thornes	Orange Set A	6
Big-head & The Greedy Dog	New Way	Nelson Thornes	Green Easy Start Set B	6
Bike for Alex, A	PM Plus	Nelson Thornes	Orange Level	6
Bike for Brad, A	PM Storybooks	Nelson Thornes	Purple Set B	8
Bike Race, The	Sails Foundation	Heinemann	Pink C – Go	1A
Billie the Hippo	Skyrider LM Chapters	Gardner	Set 1	8
Billy at School	PM Plus	Nelson Thornes	Blue Level	4
Billy Banana	Alphakids Plus	Gardner	Early Level 11	4
Billy Beetle	Web Fiction	OUP	Stage 4 (Variety)	3
Billy Can Count	PM Plus	Nelson Thornes	Yellow Level	3
Billy is Hiding	PM Plus	Nelson Thornes	Red Level	2
Billy's Baby	Story Street	Pearson	Step 4	4
Bingo and the Bone	Storyworlds	Heinemann	Stage 2 Animal World	2
Bingo and the Ducks	PM Gems	Nelson Thornes	Yellow 6	3
Bingo Goes to School	PM Plus	Nelson Thornes	Blue Level	4
Bingo Wants to Play	Storyworlds	Heinemann	Stage 2 Animal World	2

TITLE	SERIES	PUBLISHER	SET (OR AUTHOR)	BAND
Bingo's Birthday	PM Plus	Nelson Thornes	Yellow Level	3
Bingo's Ice-Cream	PM Plus	Nelson Thornes	Red Level	2
Bird Families	Alphakids Plus	Gardner	Extending Level 18	8
Bird Hide, The	Alphakids	Gardner	Extending Level 20	7
Bird in the Bush, A	Web Guided Reading	OUP	Stage 7 (Duck Green)	7
Bird Lady, The	Kingscourt Reading, Core	Kingscourt	Level 20 Little Books	8
Bird Song	Kingscourt Reading, Extension	Kingscourt	Set 5	5
Bird That Could Think, The	PM Plus	Nelson Thornes	Turquoise Level	7
Bird Watchers	Kingscourt Reading, Extension	Kingscourt	Set 9	9
Bird Watching	PM Plus	Nelson Thornes	Purple Level	8
Bird, The	Sails Foundation	Heinemann	Pink B – Was	1A
Birds	Go Facts	A&C Black	Animals	8
Bird's Eye View	PM Storybooks	Nelson Thornes	Turquoise Set B	7
Birds of Prey	Kingscourt Reading, Extension	Kingscourt	Set 9	9
Birthday Balloons	PM Storybooks	Nelson Thornes	Blue Set B	4
Birthday Bug, The	Kingscourt Reading, Core	Kingscourt	Level 2 Little Books	1B
Birthday Cake For Ben, A	PM Storybooks	Nelson Thornes	Red Set B	2
Birthday Cake, The	Story Chest	Kingscourt	Stage 2	5
Birthday Cakes	Alphakids	Gardner	Emergent Level 4	2
Birthday For Bluebell, A	Crunchies	Orchard	Colour Crackers	9
Birthday Kitten, The	PM Photo Stories	Nelson Thornes	Yellow 8	3
Birthday Presents	PM Plus	Nelson Thornes	Blue Level	4
Birthday Surprise	Spotty Zebra	Nelson Thornes	Red – Change	2
Birthday Treasure Hunt, The	Info Trail	Pearson	Emergent Geography	8
Birthday, The	Sails Foundation	Heinemann	Pink C – Going	1A
Black and White	Kingscourt Reading, Extension	Kingscourt	Set 2	2
Blackberries	PM Storybooks	Nelson Thornes	Yellow Set A	3
Blink-off, The	Dragonflies	Gardner	Turquoise/Purple	8
Blow, Wind, Blow!	Kingscourt Reading, Core	Kingscourt	Level 4 Collection	2
Blow-away Kite, The	PM Plus	Nelson Thornes	Orange Level	6
Blue Eye, The	Oxford Reading Tree	OUP	Stage 9 More Stories A	8
Blue Jackal, The	Genre Range	Pearson	Emergent Traditional Tales	6
Blue Rabbit & other stories, The	New Way	Nelson Thornes	Blue Parallel Books	6
Blueberry Muffins	Story Chest	Kingscourt	Ready-set-go Set DD	4
BMX Billy	Literacy Links Plus	Kingscourt	Early C	4
Boat Ride, The	PM Gems	Nelson Thornes	Magenta 2/3	1B
Boat, A	Sails Foundation	Heinemann	Pink B – See	1A
Body Parts	Badger NF Guided Reading	Neate Publishing	Literacy and Science	8
Body Parts	Literacy and Science	Neate Publishing		8
Body Talk	Kingscourt Reading, Core	Kingscourt	Level 13 Little Books	6
Boogie-Woogie Man, The	Story Chest	Kingscourt	Get-ready Set DD	2
Boogly, The	Literacy Links Plus	Kingscourt	Emergent D	3
Book of Space	Four Corners	Pearson	Year 2	9
Book Week	Oxford Reading Tree	OUP	Stage 3 More Stories B	3
Book Week Goes With a Bang – Part 1	Story Street	Pearson	Step 9	10
Book Week Goes With a Bang – Part 2	Story Street	Pearson	Step 9	10
Boomerangs	Kingscourt Reading, Core	Kingscourt	Level 11 Little Books	5
Boots and Shoes	Oxford Reading Tree	OUP	Fireflies, More – Stage 2	2
Boring Old Bed	Lighthouse	Ginn	Turquoise: 2	7
Boris the Brainiest Baby	Crunchies	Orchard	The One And Only	8
Bossy Bettina	Literacy Links Plus	Kingscourt	Early C	5

TITLE	SERIES	PUBLISHER	SET (OR AUTHOR)	BAND
Bounce, Catch, Kick, Throw	Big Cat	Collins	Orange	6
Bouncer Comes to Stay	Storyworlds	Heinemann	Stage 7 Our World	6
Box, The	First Stories	Gardner	Emergent C	1A
Box, The	Web Guided Reading	OUP	Stage 2 (Duck Green)	2
Boxes	Literacy Links Plus	Kingscourt	Early C	6
Boxes of Fun	Kingscourt Reading, Core	Kingscourt	Level 5 Little Books	2
Boxes, Tins and Balls	PM Maths	Nelson Thornes	Stage B	3
Boy Who Cried Wolf, The	PM Traditional Tales	Nelson Thornes	Purple Level	8
Boy Who Cried Wolf, The	Storyworlds	Heinemann	Stage 3 Once Upon a Time	2
Boy Who Talked to the Birds, The	Web Fiction	OUP	Stage 7 (Variety)	7
Boy Who Tried to Hide, The	Kingscourt Reading, Extension	Kingscourt	Set 5	5
Boy Who Wanted to be Famous, The	Alphakids Plus	Gardner	Extending Level 22	9
Boy Who Went to the North Wind, The	Literacy Links Plus	Kingscourt	Fluent D	7
Brad's Birthday Cake	PM Gems	Nelson Thornes	Green 13	5
Brand-new Butterfly, A	Literacy Links Plus	Kingscourt	Early C	7
Brave Baby, The	Big Cat	Collins	Orange	5
Brave Father Mouse	PM Storybooks	Nelson Thornes	Yellow Set A	3
Brave Little Mouse	Kingscourt Reading, Core	Kingscourt	Level 16 Little Books	6
Brave Little Tailor, The	PM Traditional Tales	Nelson Thornes	Turquoise Level	7
Brave Mouse Part 1	Story Street	Pearson	Step 3	3
Brave Mouse Part 2	Story Street	Pearson	Step 3	3
Brave Triceratops	PM Storybooks	Nelson Thornes	Green Set A	5
Bread for the Ducks	PM Plus	Nelson Thornes	Yellow Level	3
Breakfast on the Farm	Kingscourt Reading, Extension	Kingscourt	Set 2	2
Brementown Musicians, The	Spotlight on Plays	Collins	Age 7+	10
Brer Rabbit's Trickbag	Oxford Reading Tree	OUP	All Stars Pack 3	10
Bridge, The	Story Chest	Kingscourt	Get-ready Set BB	2
Bridges	AlphaWorld	Gardner	Level 21 (ext)	9
Bringing the Sea Back Home	Literacy Links Plus	Kingscourt	Fluent C	10
Broad Bean	Stopwatch	A&C Black		7
Broken Flower Pot, The	PM Plus	Nelson Thornes	Blue Level	4
Broken Roof, The	Oxford Reading Tree	OUP	Stage 6 & 7 Stories	7
Bronwen The Brave	Pathways	Collins	Year 2	8
Brother Trouble	Skyrider LM Chapters	Gardner	Set 1	9
Brown Bears	PM Non-fiction	Nelson Thornes	Turquoise Level	8
Brown Mouse Gets Some Corn	PM Plus	Nelson Thornes	Blue Level	4
Brown Mouse Plays a Trick	PM Plus	Nelson Thornes	Blue Level	4
Bruno the Bravest Man	Crunchies	Orchard	The One And Only	7
Bubbles in the Sky	PM Gems	Nelson Thornes	Magenta 2/3	2
Budgies	PM Non-fiction	Nelson Thornes	Orange Level	6
Buffy's Tricks	Literacy Links Plus	Kingscourt	Early C	4
Bug Athletes	Badger NF Guided Reading	Chrysalis	Bug Zone	9
Bug Watch	I Love Reading	Ticktock	Blue Level	4
Bug Watch	I Love Reading	Ticktock	Orange Level	6
Bug Watch	I Love Reading	Ticktock	Purple Level	8
Bugs	Kingscourt Reading, Core	Kingscourt	Level 9 Collection	4
Bugs for Breakfast	PM Plus	Nelson Thornes	Blue Level	4
Building a House	PM Plus Non-Fiction	Nelson Thornes	Blue Level	5
Building a Road	Oxford Reading Tree	OUP	Fireflies, More – Stage 3	3
Building Site, The	Web Weavers Non-fiction	OUP	Stage 2 First Words NF	4
Buildings for a Purpose	First Explorers	Kingscourt	Level 2	9

TITLE	SERIES	PUBLISHER	SET (OR AUTHOR)	BAND
Bull in a China Shop, A	Literacy Links Plus	Kingscourt	Fluent B	9
Bull's-eye	Oxford Reading Tree	OUP	Stage 3 More Stories B	3
Bully Bear	Rigby Star	Rigby	Blue Level	4
Bully, The	Oxford Reading Tree	OUP	Stage 7 More Stories A	7
Bully, The	PM Plus	Nelson Thornes	Silver Level	10
Bumper Cars, The	PM Storybooks	Nelson Thornes	Red Set B	2
Bumper Cars, The	Sails Foundation	Heinemann	Pink C – Me	1A
Bun, The	Kingscourt Reading, Extension	Kingscourt	Set 7	7
Burrows	Kingscourt Reading, Extension	Kingscourt	Set 2	2
Bus Ride, The	Kingscourt Reading, Extension	Kingscourt	Set 3	3
Bushfire in the Koala Reserve	PM Plus	Nelson Thornes	Gold Level	9
Busking	Sunshine Readers	Gardner	Orange Level Supplementary	5
Busy Beavers, The	PM Storybooks	Nelson Thornes	Orange Set C	6
Busy Bird	Alphakids Plus	Gardner	Transitional Level 13	5
Busy Trucks	I Love Reading	Ticktock	Blue Level	4
Butterfly	Alphakids	Gardner	Emergent Level 3	2
Butterfly and Caterpillar	Stopwatch	A&C Black		9
Butterfly Garden	Alphakids Plus	Gardner	Extending Level 20	8
Butterfly Net, The	Kingscourt Reading, Extension	Kingscourt	Set 3	3
Butterfly, the Bird, the Beetle and Me, The	Alphakids	Gardner	Transitional Level 15	6
Buttons	First Stories	Gardner	Emergent F	1B
Buzz and Bingo in the Fairytale Forest	Big Cat	Collins	Gold	9
Buzz and Bingo in the Monster Maze	Big Cat	Collins	Purple	8
By Land, Sea and Air	AlphaWorld	Gardner	Level 24 (ext)	10
By the Stream	Oxford Reading Tree	OUP	Stage 3 Storybooks	3

C

Cabbage Princess, The	Literacy Links Plus	Kingscourt	Fluent D	8
Cabin in the Hills, The	PM Storybooks	Nelson Thornes	Turquoise Set A	7
Cake, The	Kingscourt Reading, Core	Kingscourt	Level 6 Little Books	3
Camcorder, The	Oxford Reading Tree	OUP	Stage 4 More Stories A	5
Camels and Their Cousins	Kingscourt Reading, Extension	Kingscourt	Set 8	8
Camping	Alphakids Plus	Gardner	Early Level 9	4
Camping	Kingscourt Reading, Extension	Kingscourt	Set 3	3
Camping	Rigby Star Non-fiction	Rigby	Green Level	5
Camping Adventure	Oxford Reading Tree	OUP	Stage 5 More Stories B	5
Camping At School	Kingscourt Reading, Core	Kingscourt	White	9
Camping Holiday & other stories, The	New Way	Nelson Thornes	Green Platform Books	5
Can I Have a Pet?	Web Fiction	OUP	Stage 1 (Variety)	2
Can I Play Outside?	Literacy Links Plus	Kingscourt	Early A	4
Can You See?	Sails Foundation	Heinemann	Pink C – You	1A
Can You See Me?	Alphakids	Gardner	Emergent Level 1	1A
Can You See The Eggs?	PM Storybook Starters	Nelson Thornes	Set 2	1B
Canal Boat Cat	Storyworlds	Heinemann	Stage 9 Animal World	7
Candlelight	PM Storybooks	Nelson Thornes	Green Set A	5
Captain Bumble	Story Chest	Kingscourt	Stage 5	7
Captain Motley and the Pirate's Gold	Rockets	A&C Black	Ryan, Margaret	10
Car Trouble	PM Storybooks	Nelson Thornes	Gold Set B	9
Careful Crocodile, The	PM Storybooks	Nelson Thornes	Orange Set C	6

TITLE	SERIES	PUBLISHER	SET (OR AUTHOR)	BAND
Caribou (Reindeer)	PM Non-fiction	Nelson Thornes	Silver Level	10
Caring For Our World	Rigby Star Non-fiction	Rigby	Gold Level	9
Caring For Pets	First Facts	Badger	Level 1	1B
Caring For Plants	First Facts	Badger	Level 1	2
Carl's High Jump	PM Plus	Nelson Thornes	Gold Level	9
Carnival Horse, The	PM Plus	Nelson Thornes	Purple Level	8
Carnival, The	Oxford Reading Tree	OUP	Stage 3 More Stories B	4
Carnival, The	Story Street	Pearson	Step 6	8
Carnivals Around The World	Lighthouse	Ginn	Yellow: 7	3
Castle Adventure	Oxford Reading Tree	OUP	Stage 5 Storybooks	5
Castle, The	Storyworlds	Heinemann	Stage 6 Our World	6
Castles	Big Cat	Collins	Turquoise	7
Cat and Dog	Alphakids	Gardner	Extending Level 19	8
Cat and Mouse	PM Storybook Starters	Nelson Thornes	Set 2	1B
Cat and Rat Fall Out	Lighthouse	Ginn	Turquoise: 4	7
Cat and the Mouse, The	Alphakids Plus	Gardner	Early Level 8	4
Cat and the Stars, The	Dragonflies	Gardner	Gold	9
Cat Called Tim, A	New Way	Nelson Thornes	Orange Platform Books	8
Cat Concert	Literacy Links Plus	Kingscourt	Fluent A	8
Cat in the Hat, The	Beginner Books	Collins	Seuss, Dr	7
Cat in the Tree, A	Oxford Reading Tree	OUP	Stage 3 Storybooks	4
Cat on the Roof	Story Chest	Kingscourt	Stage 5	8
Catch It!	Rigby Star	Rigby	Pink Level	1A
Catching the Wind	Four Corners	Pearson	Year 2	7
Caterpillar Story, The	Badger NF Guided Reading	Evans Bros	Rainbows	6
Cat-Flap Trap, The	Kingscourt Reading, Core	Kingscourt	Level 15 Little Books	6
Cats	Alphakids Plus	Gardner	Emergent Level 3	1B
Cats	Big Cat	Collins	Pink B	1A
Cats	Kingscourt Reading, Core	Kingscourt	Level 20 Collection	8
Cats	PM Non-fiction	Nelson Thornes	Orange Level	6
Cats and Dogs	Genre Range	Pearson	Beginner Comics	3
Cattle	PM Non-fiction	Nelson Thornes	Purple Level	9
Caves	Kingscourt Reading, Extension	Kingscourt	Set 9	9
Cecil the Caterpillar	Lighthouse	Ginn	Yellow: 1	3
Celebrations	Kingscourt Reading, Extension	Kingscourt	Set 5	5
Cephalopods	Skyrider LM Chapters	Gardner	Set 2	8
Chairs	Alphakids Plus	Gardner	Emergent Level 1	1A
Chalk Talk	Kingscourt Reading, Extension	Kingscourt	Set 1	1B
Chameleons of the Rain Forest	Skyrider LM Chapters	Gardner	Set 2	9
Changes	Web Weavers Non-fiction	OUP	Stage 1 First Words NF	1B
Changing Earth, The	Four Corners	Pearson	Year 2	10
Changing Materials	Discovery World Links	Heinemann	Stage E	10
Changing Shape	Rigby Star Non-fiction	Rigby	Turquoise Level	9
Changing Shores	Four Corners	Pearson	Year 2	8
Charlie	Literacy Links Plus	Kingscourt	Fluent D	10
Charlie Stories	Oxford Reading Tree	OUP	More Allstars Pack 1a	9
Charlie the Bridesmaid	Rigby Star	Rigby	White Level	10
Charlie's Great Race	PM Plus	Nelson Thornes	Silver Level	10
Charlie's PE Kit	Lighthouse	Ginn	Yellow: 3	3
Chase, The	Oxford Reading Tree	OUP	Stage 2 More Stories B	3
Check-up, The	Spotty Zebra	Nelson Thornes	Pink B – Ourselves	2

TITLE	SERIES	PUBLISHER	SET (OR AUTHOR)	BAND
Cheerful Cricket, The	Alphakids Plus	Gardner	Extending Level 18	6
Cheese, Please!	Kingscourt Reading, Core	Kingscourt	Level 4 Little Books	2
Cherokee Little People, The	Rigby Star	Rigby	Purple Level	8
Cherry Blossom Cat	Storyworlds	Heinemann	Stage 9 Animal World	10
Chick	Badger NF Guided Reading	Chrysalis	Baby Animals	6
Chicken and Egg	Stopwatch	A&C Black		7
Chicken For Dinner	Story Chest	Kingscourt	Ready-set-go Set AA	2
Chicken-Licken	PM Traditional Tales	Nelson Thornes	Orange Level	6
Chickens	PM Non-fiction	Nelson Thornes	Purple Level	9
Chicks Hatching	Spotty Zebra	Nelson Thornes	Red – Change	2
Children's Farm, The	AlphaWorld	Gardner	Level 13 (trans)	5
Chinese Adventure	Oxford Reading Tree	OUP	Stage 7 More Stories A	7
Chloe the Chameleon	Rigby Star	Rigby	Orange Level	6
Chocolate Cake, The	PM Plus	Nelson Thornes	Purple Level	8
Chocolate Tree, The	Alphakids Plus	Gardner	Extending Level 20	8
Choice for Sarah, A	PM Plus	Nelson Thornes	Silver Level	10
Choices	Oxford Reading Tree	OUP	Fireflies Stage 3	3
Chooky	PM Plus	Nelson Thornes	Orange Level	6
Choose the Shoes	Web Guided Reading	OUP	Stage 3 (Duck Green)	2
Choosing a Puppy	PM Storybooks	Nelson Thornes	Yellow Set B	3
Choosing Toys	Spotlight on Fact	Collins	Y1 Toys and Games	3
Christmas Adventure	Oxford Reading Tree	OUP	Stage 6 More Stories A	6
Christmas Disco, The	Story Street	Pearson	Step 6	8
Christmas Fair, The	Oxford Reading Tree	OUP	Citizenship Stories Stage 9/10	9
Christmas Tree, The	PM Storybooks	Nelson Thornes	Blue Set A	4
Chug the Tractor	PM Storybooks	Nelson Thornes	Blue Set B	4
Cinderella	Pelican Big Bks	Pearson	Cullimore, Stan	8
Cinderella	PM Traditional Tales	Nelson Thornes	Gold Level	9
Circle Magic	Rockets	A&C Black	Smith, Wendy	9
Circus	Alphakids Plus	Gardner	Emergent Level 1	1A
Circus Boy	Alphakids Plus	Gardner	Early Level 11	5
City and Country	Alphakids Plus	Gardner	Extending Level 18	7
City Cat	Storyworlds	Heinemann	Stage 9 Animal World	10
City, Farm and Sea	First Facts	Badger	Level 2	2
Clang!	Story Street	Pearson	Step 5	6
Clarence the Crocodile	New Way	Nelson Thornes	Violet Platform Books	7
Classroom Animals	AlphaWorld	Gardner	Band 7: Turquoise	7
Classroom Caterpillars, The	PM Plus	Nelson Thornes	Green Level	5
Clay Creatures	Rigby Star Non-fiction	Rigby	Orange Level	6
Clay Dog, The	Lighthouse	Ginn	Turquoise: 5	7
Cleaner Genie	Oxford Reading Tree	OUP	More Allstars Pack 2a	9
Clever Chick, The	Rigby Star	Rigby	Green Level	5
Clever Coyote and Other Wild Dogs	Kingscourt Reading, Extension	Kingscourt	Set 9	9
Clever Fox	PM Plus	Nelson Thornes	Yellow Level	3
Clever Invention, A	Oxford Reading Tree	OUP	Citizenship Stories Stage 9/10	9
Clever Jackals, The	PM Gems	Nelson Thornes	Green 14	5
Clever Joe	Storyworlds	Heinemann	Stage 2 Our World	2
Clever Little Bird	Kingscourt Reading, Extension	Kingscourt	Set 3	3
Clever Monkey	Oxford Reading Tree	OUP	All Stars Pack 3	10
Clever Mr Brown	Story Chest	Kingscourt	Stage 4	7
Clever Penguins, The	PM Storybooks	Nelson Thornes	Green Set A	5

TITLE	SERIES	PUBLISHER	SET (OR AUTHOR)	BAND
Climbing	Literacy Links Plus	Kingscourt	Emergent C	1A
Climbing	PM Storybook Starters	Nelson Thornes	Set 1	1A
Clothes	First Facts	Badger	Level 2	2
Clothes For Rain	Oxford Reading Tree	OUP	Fireflies, More – Stage 1+	1A
Clouds	Four Corners	Pearson	Year 1	7
Clown and Elephant	Story Chest	Kingscourt	Get-ready Set C	1B
Clown in the Well	Story Chest	Kingscourt	Ready-set-go Set DD	4
Clown, The	First Stories	Gardner	Emergent B	1A
Clubhouse, The	PM Storybooks	Nelson Thornes	Gold Set A	9
Clumsy Tiger, The	Dragonflies	Gardner	Turquoise/Purple	8
Coastlines	Alphakids Plus	Gardner	Transitional Level 15	8
Cobra Cat	Storyworlds	Heinemann	Stage 9 Animal World	10
Coconut Lunches	Sunshine Readers	Gardner	Purple Level Supplementary	9
Coconut: Seed or Fruit?	Four Corners	Pearson	Year 1	7
Coco's Bell	PM Plus	Nelson Thornes	Green Level	5
Cold Day, The	Oxford Reading Tree	OUP	Stage 3 More Stories B	4
Colour it My Way	Kingscourt Reading, Core	Kingscourt	Level 8 Little Books	4
Colours Around Us	Literacy and Science	Neate Publishing		8
Come	Sails Foundation	Heinemann	Pink C – Come	1A
Come and Play	Kingscourt Reading, Core	Kingscourt	Level 5 Little Books	2
Come and Visit the Moon!	Info Trail	Pearson	Emergent Science	5
Come Back, Pip!	PM Plus	Nelson Thornes	Turquoise Level	7
Come in the Grass	Sails Foundation	Heinemann	Pink C – Come	1A
Come In!	Oxford Reading Tree	OUP	Stage 4 Storybooks	4
Come On, Tim	PM Storybooks	Nelson Thornes	Blue Set A	4
Come to My Party!	Info Trail	Pearson	Emergent Geography	6
Come to the Circus	Big Cat	Collins	Pink B	1A
Comic Illustrators	Oxford Reading Tree	OUP	Fireflies Stage 9	9
Competition, The	Dragonflies	Gardner	Turquoise/Purple	8
Computer Game, The	Rigby Star	Rigby	Yellow Level	3
Concert, The	Oxford Reading Tree	OUP	Citizenship Stories Stage 9/10	10
Concrete	Alphakids	Gardner	Early Level 9	4
Concrete Jungle	Skyrider LM Chapters	Gardner	Set 2	8
Contest, The	PM Plus	Nelson Thornes	Silver Level	10
Cooking	Sails Foundation	Heinemann	Pink C – Get	1A
Cooking Dinner	National Geographic	Rigby	Blue Level	4
Cooking Pot	Story Chest	Kingscourt	Stage 6	9
Cooking Pot, The	Storyworlds	Heinemann	Stage 6 Once Upon a Time	5
Cooped Up	Skyrider LM Chapters	Gardner	Set 1	9
Copy-Cat	Story Chest	Kingscourt	Ready-set-go Set B	1B
Coral Reef Diary	AlphaWorld	Gardner	Level 16 (trans)	6
Corker, The	Web Guided Reading	OUP	Stage 7 (Duck Green)	6
Corn	National Geographic	Rigby	Turquoise Level	8
Cosmo for Captain	Oxford Reading Tree	OUP	All Stars Pack 1	8
Costume Parade, The	Web Fiction	OUP	Stage 7 (Variety)	8
Could We Live on the Moon?	Four Corners	Pearson	Year 2	7
Count on Your Body	Rigby Star Non-fiction	Rigby	White Level	10
Countdown	Story Chest	Kingscourt	Stage 7	10
Counting Down	PM Maths	Nelson Thornes	Stage A	1B
Cow Up a Tree	Kingscourt Reading, Core	Kingscourt	Level 11 Benchmark Bk	4
Cows in the Garden	PM Storybooks	Nelson Thornes	Blue Set A	4

TITLE	SERIES	PUBLISHER	SET (OR AUTHOR)	BAND
Coyote in Trouble	Skyrider LM Chapters	Gardner	Set 1	7
Coyote, Fox, and Wolf Tales	Kingscourt Reading, Extension	Kingscourt	Set 8	8
Crab at the Bottom of the Sea, The	Literacy Links Plus	Kingscourt	Early C	6
Crab Hunt, The	PM Photo Stories	Nelson Thornes	Blue 11	4
Crabs	Alphakids Plus	Gardner	Transitional Level 16	7
Crash!	First Stories	Gardner	Emergent A	1A
Crazy Miss Maisey's Alphabet Pets	Kingscourt Reading, Extension	Kingscourt	Set 10	10
Creepy Castle, The	Storyworlds	Heinemann	Stage 5 Fantasy World	4
Creepy Crawly	Oxford Reading Tree	OUP	Stage 2 Patterned Stories	2
Cricket Bat Mystery, The	Storyworlds	Heinemann	Stage 7 Our World	6
Crocodile and a Whale, A	PM Plus	Nelson Thornes	Yellow Level	3
Crocodile Watching	Alphakids Plus	Gardner	Transitional Level 15	7
Crocodile's Bag	Kingscourt Reading, Extension	Kingscourt	Set 7	7
Crosby Crocodile's Disguise	Literacy Links Plus	Kingscourt	Fluent D	8
Cross Country Race	PM Storybooks	Nelson Thornes	Green Set A	5
Crossing the Atlantic	Four Corners	Pearson	Year 2	8
Crow and the Pot, The	PM Plus	Nelson Thornes	Green Level	5
Crown Jewels, The	Rockets	A&C Black	Rodgers, Frank	9
Cup of Tea, A	New Way	Nelson Thornes	Green Easy Start Set B	5
Cup Run	Walker Starters	Walker	Waddell, Martin	9
Curly is Hungry	Rigby Star	Rigby	Red Level	1B
Curly to the Rescue	Rigby Star	Rigby	Yellow Level	3

D

TITLE	SERIES	PUBLISHER	SET (OR AUTHOR)	BAND
Dad	PM Storybook Starters	Nelson Thornes	Set 1	1A
Dad and the Mosquito	Sunshine Readers	Gardner	Orange Level Supplementary	6
Dad Didn't Mind at All	Literacy Links Plus	Kingscourt	Early C	5
Dad's Bathtime	Literacy Links Plus	Kingscourt	Early C	5
Dad's Coming Home	Spotty Zebra	Nelson Thornes	Red – Change	2
Dad's Grand Plan	Oxford Reading Tree	OUP	Stage 6 & 7 More Stories B	6
Dad's Jacket	Oxford Reading Tree	OUP	Stage 4 More Stories C	4
Dad's Run	Oxford Reading Tree	OUP	Stage 5 More Stories C	5
Dad's Ship	PM Gems	Nelson Thornes	Magenta 2/3	2
Dan Gets Dressed	Story Chest	Kingscourt	Get-ready Set CC	2
Dance to the Beat	Big Cat	Collins	Yellow	3
Dancing Dudley	Alphakids Plus	Gardner	Transitional Level 17	6
Dancing Gingerbread	PM Photo Stories	Nelson Thornes	Green 13	5
Dandelion	Kingscourt Reading, Core	Kingscourt	Level 18 Collection	7
Danger	Story Chest	Kingscourt	Ready-set-go Set D	3
Danger at the Car Park	PM Plus	Nelson Thornes	Turquoise Level	7
Dangerous Plants	AlphaWorld	Gardner	Band 5: Green	5
Daniel	Literacy Links Plus	Kingscourt	Early D	5
Dash, the Young Meercat	PM Plus	Nelson Thornes	Gold Level	9
Daughter of the Sun	Kingscourt Reading, Extension	Kingscourt	Set 5	5
Davina and the Dinosaurs	Pathways	Collins	Year 1	6
Day at the Beach, A, Part 1	Story Street	Pearson	Step 5	5
Day at the Beach, A, Part 2	Story Street	Pearson	Step 5	5
Day at the Eden Project, A	Big Cat	Collins	Green	5
Day at the Market, A	AlphaWorld	Gardner	Level 14 (trans)	6

TITLE	SERIES	PUBLISHER	SET (OR AUTHOR)	BAND
Day I Felt Ill, The	Info Trail	Pearson	Beginner Science	5
Day in London, A	Oxford Reading Tree	OUP	Stage 8 Stories	8
Day in the Life of a Victorian Child, A	Discovery World	Heinemann	Stage C	8
Day in Town, A	Story Chest	Kingscourt	Stage 5	8
Day Out, A	Big Cat	Collins	Red A	1B
Day the Gorilla Came to School, The	Sunshine Readers	Gardner	Light Blue Level Supplementary	6
Day the Sky Fell Down, The	Lighthouse	Ginn	Green: 7	5
Daylight Robbery	Web Fiction	OUP	Stage 9 (Variety)	7
Days of the Week	PM Maths	Nelson Thornes	Stage B	3
Dear Daddy ...	Pelican Big Bks	Pearson	Dupasquier, Philippe	6
Dear Grandma	Kingscourt Reading, Extension	Kingscourt	Set 6	6
Dear Santa	Literacy Links Plus	Kingscourt	Emergent C	2
Deb's Secret Wish & other stories	New Way	Nelson Thornes	Green Platform Books	5
Deer and the Crocodile, The	Literacy Links Plus	Kingscourt	Early D	6
Den, The	Oxford Reading Tree	OUP	Stage 4 More Stories C	4
Den, The	Rigby Star	Rigby	Red Level	2
Dentist, The	PM Non-fiction	Nelson Thornes	Blue Level	5
Dentist, The	Rigby Star	Rigby	Yellow Level	3
Deserts	PM Plus Non-fiction	Nelson Thornes	Gold Level	9
Diamonds	Oxford Reading Tree	OUP	Fireflies Stage 9	9
Diary of a Sunflower	Kingscourt Reading, Core	Kingscourt	Level 18 Little Books	7
Dick Whittington	Oxford Reading Tree	OUP	More Allstars Pack 3a	10
Dick Whittington	PM Traditional Tales	Nelson Thornes	Silver Level	10
Did a Hamster Go into Space?	Info Trail	Pearson	Beginner History	7
Did Vikings Eat Chips?	Info Trail	Pearson	Emergent History	9
Dig In	Four Corners	Pearson	Year 1	5
Diggers	Oxford Reading Tree	OUP	Fireflies, More – Stage 2	2
Dilly Duck and Dally Duck	PM Plus	Nelson Thornes	Yellow Level	3
Ding Dong Bell, What's That Funny Smell?	Crunchies	Orchard	Seriously Silly Rhymes	8
Dinner	Sails Foundation	Heinemann	Pink B – For	1A
Dinner Time	Storyworlds	Heinemann	Stage 2 Our World	2
Dino at the Park	PM Photo Stories	Nelson Thornes	Yellow 7	3
Dinosaur Alphabet	Web Weavers Non-fiction	OUP	Non-fiction – Animals	7
Dinosaur Chase	PM Storybooks	Nelson Thornes	Orange Set A	6
Dinosaur Danger!	Web Guided Reading	OUP	Stage 8 (Duck Green)	7
Dinosaur Detectives	Skyrider LM Chapters	Gardner	Set 2	7
Dinosaur Discovery	Kingscourt Reading, Core	Kingscourt	Level 16 Little Books	6
Dinosaur Hunters	I Love Reading	Ticktock	Blue Level	4
Dinosaur Plant-eaters	I Love Reading	Ticktock	Blue Level	4
Dinosaurs	Alphakids Plus	Gardner	Emergent Level 4	3
Dinosaurs	Badger NF Guided Reading	Aladdin/Watts	Reading About	7
Dinosaurs	Oxford Reading Tree	OUP	Fireflies Stage 6	9
Dinosaur's Cold, The	Literacy Links Plus	Kingscourt	Early D	6
Dipper and the Old Wreck	Storyworlds	Heinemann	Stage 5 Animal World	3
Dipper Gets Stuck	Storyworlds	Heinemann	Stage 5 Animal World	4
Dipper in Danger	Storyworlds	Heinemann	Stage 5 Animal World	4
Dipper to the Rescue	Storyworlds	Heinemann	Stage 5 Animal World	4
Discovery, The	Oxford Reading Tree	OUP	Robins Pack 3	10
Disgusting Denzil	Oxford Reading Tree	OUP	All Stars Pack 2	9
Divali	Badger NF Guided Reading	Raintree	Read and Learn	6
Divali Party, The	Pathways	Collins	Year 1	5

TITLE	SERIES	PUBLISHER	SET (OR AUTHOR)	BAND
Divers' Dream	Skyrider LM Chapters	Gardner	Set 1	8
Divers of the Deep Sea	National Geographic	Rigby	White Level	10
Diving at the Pool	PM Plus	Nelson Thornes	Purple Level	8
Do All Rivers Go to the Sea?	Info Trail	Pearson	Beginner Geography	7
Doctor and Dentist	First Facts	Badger	Level 4	7
Doctor Boondoggle	Story Chest	Kingscourt	Ready-set-go Set BB	3
Doctor Ravi	Story Street	Pearson	Step 2	3
Doctor, The	PM Non-fiction	Nelson Thornes	Blue Level	5
Does Cheese Come From Cows?	Info Trail	Pearson	Beginner Science	8
Does Chocolate Grow on Trees?	Info Trail	Pearson	Emergent Science	9
Dog Called Bear, A	PM Storybooks	Nelson Thornes	Purple Set A	8
Dog Family, The	Kingscourt Reading, Core	Kingscourt	Level 17 Little Books	7
Dog From Outer Space, The	Lighthouse	Ginn	Orange: 6	6
Dog in School	Story Street	Pearson	Step 6	6
Dog on Holiday	First Stories	Gardner	Emergent D	1A
Dog School	AlphaWorld	Gardner	Band 4: Blue	4
Dog School	Kingscourt Reading, Core	Kingscourt	Level 17 Little Books	6
Dog Show, The	Rigby Star	Rigby	Pink Level	1A
Dogs	Alphakids	Gardner	Emergent Level 1	1A
Dogs	Oxford Reading Tree	OUP	Fireflies Stage 1+	1B
Dogs	PM Non-fiction	Nelson Thornes	Orange Level	6
Dogs and Cats	First Facts	Badger	Level 1	1B
Dogstar	Literacy Links Plus	Kingscourt	Fluent B	7
Dolphin in the Net, A	Sunshine Readers	Gardner	Orange Level	6
Dolphin on the Wall, The	PM Storybooks	Nelson Thornes	Silver Set B	10
Dolphin Pool, The	Oxford Reading Tree	OUP	Stage 3 Storybooks	3
Dolphins, The	PM Storybooks	Nelson Thornes	Gold Set C	9
Donkey in the Lion's Skin, The	PM Plus	Nelson Thornes	Green Level	5
Donkey That Sneezed, The	Oxford Reading Tree	OUP	Traditional Tales 5–7	6
Don't Be a Beetroot!	Info Trail	Pearson	Emergent Science	7
Don't Be Silly	Oxford Reading Tree	OUP	Stage 6 & 7 More Stories B	6
Don't Bite the Bottom Off Your Ice-cream Cone!	Info Trail	Pearson	Beginner Science	5
Don't Forget Grandma	Dragonflies	Gardner	Blue	4
Don't Look Down!	Kingscourt Reading, Extension	Kingscourt	Set 5	5
Don't Throw it Away	Info Trail	Pearson	Emergent Geography	4
Don't Throw That Out	Dragonflies	Gardner	Yellow/Blue	3
Don't Worry	Alphakids Plus	Gardner	Transitional Level 12	5
Don't Worry	Literacy Links Plus	Kingscourt	Fluent A	7
Doris Bean and the Queen	Oxford Reading Tree	OUP	All Stars Pack 2	10
Doris's Brilliant Birthday	Rockets	A&C Black	Ryan, Margaret	10
Dormouse Pot, The	Web Fiction	OUP	Stage 9 (Variety)	7
Down by the Sea	PM Plus	Nelson Thornes	Blue Level	4
Down in the Woods	Kingscourt Reading, Extension	Kingscourt	Set 6	6
Down the Side of the Sofa	Lighthouse	Ginn	Pink B: 1	1B
Down the Track	Kingscourt Reading, Core	Kingscourt	Level 11 Little Books	4
Drag Racing	Alphakids	Gardner	Extending Level 21	10
Dragon Dance, The	Oxford Reading Tree	OUP	Stage 4 More Stories B	4
Dragon Kite	Web Guided Reading	OUP	Stage 5 (Duck Green)	5
Dragon Test, The	Walker Starters	Walker	Crebbin, June	8
Dragon Tree, The	Oxford Reading Tree	OUP	Stage 5 Storybooks	5
Dragon, The	Alphakids	Gardner	Transitional Level 15	5

TITLE	SERIES	PUBLISHER	SET (OR AUTHOR)	BAND
Dragon, The	Story Chest	Kingscourt	Stage 3	6
Dragonfly Dreams	Kingscourt Reading, Core	Kingscourt	Level 19 Collection	8
Dragons	Alphakids Plus	Gardner	Extending Level 22	8
Dragon's Egg, The	Dragonflies	Gardner	Gold	9
Dragon's Rescue, The	Alphakids Plus	Gardner	Extending Level 19	8
Dragon's Tooth, The	Rockets	A&C Black	Rodgers, Frank	9
Drawing Adventure	Oxford Reading Tree	OUP	Stage 5 More Stories C	5
Dream Catchers	Kingscourt Reading, Extension	Kingscourt	Set 8	8
Dream Team, The	Lighthouse	Ginn	Orange: 7	6
Dream, The	Oxford Reading Tree	OUP	Stage 2 Storybooks	4
Dressing Up	Badger NF Guided Reading	Wayland	Changes	9
Dressing Up	PM Storybook Starters	Nelson Thornes	Set 1	1A
Dressing Up & other stories	New Way	Nelson Thornes	Blue Core Book	6
Dress-up Parade, The	Alphakids	Gardner	Transitional Level 17	7
Dress-ups	Alphakids Plus	Gardner	Early Level 6	3
Drums and Shakers	First Facts	Badger	Level 2	3
Duck In The Hat, The	Pelican Big Bks	Pearson	Waddell, Martin	6
Duck Pond	Genre Range	Pearson	Emergent Plays	5
Duck With the Broken Wing, The	PM Storybooks	Nelson Thornes	Blue Set B	4
Duckling, The	Alphakids	Gardner	Transitional Level 14	5
Ducks	Story Chest	Kingscourt	Ready-set-go Set BB	2
Ducks on the Run!	PM Plus	Nelson Thornes	Turquoise Level	7
Duma and the Lion	Storyworlds	Heinemann	Stage 7 Animal World	4
Dutch Adventure	Oxford Reading Tree	OUP	Stage 9 More Stories A	7

E

TITLE	SERIES	PUBLISHER	SET (OR AUTHOR)	BAND
Early One Morning	Alphakids	Gardner	Transitional Level 13	5
Earth and Space	Badger NF Guided Reading	Chrysalis	Start Science	9
Earth Materials	First Explorers	Kingscourt	Level 1	10
Earth's Riches	Kingscourt Reading, Core	Kingscourt	White	10
Eat Your Vegetables!	Four Corners	Pearson	Year 1	6
Eating	Badger NF Guided Reading	Chrysalis	My Healthy Body	8
Ebenezer and the Sneeze	Story Chest	Kingscourt	Ready-set-go Set BB	2
Eclipse	Kingscourt Reading, Core	Kingscourt	Level 12 Little Books	5
Edmond Went Splash!	First Stories	Gardner	Emergent F	1B
Eggs and Dandelions	PM Gems	Nelson Thornes	Blue 10	4
Eggs For Breakfast	PM Non-fiction	Nelson Thornes	Red Level	3
Egyptian Adventure	Oxford Reading Tree	OUP	Stage 8 More Stories A	8
Electricity Makes Things Work	PM Plus Non-fiction	Nelson Thornes	Purple Level	8
Elephant Diary	Web Weavers Non-fiction	OUP	Non-fiction – Animals	7
Elephant in the House, An	Kingscourt Reading, Core	Kingscourt	Level 19 Benchmark Bk	8
Elephant That Forgot, The	Storyworlds	Heinemann	Stage 8 Animal World	6
Elephant Trick	Sails Foundation	Heinemann	Pink C – You	1A
Elephant Walk	Kingscourt Reading, Extension	Kingscourt	Set 8	8
Elephant Walk	Rigby Star	Rigby	Red Level	2
Elephants	Badger NF Guided Reading	QED	Animal Lives	10
Elephants	PM Non-fiction	Nelson Thornes	Turquoise Level	8
Ella and the Toy Rabbit	PM Gems	Nelson Thornes	Yellow 6	3
Ellie and Sam	Spotty Zebra	Nelson Thornes	Pink A – Ourselves	1B

TITLE	SERIES	PUBLISHER	SET (OR AUTHOR)	BAND
Elves and the Shoemaker, The	Alphakids	Gardner	Transitional Level 14	6
Elves and the Shoemaker, The	PM Traditional Tales	Nelson Thornes	Turquoise Level	7
Elves and the Shoemaker, The	Rigby Star	Rigby	Purple Level	8
Elves and the Shoemaker, The	Storyworlds	Heinemann	Stage 7 Once Upon a Time	6
E-mails Home	Oxford Reading Tree	OUP	Fireflies Stage 5	6
Emergencies	Oxford Reading Tree	OUP	Cross-curricular Jackdaws	10
Emergency!	Web Weavers Non-fiction	OUP	Stage 2 First Words NF	4
Emergency, The	Oxford Reading Tree	OUP	Robins Pack 1	9
Emma's Photo Album	Info Trail	Pearson	Beginner History	3
Emma's Problem	Literacy Links Plus	Kingscourt	Early C	7
Emperor's New Clothes, The	Rigby Star	Rigby	Gold Level	9
Empty Lunchbox, The	Storyworlds	Heinemann	Stage 3 Our World	2
Encyclopaedia of Fantastic Fish	Rigby Star Non-fiction	Rigby	White Level	10
Energy	Badger NF Guided Reading	Chrysalis	Science Around Us	9
Enjoy! Enjoy!	Alphakids	Gardner	Transitional Level 17	7
Environmental Disasters	Oxford Reading Tree	OUP	Fireflies Stage 9	10
Enzo in the Park	Spotty Zebra	Nelson Thornes	Pink B – Change	1B
Eric's Talking Ears	Oxford Reading Tree	OUP	All Stars Pack 2	9
Erin Meets Tiffy	PM Photo Stories	Nelson Thornes	Red 5	2
Erin Rides Tiffy	PM Photo Stories	Nelson Thornes	Yellow 8	3
Erosion	AlphaWorld	Gardner	Level 23 (ext)	10
Escalator, The	Story Chest	Kingscourt	Get-ready Set AA	1B
Eva the Beekeeper	Four Corners	Pearson	Year 1	6
Everyday Forces	Discovery World	Heinemann	Stage E	7
Everyone Got Wet	Oxford Reading Tree	OUP	Stage 4 More Stories B	3
Evil Genie, The	Oxford Reading Tree	OUP	Stage 8 More Stories A	8
Eye Book, The	Bright and Early Books	Collins	Le Seig, Theo	3
Eyes	AlphaWorld	Gardner	Band 7: Turquoise	7

F

Face in the Dark, The	Kingscourt Reading, Extension	Kingscourt	Set 2	2
Face Painting	Alphakids Plus	Gardner	Emergent Level 1	1A
Fair Swap, A	PM Storybooks	Nelson Thornes	Silver Set A	10
Fair, The	First Stories	Gardner	Emergent B	1A
Fairy-Tale Flowers	Kingscourt Reading, Core	Kingscourt	Level 17 Benchmark Bk	7
Families	Kingscourt Reading, Extension	Kingscourt	Set 6	6
Families and Feasts	PM Plus Non-fiction	Nelson Thornes	Green Level	5
Families Help Each Other	First Facts	Badger	Level 2	3
Family Festivals	Badger NF Guided Reading	Chrysalis	World Of Festivals	9
Family Photos	Literacy Links Plus	Kingscourt	Early B	4
Family Tree, The	Kingscourt Reading, Core	Kingscourt	Level 6 Little Books	3
Family Tree, The	PM Plus	Nelson Thornes	Gold Level	9
Family, The	Sails Foundation	Heinemann	Pink A – He	1A
Fancy Dress	Rigby Star	Rigby	Pink Level	1A
Fancy That!	Alphakids Plus	Gardner	Early Level 7	3
Fangtastic Raps	Crunchies	Orchard	Raps	9
Fantastic Cake	Story Chest	Kingscourt	Ready-set-go Set CC	2
Fantastic Flying Squirrel, The	Big Cat	Collins	Blue	4
Fantastic Four and the Winter Games, The	Web Fiction	OUP	Stage 6 (Variety)	8

TITLE	SERIES	PUBLISHER	SET (OR AUTHOR)	BAND
Fantastic Four at Frog Farm, The	Web Fiction	OUP	Stage 6 (Variety)	8
Fantastic Four at the Seaside, The	Web Fiction	OUP	Stage 6 (Variety)	8
Fantastic Frog Facts	Alphakids Plus	Gardner	Transitional Level 14	5
Fantastic Pumpkin, The	Rigby Star	Rigby	Green Level	5
Farm Animals	First Facts	Badger	Level 3	4
Farm Day	First Facts	Badger	Level 3	4
Farm in Spring, The	PM Storybook Starters	Nelson Thornes	Set 2	1B
Farmer Skiboo	Oxford Reading Tree	OUP	All Stars Pack 1	8
Farmyard Friends	Alphakids Plus	Gardner	Extending Level 18	7
Fast Food for Butterflies	Kingscourt Reading, Extension	Kingscourt	Set 7	7
Fastest Gazelle, The	Literacy Links Plus	Kingscourt	Early D	6
Fat Cat's Chair	PM Gems	Nelson Thornes	Blue 9	4
Fatcat and the Mouse	Genre Range	Pearson	Emergent Comics	5
Father Bear Goes Fishing	PM Storybooks	Nelson Thornes	Red Set A	2
Father Bear's Surprise	PM Storybooks	Nelson Thornes	Green Set B	5
Favourite Places	AlphaWorld	Gardner	Band 3: Yellow	3
Fawn in the Forest, The	PM Plus	Nelson Thornes	Green Level	5
Feathers	Kingscourt Reading, Extension	Kingscourt	Set 8	8
Feeding the Lambs	PM Plus Non-fiction	Nelson Thornes	Green Level	5
Feet	Info Trail	Pearson	Beginner Science	7
Festival Food	Discovery World Links	Heinemann	Stage E	9
Festivals	Web Weavers Non-fiction	OUP	Stage 2 First Words NF	3
Fiddle-dee-dee	Story Chest	Kingscourt	Stage 6	9
Fierce Creatures	Web Weavers Non-fiction	OUP	Stage 1 First Words NF	1B
Fight on the Hill, The	Kingscourt Reading, Core	Kingscourt	Level 16 Benchmark Bk	6
Film Star, The	New Way	Nelson Thornes	Green Easy Start Set A	4
Finding Rainbow	Alphakids Plus	Gardner	Extending Level 20	7
Finding Tibs	Dragonflies	Gardner	Orange	6
Finest in the Land, The	Oxford Reading Tree	OUP	Stage 9 More Stories A	8
Finger Puppets, Finger Plays	Kingscourt Reading, Extension	Kingscourt	Set 5	5
Finn MacCool & Big Head MacTavish	Lighthouse	Ginn	Gold: 7	9
Fins, Wings and Legs	Four Corners	Pearson	Year 1	5
Fire	Oxford Reading Tree	OUP	Fireflies Stage 7	9
Fire and Water	Story Chest	Kingscourt	Ready-set-go Set DD	4
Fire and Wind	PM Storybooks	Nelson Thornes	Silver Set B	10
Fire Engine, The	Oxford Reading Tree	OUP	Fireflies, More – Stage 1+	1A
Fire in Wild Wood	Storyworlds	Heinemann	Stage 5 Fantasy World	4
Fire on Toytown Hill, The	PM Plus	Nelson Thornes	Blue Level	4
Fire! Fire!	Big Cat	Collins	Orange	7
Fire! Fire!	Kingscourt Reading, Extension	Kingscourt	Set 8	8
Fire! Fire!	PM Storybooks	Nelson Thornes	Yellow Set A	3
Firefighters	Alphakids Plus	Gardner	Extending Level 24	10
Firefighters	Pathways	Collins	Year 1	5
First Flight	PM Plus	Nelson Thornes	Turquoise Level	7
Fish	Rigby Star Non-fiction	Rigby	White Level	10
Fish Called Goggles, A	PM Photo Stories	Nelson Thornes	Green 13	5
Fish Picture, A	First Stories	Gardner	Emergent D	1A
Fisherman and His Wife, The	Literacy Links Plus	Kingscourt	Traditional Tale	8
Fishing	Alphakids Plus	Gardner	Early Level 7	3
Fishing	PM Storybook Starters	Nelson Thornes	Set 2	1B
Fishing	Story Chest	Kingscourt	Get-ready Set BB	2

TITLE	SERIES	PUBLISHER	SET (OR AUTHOR)	BAND
Fishing Trip, The	PM Plus	Nelson Thornes	Gold Level	9
Five and Five Are Ten	PM Maths	Nelson Thornes	Stage B	3
Five Birds and Five Mice	PM Maths	Nelson Thornes	Stage A	2
Five Little Men	Pathways	Collins	Year 1	4
Fixing Things	AlphaWorld	Gardner	Level 22 (ext)	9
Fizz and Splutter	Story Chest	Kingscourt	Ready-set-go Set D	3
Fizzkid Liz	Rigby Star	Rigby	Orange Level	6
Flat Shapes, Fat Shapes	Spotty Zebra	Nelson Thornes	Pink A – Ourselves	1A
Flicking the Switch	Skyrider LM Chapters	Gardner	Set 1	8
Floating and Sinking	Alphakids	Gardner	Early Level 11	4
Floating Boats	Oxford Reading Tree	OUP	Fireflies, More – Stage 3	3
Flock Watch	Kingscourt Reading, Core	Kingscourt	Level 10 Little Books	4
Flood!	Oxford Reading Tree	OUP	Stage 8 More Stories A	7
Flood, The	PM Storybooks	Nelson Thornes	Green Set A	5
Floppy Floppy	Oxford Reading Tree	OUP	Stage 1 First Words	1A
Floppy the Hero	Oxford Reading Tree	OUP	Stage 2 More Stories B	4
Floppy's Bath	Oxford Reading Tree	OUP	Stage 2 More Stories A	3
Flora to the Rescue	Storyworlds	Heinemann	Stage 6 Fantasy World	6
Florence Nightingale and the Crimean War	Badger NF Guided Reading	Heinemann Library	How Do We Know About ...?	10
Flower Girl, The	PM Storybooks	Nelson Thornes	Red Set B	2
Flower Petals	First Facts	Badger	Level 1	2
Flowers	AlphaWorld	Gardner	Band 1A: Pink	1B
Flowers for Grandma	PM Gems	Nelson Thornes	Yellow 7	3
Flutey Family Fruit Cake, The	Kingscourt Reading, Extension	Kingscourt	Set 9	9
Fly Away Home	Big Cat	Collins	Pink B	1A
Fly Away, Cheep	Web Guided Reading	OUP	Stage 4 (Duck Green)	3
Fly Facts	Big Cat	Collins	Turquoise	7
Fly, The	Kingscourt Reading, Core	Kingscourt	Level 5 Benchmark Bk	2
Flyers	Rigby Star	Rigby	Turquoise Level	7
Flying Carpet, The	Oxford Reading Tree	OUP	Stage 8 Stories	8
Flying Elephant, The	Oxford Reading Tree	OUP	Stage 4 More Stories B	3
Flying Fish, The	PM Storybooks	Nelson Thornes	Green Set B	5
Flying Footballs	Web Guided Reading	OUP	Stage 4 (Duck Green)	4
Flying Machine, The	Oxford Reading Tree	OUP	Stage 9 More Stories A	7
Flying Machines	Alphakids Plus	Gardner	Early Level 11	6
Flying Tea Tray, The	Web Guided Reading	OUP	Stage 8 (Duck Green)	9
Foggy Day, The	Oxford Reading Tree	OUP	Stage 2 More Stories B	3
Follow a River	Four Corners	Pearson	Year 1	6
Follow Me	Alphakids Plus	Gardner	Emergent Level 4	2
Follow the Leader	First Stories	Gardner	Emergent F	1B
Food as Art	Oxford Reading Tree	OUP	Fireflies Stage 6	8
Food For All	First Explorers	Kingscourt	Level 1	8
Food For Animals	AlphaWorld	Gardner	Band 7: Turquoise	8
Food For Festivals	Pelican Big Bks	Pearson	Witherington, Anne	8
Food For Fred	Spotty Zebra	Nelson Thornes	Red – Ourselves	3
Food is Fun	PM Plus Non-fiction	Nelson Thornes	Green Level	6
Foot Book, The	Bright and Early Books	Collins	Seuss, Dr	5
Football at the Park	PM Storybooks	Nelson Thornes	Yellow Set B	3
Football, Football!	Oxford Reading Tree	OUP	Fireflies Stage 3	3
For My Birthday	Lighthouse	Ginn	Pink A: 6	1A
Forces of Nature	First Explorers	Kingscourt	Level 2	10

TITLE	SERIES	PUBLISHER	SET (OR AUTHOR)	BAND
Forest Giants, The	Web Fiction	OUP	Stage 5 (Variety)	5
Forests	PM Plus Non-fiction	Nelson Thornes	Gold Level	9
Forgetful Giraffe	Sunshine Readers	Gardner	Light Blue Level	6
Fortune for Yo-Yo, A	Crunchies	Orchard	Colour Crackers	9
Fossils	National Geographic	Rigby	Purple Level	9
Four Cars	PM Maths	Nelson Thornes	Stage A	2
Four Friends & other stories, The	New Way	Nelson Thornes	Yellow Platform Books	8
Four Ice Creams	PM Storybook Starters	Nelson Thornes	Set 2	1B
Fowler's Family Tree	Kingscourt Reading, Extension	Kingscourt	Set 7	7
Fox and the Crow, The	Alphakids	Gardner	Early Level 9	4
Fox and the Crow, The	PM Plus	Nelson Thornes	Turquoise Level	7
Fox and the Rabbit, The	Storyworlds	Heinemann	Stage 2 Once Upon a Time	2
Fox and the Snail, The	Alphakids Plus	Gardner	Early Level 9	4
Fox and the Stork, The	Storyworlds	Heinemann	Stage 2 Once Upon a Time	2
Fox Who Foxed, The	PM Storybooks	Nelson Thornes	Green Set A	5
Foxes	PM Non-fiction	Nelson Thornes	Gold Level	9
Freaky Fish	Oxford Reading Tree	OUP	Fireflies Stage 8	8
Fred's Super Scooter	Sunshine Readers	Gardner	Purple Level	7
Freeway Turtles, The	PM Plus	Nelson Thornes	Gold Level	9
Freeze, Goldilocks!	Skyrider LM Chapters	Gardner	Set 1	9
Fried Piper of Hamstring, The	Crunchies	Orchard	Seriously Silly Stories	10
Friend for Little White Rabbit, A	PM Storybooks	Nelson Thornes	Yellow Set A	3
Friend for Max, A	PM Plus	Nelson Thornes	Green Level	5
Friend for Me, A	First Stories	Gardner	Emergent C	1A
Friends	Badger NF Guided Reading	Badger	First Facts	4
Friends	First Facts	Badger	Level 3	4
Friends	Rigby Star Non-fiction	Rigby	Pink Level	!A
Fright in the Night, A	Oxford Reading Tree	OUP	Stage 6 More Stories A	6
Frisky and the Cat	Storyworlds	Heinemann	Stage 3 Animal World	2
Frisky and the Ducks	Storyworlds	Heinemann	Stage 3 Animal World	2
Frisky plays a Trick	Storyworlds	Heinemann	Stage 3 Animal World	2
Frisky Wants to Sleep	Storyworlds	Heinemann	Stage 3 Animal World	2
Frog Alert	AlphaWorld	Gardner	Level 18 (ext)	7
Frog Bog	AlphaWorld	Gardner	Level 20 (ext)	8
Frog Day	Kingscourt Reading, Extension	Kingscourt	Set 8	8
Frog Goes on Holiday	Genre Range	Pearson	Emergent Comics	5
Frog Prince, The	Genre Range	Pearson	Beginner Traditional Tales	4
Frog Prince, The	Storyworlds	Heinemann	Stage 7 Once Upon a Time	6
Frog Princess, The	Literacy Links Plus	Kingscourt	Early D	6
Frog Under the Tree, The	PM Photo Stories	Nelson Thornes	Green 13	5
Frogs	Kingscourt Reading, Extension	Kingscourt	Set 4	4
From a Bean to a Bar	Lighthouse	Ginn	Turquoise: 3	7
From an Acorn to an Oak Tree	Info Trail	Pearson	Emergent Science	4
From Curry to Rice	Oxford Reading Tree	OUP	Fireflies Stage 4	6
From One to Eight	PM Maths	Nelson Thornes	Stage B	3
From Seedling to Tree	Rigby Star Non-fiction	Rigby	Yellow Level	3
Fruit	Web Weavers Non-fiction	OUP	First Non-fiction: Pack B	4
Fruit Salad	Alphakids	Gardner	Emergent Level 1	1A
Fruits and Seeds	Oxford Reading Tree	OUP	Cross-curricular Jackdaws	9
Fun at the Beach	Oxford Reading Tree	OUP	Stage 1 First Words	1B
Fun Things to Make and Do	Discovery World	Heinemann	Stage D	4

TITLE	SERIES	PUBLISHER	SET (OR AUTHOR)	BAND
Fun With Fruit	Kingscourt Reading, Extension	Kingscourt	Set 1	1B
Fun With Shadows	Four Corners	Pearson	Year 2	6
Funny Ears	Rigby Star Non-fiction	Rigby	Yellow Level	2
Funny Fish	Big Cat	Collins	Blue	4
Fussy Heron	PM Gems	Nelson Thornes	Blue 10	4

G

Gallo and Zorro	Literacy Links Plus	Kingscourt	Early D	8
Game With Shapes, A	PM Maths	Nelson Thornes	Stage A	2
Games We Play	PM Plus Non-fiction	Nelson Thornes	Orange Level	6
Gardener and the Scarecrow, The	Dragonflies	Gardner	Blue	4
Gardener's Maze, The	Dragonflies	Gardner	Green	5
Gelati	Alphakids Plus	Gardner	Extending Level 19	8
Genie in the Bottle, The	Web Fiction	OUP	Stage 5 (Variety)	5
Getting Around	Alphakids Plus	Gardner	Transitional Level 13	6
Getting Bigger	Spotty Zebra	Nelson Thornes	Pink B – Change	1B
Getting Ready	Web Guided Reading	OUP	Stage 1 (Duck Green)	1B
Getting Ready For Football	Spotty Zebra	Nelson Thornes	Pink A – Ourselves	1A
Ghost and the Sausage, The	Story Chest	Kingscourt	Stage 6	9
Ghost Tricks	Oxford Reading Tree	OUP	Robins Pack 3	10
Ghost, The	Story Chest	Kingscourt	Get-ready Set A	1A
Ghostyshocks and the Three Scares	Crunchies	Orchard	Seriously Silly Stories	8
Giant and the Frippit, The	Rigby Star	Rigby	Orange Level	6
Giant Gingerbread Man, The	Alphakids	Gardner	Early Level 9	4
Giant Grass	Kingscourt Reading, Core	Kingscourt	Level 18 Little Books	7
Giant Jumperee, The	Rigby Star	Rigby	Turquoise Level	7
Giant Seeds, The	PM Plus	Nelson Thornes	Purple Level	8
Giant's Diary, The	Alphakids Plus	Gardner	Extending Level 22	8
Giants, The	Web Guided Reading	OUP	Stage 6 (Duck Green)	7
Gibbon Island	PM Plus	Nelson Thornes	Turquoise Level	7
Gifts, The	Story Chest	Kingscourt	Get-ready Set DD	2
Gigantic Bell, The	PM Plus	Nelson Thornes	Gold Level	9
Giggle Box, The	Story Chest	Kingscourt	Ready-set-go Set DD	4
Ginger, Where Are You?	Pathways	Collins	Year 2	8
Gingerbread Man, The	PM Traditional Tales	Nelson Thornes	Orange Level	6
Gingerbread Man, The	Storyworlds	Heinemann	Stage 6 Once Upon a Time	5
Gizmos' Party, The	Rigby Star	Rigby	White Level	10
Gizmos' Trip, The	Rigby Star	Rigby	White Level	10
Glasses	Alphakids	Gardner	Emergent Level 1	1A
Glide, Wriggle, Zoom	Skyrider LM Chapters	Gardner	Set 2	9
Glorious Mud	Oxford Reading Tree	OUP	Fireflies Stage 7	9
Go Back to Sleep	Literacy Links Plus	Kingscourt	Emergent D	3
Go Cart, The	PM Storybook Starters	Nelson Thornes	Set 1	1A
Go, Annie, Go!	Skyrider LM Chapters	Gardner	Set 1	9
Goal!	Lighthouse	Ginn	Green: 6	5
Goat Monster & other stories, The	New Way	Nelson Thornes	Violet Platform Books	7
Goat, The	Alphakids Plus	Gardner	Emergent Level 4	2
Goat, The	Sails Foundation	Heinemann	Pink A – He	1A
Goats	PM Non-fiction	Nelson Thornes	Purple Level	9

TITLE	SERIES	PUBLISHER	SET (OR AUTHOR)	BAND
Goats in the Turnip Field, The	PM Plus	Nelson Thornes	Orange Level	6
Going Fishing	National Geographic	Rigby	Orange Level	5
Going on Holiday	PM Plus	Nelson Thornes	Starters One	1A
Going on Safari	Skyrider LM Chapters	Gardner	Set 2	8
Going Out	PM Plus	Nelson Thornes	Starters Two	1B
Going Places	First Explorers	Kingscourt	Level 1	9
Going Places	First Stories	Gardner	Emergent A	1A
Going Shopping	Alphakids	Gardner	Emergent Level 5	3
Going Shopping	Sails Foundation	Heinemann	Pink C – Are	1A
Going Somewhere	Oxford Reading Tree	OUP	Fireflies Stage 3	2
Going Swimming	AlphaWorld	Gardner	Level 13 (trans)	5
Going to Bed	Sails Foundation	Heinemann	Pink C – Going	1A
Going to School	Four Corners	Pearson	Year 2	7
Going to School	Story Chest	Kingscourt	Get-ready Set C	1B
Going Up the Wall	Skyrider LM Chapters	Gardner	Set 2	8
Going Up!	Walker Starters	Walker	Waddell, Martin	9
Go-kart Race, The	Oxford Reading Tree	OUP	Stage 6 More Stories A	6
Golden Touch, The	Kingscourt Reading, Core	Kingscourt	White	9
Goldfish	Badger NF Guided Reading	Franklin Watts	Let's Read About Pets	4
Goldfish	PM Non-fiction	Nelson Thornes	Orange Level	6
Goldilocks and the Three Bears	Alphakids Plus	Gardner	Early Level 9	4
Goldilocks and the Three Bears	Genre Range	Pearson	Emergent Traditional Tales	5
Goldilocks and the Three Bears	Kingscourt Reading, Extension	Kingscourt	Set 4	4
Goldilocks and the Three Bears	Literacy Links Plus	Kingscourt	Traditional Tale	4
Goldilocks and the Three Bears	Oxford Reading Tree	OUP	Traditional Tales 5-7	4
Goldilocks and the Three Bears	PM Traditional Tales	Nelson Thornes	Turquoise Level	7
Gonna Bird, The	Kingscourt Reading, Extension	Kingscourt	Set 5	5
Good Fun Farm	Big Cat	Collins	Turquoise	7
Good Morning, Who's Snoring?	Kingscourt Reading, Core	Kingscourt	Level 9 Little Books	4
Good Old Mum!	Oxford Reading Tree	OUP	Stage 1+ Patterned Stories	2
Good Old Wood	Kingscourt Reading, Core	Kingscourt	White	10
Good to Eat	Alphakids Plus	Gardner	Extending Level 23	9
Good Trick, A	Oxford Reading Tree	OUP	Stage 1 First Words	1A
Goodbye, Ebony	Sunshine Readers	Gardner	Light Blue Level	7
Goodness Gracious!	Literacy Links Plus	Kingscourt	Early C	7
Gordon Gets Even	Lighthouse	Ginn	White 1	10
Gordon the Clever Goat	Web Fiction	OUP	Stage 4 (Variety)	4
Gorgo Meets Her Match	PM Storybooks	Nelson Thornes	Purple Set C	8
Gorillas	Alphakids Plus	Gardner	Early Level 11	6
Gotcha Box, The	Story Chest	Kingscourt	Get-ready Set BB	1A
Grabber	Pathways	Collins	Year 2	6
Graeme Base, Writer and Illustrator	Alphakids	Gardner	Extending Level 23	10
Graffiti	Sunshine Readers	Gardner	Orange Level Supplementary	5
Gramps	Sunshine Readers	Gardner	Light Blue Level	7
Gran	Oxford Reading Tree	OUP	Stage 5 Storybooks	5
Grandad	Literacy Links Plus	Kingscourt	Fluent D	10
Grandad and Me	Oxford Reading Tree	OUP	Fireflies Stage 4	5
Grandad's Boneshaker Bicycle	Rockets	A&C Black	West, Colin	9
Grandad's Ears	Pathways	Collins	Year 1	4
Grandad's Mask	PM Storybooks	Nelson Thornes	Turquoise Set C	7
Grandad's Star	Sunshine Readers	Gardner	Purple Level	9

TITLE	SERIES	PUBLISHER	SET (OR AUTHOR)	BAND
Grandad's Visit	PM Gems	Nelson Thornes	Green 13	5
Grandma's Memories	Literacy Links Plus	Kingscourt	Early B	5
Grandma's Pie	Kingscourt Reading, Core	Kingscourt	Level 13 Little Books	5
Grandma's Stick	Story Chest	Kingscourt	Stage 6	9
Grandma's Surprise	Storyworlds	Heinemann	Stage 5 Our World	5
Grandpa	Rigby Star	Rigby	Yellow Level	2
Grandpa Jones & the No-company Cat	PM Plus	Nelson Thornes	Silver Level	10
Grandpa's Birthday	Literacy Links Plus	Kingscourt	Fluent A	7
Grandpa's Bright Ideas	Lighthouse	Ginn	Gold: 3	9
Grandpa's House	Alphakids	Gardner	Emergent Level 2	1B
Grandpa's Lemonade	Kingscourt Reading, Extension	Kingscourt	Set 4	4
Granny Garcia's Gifts	Kingscourt Reading, Extension	Kingscourt	Set 7	7
Granny's Jungle Garden	Rockets	A&C Black	West, Colin	9
Grass for Dinner	Sails Foundation	Heinemann	Pink C – Said	1A
Gravity and the Solar System	PM Plus Non-fiction	Nelson Thornes	Silver Level	10
Great Big Elephants	Alphakids Plus	Gardner	Extending Level 23	9
Great Day for Up!	Bright and Early Books	Collins	Seuss, Dr	6
Great Day Out	Alphakids	Gardner	Early Level 10	4
Great Fire of London, The	Badger NF Guided Reading	Heinemann Library	How Do We Know About ...?	9
Great Fire of London, The	Discovery World Links	Heinemann	Stage F	9
Great Fire of London, The	Rigby Star Non-fiction	Rigby	White Level	9
Great Inventions	Four Corners	Pearson	Year 1	7
Great Pyramid, The	Lighthouse	Ginn	White 8	10
Great Race, The	Oxford Reading Tree	OUP	Stage 5 More Stories A	5
Great Sebastian, The	Alphakids	Gardner	Extending Level 19	7
Great Stew Disaster, The	Web Fiction	OUP	Stage 9 (Variety)	9
Great Tin-rolling Race, The	Alphakids	Gardner	Extending Level 21	9
Great-aunt Gertrude & the Handbag Thief	New Way	Nelson Thornes	Orange Parallel Books	9
Great-aunt Gertrude Comes to Stay	New Way	Nelson Thornes	Violet Parallel Books	8
Greedy Cat's Door	Dragonflies	Gardner	Blue	4
Greedy Guts and Belly Busters	Crunchies	Orchard	Twice Upon a Time	8
Greedy King, The	Lighthouse	Ginn	Orange: 3	6
Green Dragons, The	PM Storybooks	Nelson Thornes	Purple Set B	8
Green Eggs and Ham	Beginner Books	Collins	Seuss, Dr	6
Green Foods	Badger NF Guided Reading	Raintree	Read and Learn	4
Green Grass	Story Chest	Kingscourt	Get-ready Set BB	2
Green Island	Oxford Reading Tree	OUP	Stage 9 Stories	8
Gregor, The Grumblesome Giant	Literacy Links Plus	Kingscourt	Early C	6
Grizzlegrots, The	Alphakids Plus	Gardner	Transitional Level 13	5
Grow your Own Bean Plant!	Rigby Star Non-fiction	Rigby	Purple Level	7
Growing	Kingscourt Reading, Core	Kingscourt	Level 3 Little Books	2
Growing Mr Greenhead	Web Weavers Non-fiction	OUP	First Non-fiction: Pack B	3
Growing Strawberries	Alphakids Plus	Gardner	Transitional Level 13	5
Growing Tomatoes	Alphakids	Gardner	Early Level 8	3
Grown-ups Make You Grumpy	Lighthouse	Ginn	Turquoise: 1	7
Grump, The	Literacy Links Plus	Kingscourt	Early B	5
Grumpy Elephant	Story Chest	Kingscourt	Ready-set-go Set D	3
Guard Dog Diggory	Skyrider LM Chapters	Gardner	Set 2	8
Guess What I Am?	Badger NF Guided Reading	Walker Books	Peep-hole Books	5
Guess Who?	Rigby Star	Rigby	Red Level	1A
Guide to Growing	Four Corners	Pearson	Year 1	3

TITLE	SERIES	PUBLISHER	SET (OR AUTHOR)	BAND
Guinea Pigs	PM Non-fiction	Nelson Thornes	Orange Level	6
Gulp!	Story Chest	Kingscourt	Ready-set-go Set DD	4
Gymnastics	Alphakids Plus	Gardner	Early Level 7	3

H

TITLE	SERIES	PUBLISHER	SET (OR AUTHOR)	BAND
Hailstorm, The	PM Storybooks	Nelson Thornes	Turquoise Set B	7
Haircut Letters, The	Genre Range	Pearson	Emergent Letters	5
Hairdresser, The	PM Non-fiction	Nelson Thornes	Blue Level	5
Hairy Harry	National Geographic	Rigby	Blue Level	4
Hairy Toe, The	Spotlight on Plays	Collins	Age 7+	10
Hairy Toes and Scary Bones	Crunchies	Orchard	Twice Upon a Time	9
Hal the Highwayman	Walker Starters	Walker	Crebbin, June	8
Half for You, Half for Me	Literacy Links Plus	Kingscourt	Early D	7
Halfmoon Bay	Dragonflies	Gardner	Blue	4
Halloween	Story Chest	Kingscourt	Get-ready Set CC	1B
Hamburger	Alphakids Plus	Gardner	Emergent Level 3	2
Hamid Does His Best	Oxford Reading Tree	OUP	Robins Pack 3	9
Handle with Care	First Explorers	Kingscourt	Level 2	8
Hands	Big Cat	Collins	Yellow	3
Hands Up Wolf!	Skyrider LM Chapters	Gardner	Set 2	9
Hansel and Gretel	New Way	Nelson Thornes	Yellow Platform Books	8
Hansel and Gretel	Storyworlds	Heinemann	Stage 9 Once Upon a Time	9
Happily Ever After	Kingscourt Reading, Extension	Kingscourt	Set 8	8
Happy Birthday	Dragonflies	Gardner	Red	2
Happy Birthday, Frog	Story Chest	Kingscourt	Get-ready Set DD	2
Happy Diwali	Spotty Zebra	Nelson Thornes	Pink B – Ourselves	1B
Happy Prince & The Selfish Giant, The	New Way	Nelson Thornes	Orange Platform Books	10
Hare and the Tortoise, The	Genre Range	Pearson	Beginner Traditional Tales	4
Hare and the Tortoise, The	Literacy Links Plus	Kingscourt	Fluent B	8
Hare and the Tortoise, The	PM Traditional Tales	Nelson Thornes	Purple Level	8
Hare and the Tortoise, The	Storyworlds	Heinemann	Stage 3 Once Upon a Time	2
Harold the Hairiest Man	Crunchies	Orchard	The One And Only	8
Harry the Clever Spider	Big Cat	Collins	Turquoise	7
Harry's New Hat	PM Gems	Nelson Thornes	Blue 10	4
Harry's Elephant	Storyworlds	Heinemann	Stage 6 Animal World	6
Harry's Monkey	Storyworlds	Heinemann	Stage 6 Animal World	6
Harry's Seal	Storyworlds	Heinemann	Stage 6 Animal World	6
Harry's Snake	Storyworlds	Heinemann	Stage 6 Animal World	6
Hat Chat	Kingscourt Reading, Extension	Kingscourt	Set 7	7
Hat Trick, The	Literacy Links Plus	Kingscourt	Emergent B	2
Hats	Sails Foundation	Heinemann	Pink B – And	1A
Hats for the Carnival	Lighthouse	Ginn	Green: 1	5
Hattie Hates Hats	Pathways	Collins	Year 2	7
Hatupatu and the Birdwoman	Story Chest	Kingscourt	Stage 7	10
Haunted House, The	Story Chest	Kingscourt	Ready-set-go Set D	4
Have You Got Everything, Colin?	Rigby Star	Rigby	Yellow Level	3
Have You Seen My Bag?	Info Trail	Pearson	Beginner Geography	4
Hay Cart, The	Web Fiction	OUP	Stage 6 (Variety)	8
He Who Listens	Literacy Links Plus	Kingscourt	Fluent A	8

TITLE	SERIES	PUBLISHER	SET (OR AUTHOR)	BAND
Headfirst into the Porridge	Rigby Star	Rigby	Star Plus	10
Healthy Food	PM Plus Non-fiction	Nelson Thornes	Green Level	5
Heating Food	Web Weavers Non-fiction	OUP	First Non-fiction: Pack B	4
Hector and the Cello	Big Cat	Collins	Purple	8
Hedgehog is Hungry	PM Storybooks	Nelson Thornes	Red Set A	2
Helena and the Wild Man	Web Fiction	OUP	Stage 9 (Variety)	10
Hello	New Way	Nelson Thornes	Green Easy Start Set A	4
Hello	Story Chest	Kingscourt	Get-ready Set C	2
Hello Baby	Spotty Zebra	Nelson Thornes	Pink B – Ourselves	2
Hello!	Oxford Reading Tree	OUP	Fireflies, More – Stage 4	4
Hello, Bingo	PM Gems	Nelson Thornes	Magenta 2/3	2
Help Me	Story Chest	Kingscourt	Stage 2	5
Helpers	Storyworlds	Heinemann	Stage 2 Our World	2
Helpful Harry & other stories	New Way	Nelson Thornes	Violet Platform Books	9
Helping Dad	Kingscourt Reading, Extension	Kingscourt	Set 1	1A
Helping Hand, A	Sunshine Readers	Gardner	Orange Level	6
Helping Hands	Kingscourt Reading, Core	Kingscourt	Gold	9
Helping in the Garden	Alphakids Plus	Gardner	Emergent Level 3	2
Here Come the Shapes	PM Plus	Nelson Thornes	Yellow Level	3
Here Comes Little Chimp	PM Plus	Nelson Thornes	Red Level	2
Here I Am!	First Stories	Gardner	Emergent B	1A
Here is a Bird	Sails Foundation	Heinemann	Pink A – Is	1A
Hermie the Crab	PM Plus	Nelson Thornes	Turquoise Level	7
Hermit Crab	PM Storybooks	Nelson Thornes	Yellow Set A	3
Hermit Crab's New Shell	Web Fiction	OUP	Stage 3 (Variety)	2
Hey Presto!	Oxford Reading Tree	OUP	Stage 2 Patterned Stories	2
Hiccups!	Web Guided Reading	OUP	Stage 5 (Duck Green)	4
Hide and Seek	Oxford Reading Tree	OUP	Stage 1+ First Sentences	1B
Hide and Seek	Pathways	Collins	Year 1	7
Hide and Seek	PM Storybooks	Nelson Thornes	Red Set B	2
Hide-and-Seek	First Stories	Gardner	Emergent F	1A
Hiding from Bella	PM Photo Stories	Nelson Thornes	Yellow 6	3
Hiding in the Sea	Alphakids Plus	Gardner	Early Level 8	4
Hiding Places	Kingscourt Reading, Extension	Kingscourt	Set 9	9
High Five Henry	Oxford Reading Tree	OUP	All Stars Pack 2	10
High Flier	Oxford Reading Tree	OUP	Stage 9 True Stories	9
Highland Cattle, The	Storyworlds	Heinemann	Stage 8 Our World	7
Highland Games, The	Storyworlds	Heinemann	Stage 8 Our World	7
Hippos	Kingscourt Reading, Core	Kingscourt	Level 9 Little Books	4
Hippos	PM Non-fiction	Nelson Thornes	Turquoise Level	8
Hippo's Hiccups	Literacy Links Plus	Kingscourt	Early C	6
Hissing Bush, The	Dragonflies	Gardner	Green	5
History of Football, The	Info Trail	Pearson	Emergent History	8
Hole in the King's Sock, The	Dragonflies	Gardner	Orange	6
Hole, The	Sails Foundation	Heinemann	Pink B – This	1A
Holiday at Lighthouse Rock	PM Plus	Nelson Thornes	Silver Level	10
Holiday Time	PM Gems	Nelson Thornes	Red 3	2
Holiday, The	Oxford Reading Tree	OUP	Robins Pack 2	8
Holiday, The	Sails Foundation	Heinemann	Pink B – Went	1A
Holidays Then and Now	Spotlight on Fact	Collins	Y2 The Seaside	10
Home for Bonnie, A	Rigby Star Non-fiction	Rigby	Turquoise Level	7

TITLE	SERIES	PUBLISHER	SET (OR AUTHOR)	BAND
Home for Curly, A	Rigby Star	Rigby	Pink Level	1A
Home for Diggory, A	Skyrider LM Chapters	Gardner	Set 1	8
Home For Little Teddy, A	PM Storybooks	Nelson Thornes	Red Set B	2
Home for Star and Patches, A	PM Plus	Nelson Thornes	Gold Level	9
Homes	Kingscourt Reading, Extension	Kingscourt	Set 2	2
Honey for Baby Bear	PM Storybooks	Nelson Thornes	Blue Set A	4
Hop on Pop	Beginner Books	Collins	Seuss, Dr	6
Hop, Hop, Kangaroo	Pathways	Collins	Year 1	6
Hop, Skip and Jump	Oxford Reading Tree	OUP	Fireflies, More – Stage 1+	1B
Horace	Story Chest	Kingscourt	Ready-set-go Set C	2
Horns, Scales, Claws, and Tails	Kingscourt Reading, Core	Kingscourt	Level 16 Little Books	6
Horse and the Bell, The	PM Plus	Nelson Thornes	Gold Level	9
Horse Power	Skyrider LM Chapters	Gardner	Set 1	7
Horses	PM Non-fiction	Nelson Thornes	Purple Level	9
Horse's Hiccups	Kingscourt Reading, Extension	Kingscourt	Set 4	4
Horses of the Sea	Lighthouse	Ginn	White 6	10
Horses' Holiday	Big Cat	Collins	Turquoise	7
Hospital Party	PM Plus	Nelson Thornes	Green Level	5
Hot and Cold	Oxford Reading Tree	OUP	Fireflies Stage 2	3
Hot Dog Harris	Crunchies	Orchard	Colour Crackers	8
Hot Places	First Facts	Badger	Level 3	3
Hot Sunny Days	PM Plus Non-fiction	Nelson Thornes	Yellow Level	4
Hot Surprise, The	Rigby Star	Rigby	Orange Level	6
Hot-air Balloons	Alphakids	Gardner	Extending Level 18	8
Hound Gelert & Wookey Witch	New Way	Nelson Thornes	Orange Platform Books	10
House for Sale	Oxford Reading Tree	OUP	Stage 4 Storybooks	4
House in the Tree, The	PM Storybooks	Nelson Thornes	Blue Set A	4
House on the Hill, The	PM Plus	Nelson Thornes	Blue Level	4
House, A	PM Storybook Starters	Nelson Thornes	Set 1	1A
House, A	Sails Foundation	Heinemann	Pink B – See	1A
Househunting	PM Storybooks	Nelson Thornes	Green Set A	5
Houses	Story Chest	Kingscourt	Get-ready Set B	2
Houses and Homes	PM Plus Non-fiction	Nelson Thornes	Blue Level	5
Houses Then and Now	Oxford Reading Tree	OUP	Fireflies Stage 5	7
How Animals Move Around	PM Plus Non-fiction	Nelson Thornes	Purple Level	8
How Bat Learned to Fly	Kingscourt Reading, Extension	Kingscourt	Set 6	6
How Big is it?	Lighthouse	Ginn	Turquoise: 6	7
How Billy Duck Learned to Swim	Pelican Big Bks	Pearson	Waddell, Martin	5
How Do Birds Fly?	First Facts	Badger	Level 4	8
How Do Plants Grow Here?	AlphaWorld	Gardner	Level 19 (ext)	8
How Do You Sleep?	Web Weavers Non-fiction	OUP	First Non-fiction: Pack A	5
How Does it Work?	Big Cat	Collins	Gold	9
How Does it Work?	Spotty Zebra	Nelson Thornes	Red – Ourselves	3
How Does My Bike Work?	National Geographic	Rigby	Green Level	5
How Does Water Change?	Rigby Star Non-fiction	Rigby	Green Level	6
How Fire Came to Earth	Literacy Links Plus	Kingscourt	Early D	7
How Many Hot Dogs?	Story Chest	Kingscourt	Ready-set-go Set CC	4
How Many Legs?	Web Weavers Non-fiction	OUP	Stage 1 First Words NF	1B
How Music is Made	Rigby Star Non-fiction	Rigby	Turquoise Level	8
How My Bike Was Made	Web Weavers Non-fiction	OUP	Non-fiction – Toys	7
How News Travels	PM Plus Non-fiction	Nelson Thornes	Purple Level	8

TITLE	SERIES	PUBLISHER	SET (OR AUTHOR)	BAND
How People Move Around	PM Plus Non-fiction	Nelson Thornes	Purple Level	8
How Rabbit Caught the Sun	Kingscourt Reading, Core	Kingscourt	Level 12 Little Books	5
How Spiders Catch Their Food	AlphaWorld	Gardner	Level 19 (ext)	8
How the Camel Got His Hump	Kingscourt Reading, Extension	Kingscourt	Set 6	6
How the Geese Saved Rome	Kingscourt Reading, Core	Kingscourt	Level 10 Little Books	4
How to Be a Pirate in 10 Easy Stages	Big Cat	Collins	Gold	9
How to be Healthy	Oxford Reading Tree	OUP	Fireflies Stage 3	3
How to Choose a Pet	Discovery World	Heinemann	Stage E	9
How To Draw Cartoons	Big Cat	Collins	Purple	8
How to Draw Yourself	Oxford Reading Tree	OUP	Fireflies Stage 3	3
How to Dress a Knight	Info Trail	Pearson	Emergent History	3
How to Dress a Queen	Info Trail	Pearson	Emergent History	4
How to Grow a Nasturtium	Discovery World Links	Heinemann	Stage C	8
How to Have a Party	Big Cat	Collins	Yellow	3
How to Look After a Rabbit	Spotty Zebra	Nelson Thornes	Red – Ourselves	3
How to Look After a Rat	Info Trail	Pearson	Emergent Science	6
How to Make a Bird Feeder	Rigby Star Non-fiction	Rigby	Green Level	4
How to Make a Feely Box	Info Trail	Pearson	Beginner Science	5
How to Make a Fruit Salad	Oxford Reading Tree	OUP	Fireflies, More – Stage 4	4
How to Make a Hot Dog	Story Chest	Kingscourt	Get-ready Set DD	2
How to Make a Party Hat	Web Weavers Non-fiction	OUP	Stage 2 First Words NF	4
How to Make a Puppet Theatre	Oxford Reading Tree	OUP	Fireflies, More – Stage 4	4
How to Make a Wormery	Oxford Reading Tree	OUP	Fireflies, More – Stage 5	7
How to Make Can Stilts	Story Chest	Kingscourt	Ready-set-go Set BB	3
How to Make Pop-up Cards	Big Cat	Collins	Orange	7
How to Make Storybooks	Big Cat	Collins	Turquoise	7
How to Make Toys from the Past	Web Weavers Non-fiction	OUP	Non-fiction – Toys	6
How to Read the Sky	Info Trail	Pearson	Beginner Geography	6
How to Use a Computer	Oxford Reading Tree	OUP	Fireflies Stage 9	9
How to Write a Family Tree	Info Trail	Pearson	Beginner History	5
How Turtle Got His Shell	Rigby Star	Rigby	Orange Level	6
How Turtle Raced Beaver	Literacy Links Plus	Kingscourt	Early D	7
Huge and Horrible Beast, The	Oxford Reading Tree	OUP	More Allstars Pack 3a	10
Hullabaloo at the Zoo	Lighthouse	Ginn	Blue: 4	4
Hungry Baby, The	Alphakids Plus	Gardner	Transitional Level 14	5
Hungry Bear, The	Alphakids	Gardner	Transitional Level 12	5
Hungry Chickens, The	Literacy Links Plus	Kingscourt	Early C	5
Hungry Giant's Lunch, The	Story Chest	Kingscourt	Ready-set-go Set DD	3
Hungry Hedgehog	Kingscourt Reading, Core	Kingscourt	Level 3 Little Books	2
Hungry Kitten, The	PM Storybooks	Nelson Thornes	Yellow Set A	3
Hungry Monster	Story Chest	Kingscourt	Stage 3	6
Hungry Squirrel, The	PM Gems	Nelson Thornes	Red 4	2
Hunt for Gold, The	Oxford Reading Tree	OUP	Stage 7 More Stories A	7
Hunting in the Dark	Alphakids Plus	Gardner	Transitional Level 15	6
Hurry Up!	AlphaWorld	Gardner	Band 3: Yellow	3
Hut in the Old Tree, The	PM Plus	Nelson Thornes	Turquoise Level	7

I

| I Am a Bee | Sails Foundation | Heinemann | Pink A – He | 1A |

TITLE	SERIES	PUBLISHER	SET (OR AUTHOR)	BAND
I Am a Painter	Sails Foundation	Heinemann	Pink A – He	1A
I Am Frightened	Story Chest	Kingscourt	Get-ready Set C	2
I Am Here	Sails Foundation	Heinemann	Pink C – Said	1A
I Am Hot!	Spotty Zebra	Nelson Thornes	Pink B – Change	2
I Am Jumping	Sails Foundation	Heinemann	Pink A – Am	1A
I am Miss Cherry	Genre Range	Pearson	Beginner Plays	4
I Am Running	PM Plus	Nelson Thornes	Starters One	1A
I Am Working	Sails Foundation	Heinemann	Pink A – Am	1A
I Can	Sails Foundation	Heinemann	Pink A – Can	1A
I Can Fly	Lighthouse	Ginn	Pink B: 4	1B
I Can Help	Sails Foundation	Heinemann	Pink C – Get	1A
I Can Laugh	Sails Foundation	Heinemann	Pink A – Can	1A
I Can Read With My Eyes Shut	Beginner Books	Collins	Seuss, Dr	6
I Can Swim	Sails Foundation	Heinemann	Pink A – Can	1A
I Can't Find My Roller Skates	Alphakids	Gardner	Emergent Level 5	2
I Can't Open it!	Rigby Star	Rigby	Yellow Level	3
I Dig Dinosaurs	First Explorers	Kingscourt	Level 2	9
I Grew a Sunflower Big as My Dad	Info Trail	Pearson	Beginner Science	4
I Have a Question, Grandma	Literacy Links Plus	Kingscourt	Early D	5
I Like Birds	Sails Foundation	Heinemann	Pink A – Like	1A
I Like Boxes	Sails Foundation	Heinemann	Pink B – And	1A
I Like Elephants	Sails Foundation	Heinemann	Pink A – Like	1A
I Like Hats	Sails Foundation	Heinemann	Pink A – Like	1A
I Like Jam	Sails Foundation	Heinemann	Pink B – And	1A
I Like Rice	First Stories	Gardner	Emergent C	1A
I Like Riding	Sails Foundation	Heinemann	Pink A – Like	1A
I Like That Horse	First Stories	Gardner	Emergent D	1B
I Like to Jump	Rigby Star	Rigby	Red Level	2
I Love Chickens	Story Chest	Kingscourt	Ready-set-go Set BB	2
I Love the UK	Discovery World Links	Heinemann	Stage E	10
I Made a Picture	Kingscourt Reading, Extension	Kingscourt	Set 1	1B
I Spy	Kingscourt Reading, Core	Kingscourt	Level 1 Little Books	1B
I Spy in the Garden	Spotty Zebra	Nelson Thornes	Pink B – Change	2
I Spy Pancakes and Pies	Crunchies	Orchard	Twice Upon a Time	9
I Take Care of My Dog	Rigby Star Non-fiction	Rigby	Blue Level	3
I Want a Party	Pathways	Collins	Year 2	9
I Want a Pet!	Big Cat	Collins	Green	5
I Want to be an Acrobat	Alphakids Plus	Gardner	Extending Level 22	8
I Wash	First Stories	Gardner	Emergent A	1A
Ice and Snow	AlphaWorld	Gardner	Band 3: Yellow	3
Ice Cream	Alphakids	Gardner	Emergent Level 1	1A
Ice Cream	Big Cat	Collins	Gold	9
Ice Cream	Sails Foundation	Heinemann	Pink C – You	1A
Ice-Cream Factory, The	Rigby Star Non-fiction	Rigby	Gold Level	9
Ice-Cream Stick	Story Chest	Kingscourt	Get-ready Set DD	3
Ice-Maker Ice-Breaker	Oxford Reading Tree	OUP	Fireflies Stage 8	9
If I Were Invisible ...	Alphakids	Gardner	Extending Level 18	7
If Wishes Were Fishes	Crunchies	Orchard	Twice Upon a Time	9
If You Like Strawberries	Literacy Links Plus	Kingscourt	Early B	5
I'm a Chef	Literacy Links Plus	Kingscourt	Fluent D	10
I'm Brave	Alphakids	Gardner	Emergent Level 2	1A

TITLE	SERIES	PUBLISHER	SET (OR AUTHOR)	BAND
I'm in an Ad	Alphakids Plus	Gardner	Extending Level 20	8
I'm Not Scared	Web Guided Reading	OUP	Stage 4 (Duck Green)	4
I'm on the Phone	Alphakids	Gardner	Transitional Level 12	5
Important Case, An	Oxford Reading Tree	OUP	Stage 4 More Stories C	4
In a Cold, Cold Place	Alphakids Plus	Gardner	Emergent Level 4	2
In My Bed	Literacy Links Plus	Kingscourt	Emergent C	2
In My Family	AlphaWorld	Gardner	Band 1B: Pink	1B
In My Room	Literacy Links Plus	Kingscourt	Emergent C	2
In Our Classroom	PM Plus	Nelson Thornes	Starters One	1A
In Ravi's Den	Lighthouse	Ginn	Red: 7	2
In Search of Treasure	PM Plus	Nelson Thornes	Silver Level	10
In the Afternoon	PM Non-fiction	Nelson Thornes	Green Level	6
In the Car	First Stories	Gardner	Emergent C	1B
In the City of Rome	Literacy Links Plus	Kingscourt	Fluent D	5
In the Dark	Big Cat	Collins	Red A	1A
In the Garden	Dragonflies	Gardner	Pink	1B
In the Garden	First Facts	Badger	Level 2	2
In the Garden	Literacy Links Plus	Kingscourt	Early B	3
In the Garden	Oxford Reading Tree	OUP	Stage 6 & 7 Stories	5
In the Garden	PM Plus	Nelson Thornes	Starters One	1
In the Garden	Sails Foundation	Heinemann	Pink B – This	1A
In the Hen House	Story Street	Pearson	Step 2	2
In the Mirror	Story Chest	Kingscourt	Get-ready Set A	1B
In the Morning	PM Non-fiction	Nelson Thornes	Green Level	6
In the Mud	Sails Foundation	Heinemann	Pink B – Was	1A
In the Ocean	Alphakids Plus	Gardner	Emergent Level 4	2
In the Park	Literacy Links Plus	Kingscourt	Early C	5
In the Playground	AlphaWorld	Gardner	Band 5: Green	5
In the Treetops	AlphaWorld	Gardner	Level 16 (trans)	6
In the Trolley	PM Storybook Starters	Nelson Thornes	Set 1	1A
Insects	Alphakids	Gardner	Transitional Level 14	6
Insects	Go Facts	A&C Black	Animals	8
Interesting Insects	Kingscourt Reading, Core	Kingscourt	Level 18 Benchmark Bk	7
Interview with Florence Nightingale, An	Discovery World Links	Heinemann	Stage F	10
Inventing the Telephone	Four Corners	Pearson	Year 1	8
Inventions of Thomas Edison, The	Rigby Star Non-fiction	Rigby	Purple Level	9
Is it a Fruit?	Rigby Star Non-fiction	Rigby	Orange Level	5
Is It an Insect?	First Stories	Gardner	Emergent E	1B
Is it Shiny?	Badger NF Guided Reading	A&C Black	Science Buzzwords	6
Is Lightning Most Frightening?	Info Trail	Pearson	Emergent Geography	6
Is Simba Happy in the Zoo?	Info Trail	Pearson	Emergent Science	6
Is That an Earthquake?	Dragonflies	Gardner	Orange	6
Is the Wise Owl Wise?	Rigby Star	Rigby	Turquoise Level	7
Is This Too Much?	Oxford Reading Tree	OUP	Fireflies Stage 2	1B
Island Picnic, The	PM Storybooks	Nelson Thornes	Green Set A	5
It is Raining	PM Plus Non-fiction	Nelson Thornes	Yellow Level	3
It's a Gift	Lighthouse	Ginn	Blue: 5	4
It's About Time	Kingscourt Reading, Extension	Kingscourt	Set 7	7
It's Best to be Five!	Info Trail	Pearson	Beginner History	3
It's Not Fair	New Way	Nelson Thornes	Green Easy Start Set B	5
It's Not Fair	Oxford Reading Tree	OUP	Stage 5 More Stories A	6

TITLE	SERIES	PUBLISHER	SET (OR AUTHOR)	BAND
It's the Weather	Oxford Reading Tree	OUP	Stage 2 Patterned Stories	2

J

TITLE	SERIES	PUBLISHER	SET (OR AUTHOR)	BAND
Jack and Billy	PM Plus	Nelson Thornes	Red Level	2
Jack and Billy and Rose	PM Plus	Nelson Thornes	Blue Level	4
Jack and Chug	PM Storybooks	Nelson Thornes	Orange Set A	6
Jack and the Beanstalk	Alphakids Plus	Gardner	Extending Level 21	8
Jack and the Beanstalk	Literacy Links Plus	Kingscourt	Traditional Tale	6
Jack and the Beanstalk	Oxford Reading Tree	OUP	Traditional Tales 5–7	6
Jack and the Beanstalk	Storyworlds	Heinemann	Stage 9 Once Upon a Time	9
Jack and the Magic Harp	PM Traditional Tales	Nelson Thornes	Gold Level	9
Jack-in-the-Box	Story Chest	Kingscourt	Stage 3	6
Jack's Birthday	PM Plus	Nelson Thornes	Red Level	2
Jack's Boat	National Geographic	Rigby	Turquoise Level	5
Jack's Road	PM Gems	Nelson Thornes	Magenta 2/3	2
Jade Emperor and the Four Dragons, The	Lighthouse	Ginn	Purple: 4	8
Jake and the Big Fish	PM Photo Stories	Nelson Thornes	Yellow 7	3
Jake Kicks a Goal	PM Photo Stories	Nelson Thornes	Red 5	2
Jake's Car	PM Photo Stories	Nelson Thornes	Red 4	2
Jake's Plane	PM Photo Stories	Nelson Thornes	Yellow 8	3
Jamie's Food Guide	Discovery World Links	Heinemann	Stage E	10
Jane Goodall	Rigby Star Non-fiction	Rigby	Star Plus Level	10
Jane's Car	PM Storybooks	Nelson Thornes	Blue Set A	4
Japanese Garden, The	PM Plus	Nelson Thornes	Gold Level	9
Jasmine's Duck	Lighthouse	Ginn	Green: 3	5
Jellyfish	Alphakids Plus	Gardner	Extending Level 19	8
Jenny in Bed	Lighthouse	Ginn	Yellow: 2	3
Jenny the Joker	Rockets	A&C Black	West, Colin	9
Jeremy's Cake	Kingscourt Reading, Extension	Kingscourt	Set 4	4
Jessica in the Dark	PM Storybooks	Nelson Thornes	Orange Set B	6
Jets and the Rockets, The	PM Plus	Nelson Thornes	Turquoise Level	7
Jigsaw Puzzle, The	Oxford Reading Tree	OUP	Stage 7 More Stories A	7
Jo the Model Maker	Lighthouse	Ginn	Orange: 5	6
Jodie and Juggler	Big Cat	Collins	Green	5
Joe and the Bike	Oxford Reading Tree	OUP	Stage 3 Sparrows	3
Joe Makes a House	PM Plus	Nelson Thornes	Blue Level	4
Joey	PM Storybooks	Nelson Thornes	Green Set B	5
Johann and the Birds	Alphakids	Gardner	Extending Level 22	8
Jojo and the Football	Story Street	Pearson	Step 3	3
Jojo Makes the Team	Story Street	Pearson	Step 7	8
Joke Machine, The	Oxford Reading Tree	OUP	Stage 6 & 7 More Stories B	7
Jolly Hungry Jack	Lighthouse	Ginn	Orange: 4	6
Jolly Roger and the Spyglass	PM Gems	Nelson Thornes	Blue 11	4
Jolly Roger and the Treasure	PM Plus	Nelson Thornes	Yellow Level	3
Jolly Roger, the Pirate	PM Storybooks	Nelson Thornes	Yellow Set B	3
Jonathan Buys a Present	PM Storybooks	Nelson Thornes	Turquoise Set A	7
Jordan and the Northside Reps	PM Storybooks	Nelson Thornes	Silver Set C	10
Jordan at the Big Game	PM Plus	Nelson Thornes	Orange Level	6
Jordan's Catch	PM Storybooks	Nelson Thornes	Purple Set C	8

TITLE	SERIES	PUBLISHER	SET (OR AUTHOR)	BAND
Jordan's Football	PM Plus	Nelson Thornes	Green Level	5
Jordan's Lucky Day	PM Storybooks	Nelson Thornes	Turquoise Set C	7
Josh and Scruffy	PM Photo Stories	Nelson Thornes	Magenta 2/3	2
Josh and the Big Boys	PM Photo Stories	Nelson Thornes	Magenta 2/3	2
Josh and the Kite	PM Photo Stories	Nelson Thornes	Magenta 2/3	2
Josh and the Magic Beanstalk	Web Fiction	OUP	Stage 9 (Variety)	8
Josh Rides a Skateboard	PM Photo Stories	Nelson Thornes	Yellow 6	3
Josie and the Baby	Rigby Star	Rigby	Yellow Level	2
Josie and the Junk Box	Rigby Star	Rigby	Pink Level	1A
Josie and the Parade	Rigby Star	Rigby	Red Level	2
Josie and the Play	Rigby Star	Rigby	Blue Level	4
Josie Goes on Holiday	Rigby Star	Rigby	Green Level	5
Josie's New Coat	Rigby Star	Rigby	Blue Level	4
Journey Into the Earth, The	Storyworlds	Heinemann	Stage 9 Fantasy World	9
Journey to the Undersea Gardens	Four Corners	Pearson	Year 2	10
Juggling	Rigby Star	Rigby	Pink Level	1A
Julia Donaldson, A Biography	Oxford Reading Tree	OUP	Fireflies, More – Stage 5	6
Jumble Sale, The	Oxford Reading Tree	OUP	Stage 3 More Stories A	3
Jumble the Puppy	Storyworld Bridges	Heinemann	Stage 12	10
Jumbo	Genre Range	Pearson	Emergent Plays	4
Jumbo	PM Plus	Nelson Thornes	Yellow Level	3
Jump, Jump, Kangaroo	Story Chest	Kingscourt	Get-ready Set CC	2
Jumpers	Oxford Reading Tree	OUP	Fireflies, More – Stage 3	3
Jumping Jack	Rigby Star	Rigby	Purple Level	8
Jungle Frogs, The	PM Plus	Nelson Thornes	Green Level	5
Just Hanging Around	Kingscourt Reading, Extension	Kingscourt	Set 9	9
Just Like Grandpa	Literacy Links Plus	Kingscourt	Early A	4
Just Like Me	Story Chest	Kingscourt	Stage 4	7
Just Like You	Spotty Zebra	Nelson Thornes	Pink B – Change	1B
Just My Luck	Literacy Links Plus	Kingscourt	Early C	7
Just One Guinea Pig	PM Storybooks	Nelson Thornes	Orange Set B	6
Just the Bee's Knees	Kingscourt Reading, Core	Kingscourt	Level 19 Little Books	8

K

TITLE	SERIES	PUBLISHER	SET (OR AUTHOR)	BAND
Kangaroos	PM Non-fiction	Nelson Thornes	Turquoise Level	8
Kate and the Sheep	Oxford Reading Tree	OUP	Robins Pack 1	8
Katie's Butterfly	PM Plus	Nelson Thornes	Green Level	5
Katie's Caterpillar	PM Plus	Nelson Thornes	Yellow Level	3
Kayaking at the Blue Lake	PM Plus	Nelson Thornes	Gold Level	9
Keep Trying	Dragonflies	Gardner	Yellow/Blue	3
Keep Your Hamster Happy	Web Weavers Non-fiction	OUP	Non-fiction – Animals	7
Keeping Healthy	First Facts	Badger	Level 1	2
Kenji's Haircut	Lighthouse	Ginn	Red: 6	2
Kerry	PM Storybooks	Nelson Thornes	Silver Set A	10
Kerry's Double	PM Storybooks	Nelson Thornes	Silver Set A	10
Kevin and the Pirate Test	Rockets	A&C Black	Ryan, Margaret	10
Key Trouble	Oxford Reading Tree	OUP	Stage 9 More Stories A	7
Kiboko and the Water Snake	Storyworlds	Heinemann	Stage 7 Animal World	5
Kick-a-Lot Shoes, The	Story Chest	Kingscourt	Stage 2	5

TITLE	SERIES	PUBLISHER	SET (OR AUTHOR)	BAND
Kidnappers, The	Oxford Reading Tree	OUP	Stage 8 Stories	6
Killer Plants	AlphaWorld	Gardner	Level 18 (ext)	8
Kim and the Computer Giant	Storyworlds	Heinemann	Stage 8 Fantasy World	6
Kim and the Computer Mouse	Storyworlds	Heinemann	Stage 8 Fantasy World	8
Kim and the Missing Paint Pot	Storyworlds	Heinemann	Stage 8 Fantasy World	8
Kim and the Shape Dragon	Storyworlds	Heinemann	Stage 8 Fantasy World	8
Kim's Lunch	Alphakids	Gardner	Transitional Level 12	5
Kind Emma	Big Cat	Collins	Orange	6
Kind Prince & other stories, The	New Way	Nelson Thornes	Violet Core Book	8
Kindest Family, The	PM Plus	Nelson Thornes	Purple Level	8
King Midas and the Golden Touch	PM Storybooks	Nelson Thornes	Gold Set B	9
King of the Birds, The	Crunchies	Orchard	Tall Tales	9
King of the Birds, The	Rigby Star	Rigby	Purple Level	8
King of the Ostriches & other stories	New Way	Nelson Thornes	Blue Parallel Books	8
King's Birthday, The	Dragonflies	Gardner	Turquoise/Purple	7
King's Ears, The	Web Fiction	OUP	Stage 7 (Variety)	7
King's Race & other stories, The	New Way	Nelson Thornes	Yellow Platform Books	8
Kipper and the Giant	Oxford Reading Tree	OUP	Stage 6 & 7 Stories	6
Kipper and the Trolls	Oxford Reading Tree	OUP	Stage 5 More Stories C	5
Kipper the Clown	Oxford Reading Tree	OUP	Stage 3 More Stories A	3
Kipper's Balloon	Oxford Reading Tree	OUP	Stage 2 More Stories A	3
Kipper's Birthday	Oxford Reading Tree	OUP	Stage 2 More Stories A	3
Kipper's Diary	Oxford Reading Tree	OUP	Stage 1+ First Sentences	1B
Kipper's Idea	Oxford Reading Tree	OUP	Stage 3 More Stories A	4
Kipper's Laces	Oxford Reading Tree	OUP	Stage 2 More Stories B	4
Kitchen Garden	AlphaWorld	Gardner	Band 5: Green	5
Kites	AlphaWorld	Gardner	Band 8: Purple	8
Kites	Web Weavers Non-fiction	OUP	Non-fiction – Toys	7
Kites, The	Sails Foundation	Heinemann	Pink C – Going	1A
Kitty Cat	PM Plus	Nelson Thornes	Red Level	2
Kitty Cat and Fat Cat	PM Plus	Nelson Thornes	Red Level	2
Kitty Cat and the Bird	PM Gems	Nelson Thornes	Red 4	2
Kitty Cat and the Fish	PM Plus	Nelson Thornes	Red Level	2
Kitty Cat and the Paint	PM Plus	Nelson Thornes	Blue Level	4
Kitty Cat Plays Inside	PM Plus	Nelson Thornes	Yellow Level	3
Kitty Cat Runs Up a Tree	PM Gems	Nelson Thornes	Yellow 7	3
Knit, Knit, Knit, Knit	Literacy Links Plus	Kingscourt	Fluent A	6
Knitting for Penguins	Kingscourt Reading, Extension	Kingscourt	Set 7	8
Knock, Knock! Who's There?	Crunchies	Orchard	Twice Upon a Time	8
Know Where to Go	Skyrider LM Chapters	Gardner	Set 2	9
Knucklebones	Info Trail	Pearson	Beginner History	7
Korka the Mighty Elf	Rigby Star	Rigby	Turquoise Level	7

L

TITLE	SERIES	PUBLISHER	SET (OR AUTHOR)	BAND
Ladybird	Stopwatch	A&C Black		8
Ladybird, Ladybird	Kingscourt Reading, Core	Kingscourt	Level 10 Benchmark Bk	4
Ladybird, Ladybird	Web Weavers Non-fiction	OUP	First Non-fiction: Pack A	5
Lake of Stars, The	Storyworlds	Heinemann	Stage 5 Once Upon a Time	4
Lamby's Breakfast	PM Photo Stories	Nelson Thornes	Yellow 6	3

TITLE	SERIES	PUBLISHER	SET (OR AUTHOR)	BAND
Land Around Us, The	AlphaWorld	Gardner	Level 12 (trans)	5
Land of the Dinosaurs	Oxford Reading Tree	OUP	Stage 6 & 7 Stories	6
Last One Picked	Alphakids	Gardner	Transitional Level 13	5
Last Word, The	Alphakids Plus	Gardner	Transitional Level 15	6
Late For Football	PM Storybooks	Nelson Thornes	Blue Set A	4
Late For School	Web Fiction	OUP	Stage 3 (Variety)	3
Late For the Party	PM Photo Stories	Nelson Thornes	Green 14	5
Latest Dance Craze, The	Sunshine Readers	Gardner	Purple Level	9
Laughing Hyena	Lighthouse	Ginn	Green: 8	5
Laughing Place, The	Kingscourt Reading, Core	Kingscourt	Level 17 Little Books	7
Laughing Princess, The	Oxford Reading Tree	OUP	Stage 6 More Stories A	6
Lazy Giant, The	Oxford Reading Tree	OUP	More Allstars Pack 1a	9
Lazy Pig, The	PM Storybooks	Nelson Thornes	Red Set A	2
Leaf Boats, The	PM Plus	Nelson Thornes	Yellow Level	3
Leaves	AlphaWorld	Gardner	Band 2: Red	2
Leela and the Lost Shoe	Web Guided Reading	OUP	Stage 6 (Duck Green)	7
Leela's Secret Plan	Web Guided Reading	OUP	Stage 5 (Duck Green)	4
Leela's Tree	Spotty Zebra	Nelson Thornes	Pink A – Change	1B
Legs	Literacy Links Plus	Kingscourt	Early A	2
Let Me in	Story Chest	Kingscourt	Stage 3	6
Let's Build a House	Badger NF Guided Reading	Franklin Watts	Wonderwise	9
Let's Eat!	First Facts	Badger	Level 2	2
Let's Go Shopping	Big Cat	Collins	Red B	1B
Let's Go To Mars	Big Cat	Collins	Purple	8
Let's Have a Dog	Pathways	Collins	Year 1	5
Let's Make Music	Four Corners	Pearson	Year 1	6
Let's Make Pancakes	Alphakids Plus	Gardner	Transitional Level 12	5
Let's Party	AlphaWorld	Gardner	Level 18 (ext)	7
Let's Play	Four Corners	Pearson	Year 2	9
Let's Play Board Games!	Spotlight on Fact	Collins	Y1 Toys and Games	4
Let's Pretend	First Facts	Badger	Level 2	3
Let's Pretend	PM Plus	Nelson Thornes	Red Level	2
Letter to New Zealand, A	Big Cat	Collins	Orange	6
Letters From Lucy	Pathways	Collins	Year 2	8
Life Cycles	AlphaWorld	Gardner	Level 12 (trans)	4
Life in Space	First Facts	Badger	Level 4	8
Lift, The	Story Chest	Kingscourt	Ready-set-go Set CC	4
Lift-off!	First Facts	Badger	Level 4	8
Lights On	First Explorers	Kingscourt	Level 2	10
Lili's Breakfast	Kingscourt Reading, Extension	Kingscourt	Set 4	4
Lily and the Leaf Boats	PM Photo Stories	Nelson Thornes	Magenta 2/3	2
Lily's Play House	PM Photo Stories	Nelson Thornes	Red 4	2
Line Dancing	First Stories	Gardner	Emergent B	1A
Ling Lee's Surprise	Dragonflies	Gardner	Green	5
Lion and the Mouse, The	PM Storybooks	Nelson Thornes	Blue Set A	5
Lion and the Rabbit, The	PM Storybooks	Nelson Thornes	Blue Set A	4
Lion Talk	Kingscourt Reading, Extension	Kingscourt	Set 6	6
Lions and the Buffaloes, The	PM Plus	Nelson Thornes	Orange Level	6
Lions and Tigers	First Facts	Badger	Level 4	8
Lions and Tigers	PM Non-fiction	Nelson Thornes	Turquoise Level	8
Lion's Dinner, The	Rigby Star	Rigby	Yellow Level	3

TITLE	SERIES	PUBLISHER	SET (OR AUTHOR)	BAND
Lion's Lunch	Lighthouse	Ginn	Blue: 6	4
Litter Queen, The	Oxford Reading Tree	OUP	Stage 9 Stories	7
Little Adventure, A	PM Storybooks	Nelson Thornes	Silver Set A	10
Little Angels	Web Guided Reading	OUP	Stage 3 (Duck Green)	3
Little Blue Horse, The	PM Plus	Nelson Thornes	Orange Level	6
Little Blue, Big Blue	Rigby Star	Rigby	White Level	10
Little Bo Peep Has Knickers That Bleep	Crunchies	Orchard	Seriously Silly Rhymes	10
Little Brother	Story Chest	Kingscourt	Get-ready Set C	2
Little Brother's Haircut	Story Chest	Kingscourt	Stage 7	10
Little Bulldozer	PM Storybooks	Nelson Thornes	Yellow Set A	3
Little Bulldozer Helps Again	PM Storybooks	Nelson Thornes	Blue Set B	4
Little Chimp	PM Plus	Nelson Thornes	Red Level	2
Little Chimp and Baby Chimp	PM Plus	Nelson Thornes	Blue Level	4
Little Chimp and Big Chimp	PM Plus	Nelson Thornes	Red Level	2
Little Chimp and the Bees	PM Plus	Nelson Thornes	Blue Level	4
Little Chimp and the Buffalo	PM Gems	Nelson Thornes	Green 12	5
Little Chimp and the Termites	PM Plus	Nelson Thornes	Green Level	5
Little Chimp Finds Some Fruit	PM Gems	Nelson Thornes	Blue 11	4
Little Chimp is Brave	PM Gems	Nelson Thornes	Red 5	2
Little Chimp Runs Away	PM Plus	Nelson Thornes	Yellow Level	3
Little Dinosaur Escapes	PM Storybooks	Nelson Thornes	Turquoise Set B	7
Little Dragon, The	Oxford Reading Tree	OUP	Stage 2 More Patterned Stories	2
Little Duck for Lily, A	PM Photo Stories	Nelson Thornes	Magenta 2/3	2
Little Duckling	Spotty Zebra	Nelson Thornes	Red – Change	2
Little Ducklings	First Stories	Gardner	Emergent E	1B
Little Giraffe, The	PM Photo Stories	Nelson Thornes	Red 3	2
Little Girl and Her Beetle, The	Literacy Links Plus	Kingscourt	Fluent B	7
Little Girl and the Bear, The	Storyworlds	Heinemann	Stage 9 Once Upon a Time	10
Little Hearts	Story Chest	Kingscourt	Ready-set-go Set AA	2
Little Match Girl, The	Lighthouse	Ginn	White 7	10
Little Meanie's Lunch	Story Chest	Kingscourt	Ready-set-go Set AA	3
Little Monkey	Alphakids	Gardner	Early Level 11	4
Little Pig	Story Chest	Kingscourt	Ready-set-go Set B	2
Little Rabbit	Storyworlds	Heinemann	Stage 4 Once Upon a Time	3
Little Red Bus, The	PM Storybooks	Nelson Thornes	Green Set A	5
Little Red Hen & other stories	New Way	Nelson Thornes	Green Platform Books	6
Little Red Hen, The	Kingscourt Reading, Extension	Kingscourt	Set 5	5
Little Red Hen, The	Literacy Links Plus	Kingscourt	Traditional Tale	4
Little Red Hen, The	PM Traditional Tales	Nelson Thornes	Orange Level	6
Little Red Riding Hood	Kingscourt Reading, Core	Kingscourt	Level 18 Little Books	7
Little Red Riding Hood	PM Traditional Tales	Nelson Thornes	Turquoise Level	7
Little Red Riding Hood	Storyworlds	Heinemann	Stage 8 Once Upon a Time	7
Little Red Riding Wolf	Crunchies	Orchard	Seriously Silly Stories	10
Little Seeds	First Stories	Gardner	Emergent E	1B
Little Snowman, The	PM Storybooks	Nelson Thornes	Red Set B	2
Little Teddy and Monkey	PM Gems	Nelson Thornes	Red 3	2
Little Things	PM Storybook Starters	Nelson Thornes	Set 1	1A
Little White Hen, The	PM Plus	Nelson Thornes	Yellow Level	3
Little Work Plane, The	PM Plus	Nelson Thornes	Orange Level	6
Living and Growing	PM Plus Non-fiction	Nelson Thornes	Orange Level	6
Living and Non-living Things	Alphakids	Gardner	Emergent Level 2	1B

TITLE	SERIES	PUBLISHER	SET (OR AUTHOR)	BAND
Living in Space	Rigby Star Non-fiction	Rigby	Star Plus Level	10
Living or Not?	First Facts	Badger	Level 1	2
Living Together	Alphakids	Gardner	Extending Level 23	10
Living with Others	PM Plus Non-fiction	Nelson Thornes	Orange Level	7
Lizard Loses His Tail	PM Storybooks	Nelson Thornes	Red Set A	2
Lizard the Wizard	Rockets	A&C Black	Rodgers, Frank	9
Lizard's Tail	Alphakids Plus	Gardner	Early Level 8	3
Lizzie's Lizard	Kingscourt Reading, Extension	Kingscourt	Set 7	7
Locked In	PM Plus	Nelson Thornes	Green Level	5
Locked Out	PM Storybooks	Nelson Thornes	Blue Set A	5
Lollipop, the Old Car	PM Plus	Nelson Thornes	Green Level	5
London's Burning!	Info Trail	Pearson	Emergent History	5
Lonely Giant, The	Literacy Links Plus	Kingscourt	Fluent B	8
Lonely Troll, The	Alphakids	Gardner	Transitional Level 17	7
Long and Short	PM Maths	Nelson Thornes	Stage A	2
Long Bike Ride, The	PM Photo Stories	Nelson Thornes	Blue 10	4
Long Journey, The	Oxford Reading Tree	OUP	Robins Pack 1	9
Long Live Roberto	Crunchies	Orchard	Colour Crackers	9
Look at Me	Alphakids Plus	Gardner	Emergent Level 1	1A
Look at Me	Dragonflies	Gardner	Pink	1B
Look at Me	Oxford Reading Tree	OUP	Stage 1+ First Sentences	1B
Look at Me	PM Storybook Starters	Nelson Thornes	Set 1	1A
Look at Me!	Lighthouse	Ginn	Pink A: 2	1A
Look at My Weaving	First Stories	Gardner	Emergent F	1B
Look at the Animals	Sails Foundation	Heinemann	Pink B – Look	1A
Look at the Ball	Kingscourt Reading, Extension	Kingscourt	Set 1	1B
Look at the House	PM Plus	Nelson Thornes	Starters One	1A
Look at the Painting	Spotty Zebra	Nelson Thornes	Pink A – Change	1B
Look at the Robot	Sails Foundation	Heinemann	Pink B – Look	1A
Look at the Tree	National Geographic	Rigby	Pink Level	1A
Look at This Mess!	First Stories	Gardner	Emergent F	1B
Look Closer	Pathways	Collins	Year 1	8
Look For Me	Story Chest	Kingscourt	Ready-set-go Set C	2
Look in the Garden	PM Plus	Nelson Thornes	Green Level	5
Look Inside	Kingscourt Reading, Extension	Kingscourt	Set 8	8
Look Out Fish!	Lighthouse	Ginn	Pink B: 2	1B
Look Out For Bingo	PM Plus	Nelson Thornes	Yellow Level	3
Look Out for Your Tail	Literacy Links Plus	Kingscourt	Fluent C	8
Look Out of the Window	Kingscourt Reading, Core	Kingscourt	Level 4 Little Books	2
Look Out!	PM Plus	Nelson Thornes	Orange Level	6
Look Out, Dan!	Story Chest	Kingscourt	Get-ready Set CC	2
Look Smart	Oxford Reading Tree	OUP	Stage 4 More Stories C	4
Look Up	First Explorers	Kingscourt	Level 1	8
Look Up, Look Down	PM Non-fiction	Nelson Thornes	Red Level	3
Look What I Found!	Lighthouse	Ginn	Pink A: 8	1A
Look What You Can Make!	Kingscourt Reading, Core	Kingscourt	Level 6 Little Books	3
Looking After Baby	Kingscourt Reading, Extension	Kingscourt	Set 2	2
Looking After Chickens	Alphakids	Gardner	Transitional Level 15	6
Looking After Eggs	AlphaWorld	Gardner	Level 20 (ext)	8
Looking After Pip	Story Street	Pearson	Step 5	5
Looking After Their Young	Alphakids	Gardner	Extending Level 18	8

TITLE	SERIES	PUBLISHER	SET (OR AUTHOR)	BAND
Looking After Your Dog	Oxford Reading Tree	OUP	Fireflies Stage 5	7
Looking at Teddy Bears	Pelican Big Bks	Pearson	Purkis, Sallie	7
Looking Down	First Stories	Gardner	Emergent F	1B
Looking Down	PM Storybook Starters	Nelson Thornes	Set 2	1B
Looking for Fang	Alphakids	Gardner	Emergent Level 5	3
Looking for Lucky	Genre Range	Pearson	Beginner Comics	3
Looking in Mirrors	AlphaWorld	Gardner	Level 16 (trans)	6
Looking Like Plants	Alphakids Plus	Gardner	Transitional Level 12	6
Losing Lucky	Story Street	Pearson	Step 6	6
Lost	Kingscourt Reading, Core	Kingscourt	Level 13 Benchmark Bk	5
Lost	Story Chest	Kingscourt	Ready-set-go Set B	2
Lost	Story Street	Pearson	Step 3	3
Lost and Found	Web Guided Reading	OUP	Stage 2 (Duck Green)	2
Lost at the Fun Park	PM Storybooks	Nelson Thornes	Blue Set B	4
Lost Coat, The	Storyworlds	Heinemann	Stage 3 Our World	2
Lost Costume, The	Storyworlds	Heinemann	Stage 6 Our World	6
Lost in Space	Skyrider LM Chapters	Gardner	Set 1	9
Lost in the Forest	PM Storybooks	Nelson Thornes	Orange Set C	6
Lost in the Jungle	Oxford Reading Tree	OUP	Stage 6 & 7 Stories	7
Lost in the Mist	Storyworlds	Heinemann	Stage 8 Our World	7
Lost in the Park	Alphakids	Gardner	Transitional Level 13	6
Lost Key, The	Oxford Reading Tree	OUP	Stage 6 & 7 Stories	7
Lost Keys, The	PM Plus	Nelson Thornes	Green Level	5
Lost Mother, The	Alphakids	Gardner	Early Level 6	3
Lost Puppy, The	Oxford Reading Tree	OUP	Stage 2 More Patterned Stories	2
Lost Socks	PM Plus	Nelson Thornes	Blue Level	4
Loudest Sneeze, The	Alphakids	Gardner	Transitional Level 16	6
Lucky Day for Little Dinosaur, A	PM Storybooks	Nelson Thornes	Yellow Set B	3
Lucky Dip, The	PM Plus	Nelson Thornes	Red Level	2
Lucky Ducks	Web Guided Reading	OUP	Stage 6 (Duck Green)	7
Lucky Goes to Dog School	PM Storybooks	Nelson Thornes	Yellow Set A	3
Lucky the Goat	Oxford Reading Tree	OUP	Stage 4 Sparrows	4
Lucy Loses Red Ted	Storyworlds	Heinemann	Stage 4 Our World	3
Lucy Meets a Dragon	Literacy Links Plus	Kingscourt	Fluent B	10
Lucy's Luck	Sunshine Readers	Gardner	Light Blue Level	7
Luke's First Day	Pathways	Collins	Year 1	3
Luke's Go-Kart	PM Storybooks	Nelson Thornes	Gold Set A	9
Lunch Boxes	Dragonflies	Gardner	Pink	1A
Lunch Bunch, The	Kingscourt Reading, Extension	Kingscourt	Set 9	9
Lunch for Greedy Cat	Dragonflies	Gardner	Blue	4
Lunch for Tig	Web Fiction	OUP	Stage 2 (Variety)	3
Lunchtime at the Zoo	First Stories	Gardner	Emergent E	1B

M

TITLE	SERIES	PUBLISHER	SET (OR AUTHOR)	BAND
Machines Make Fun Rides	National Geographic	Rigby	Orange Level	5
Mack's Big Day	PM Plus	Nelson Thornes	Purple Level	8
Magenta and the Ghost Babies	Rockets	A&C Black	Shulman, Dee	9
Magenta and the Ghost Bride	Rockets	A&C Black	Shulman, Dee	9
Magenta and the Ghost School	Rockets	A&C Black	Shulman, Dee	9

TITLE	SERIES	PUBLISHER	SET (OR AUTHOR)	BAND
Magenta and the Scary Ghosts	Rockets	A&C Black	Shulman, Dee	9
Magic Boots, The	Storyworlds	Heinemann	Stage 7 Fantasy World	5
Magic Button, The	Story Street	Pearson	Step 3	3
Magic Carpet, The	Storyworlds	Heinemann	Stage 9 Fantasy World	9
Magic Coat, The	Storyworlds	Heinemann	Stage 7 Fantasy World	6
Magic Doctor, The	Oxford Reading Tree	OUP	Traditional Tales 5–7	8
Magic Hat, The	Storyworlds	Heinemann	Stage 7 Fantasy World	6
Magic Hotel	Rockets	A&C Black	Smith, Wendy	9
Magic Jigsaw, The	Rigby Star	Rigby	Gold Level	10
Magic Key, The	Oxford Reading Tree	OUP	Stage 5 Storybooks	4
Magic Number, The	Web Fiction	OUP	Stage 9 (Variety)	8
Magic Paintbrush, The	Web Fiction	OUP	Stage 1 (Variety)	2
Magic Pen, The	Big Cat	Collins	Green	5
Magic Porridge Pot, The	Oxford Reading Tree	OUP	All Stars Pack 1	8
Magic Puppet, The	Web Guided Reading	OUP	Stage 7 (Duck Green)	6
Magic Shoes, The	Storyworlds	Heinemann	Stage 7 Fantasy World	6
Magic Tricks	Oxford Reading Tree	OUP	Fireflies Stage 5	5
Magic Trident, The	Storyworlds	Heinemann	Stage 6 Fantasy World	6
Magnets	AlphaWorld	Gardner	Level 15 (trans)	6
Magnets	National Geographic	Rigby	Purple Level	10
Magnets	Rigby Star Non-fiction	Rigby	Gold Level	8
Magpie Tree, The	Dragonflies	Gardner	Turquoise/Purple	8
Magpie's Baking Day	PM Storybooks	Nelson Thornes	Blue Set A	4
Make a Bottle Garden	Lighthouse	Ginn	Purple: 2	8
Make a Glider	Kingscourt Reading, Extension	Kingscourt	Set 3	3
Make a Kite	Kingscourt Reading, Core	Kingscourt	Level 4 Little Books	2
Make a Milkshake	Web Weavers Non-fiction	OUP	First Non-fiction: Pack A	3
Make a Rainbow	Kingscourt Reading, Core	Kingscourt	Level 12 Benchmark Bk	5
Make a Zoo	First Facts	Badger	Level 2	2
Make Your Own Monster!	Rigby Star Non-fiction	Rigby	Blue Level	5
Making a Bird	PM Plus Non-fiction	Nelson Thornes	Starters One	1A
Making a Book	Oxford Reading Tree	OUP	Fireflies Stage 10	10
Making a Butterfly	PM Maths	Nelson Thornes	Stage A	2
Making a Cat and a Mouse	PM Plus Non-fiction	Nelson Thornes	Red Level	2
Making a Caterpillar	PM Plus Non-fiction	Nelson Thornes	Yellow Level	3
Making a Dinosaur	PM Plus Non-fiction	Nelson Thornes	Starters One	1A
Making a Picture	Alphakids Plus	Gardner	Early Level 6	3
Making a Rabbit	PM Plus Non-fiction	Nelson Thornes	Starters One	1A
Making a Space Shuttle	Oxford Reading Tree	OUP	Fireflies Stage 7	8
Making a Torch	Alphakids	Gardner	Extending Level 23	10
Making a Toy House	PM Plus Non-fiction	Nelson Thornes	Blue Level	4
Making an Animated Cartoon	Alphakids Plus	Gardner	Extending Level 23	9
Making Bread	Alphakids	Gardner	Transitional Level 12	5
Making Butter	Alphakids	Gardner	Emergent Level 4	3
Making Caterpillars and Butterflies	Literacy Links Plus	Kingscourt	Early C	6
Making Dips	Alphakids Plus	Gardner	Extending Level 21	9
Making Lunch	Alphakids	Gardner	Emergent Level 5	2
Making Muffins	Oxford Reading Tree	OUP	Fireflies Stage 1+	1B
Making Muffins	Spotty Zebra	Nelson Thornes	Red – Change	3
Making Music	Alphakids Plus	Gardner	Emergent Level 2	1A
Making Party Food	PM Plus Non-fiction	Nelson Thornes	Green Level	6

TITLE	SERIES	PUBLISHER	SET (OR AUTHOR)	BAND
Making Party Hats	PM Maths	Nelson Thornes	Stage B	3
Making Pizza	Alphakids Plus	Gardner	Emergent Level 4	2
Making Pots with Dad	Alphakids Plus	Gardner	Transitional Level 14	6
Making Prints	Oxford Reading Tree	OUP	Fireflies, More – Stage 2	1B
Making Spaghetti	Alphakids Plus	Gardner	Early Level 9	4
Making Work Easy	AlphaWorld	Gardner	Level 19 (ext)	8
Making Yoghurt	Skyrider LM Chapters	Gardner	Set 2	9
Malcolm Magpie	Kingscourt Reading, Extension	Kingscourt	Set 5	5
Mamba and the Crocodile Bird	Storyworlds	Heinemann	Stage 7 Animal World	5
Mammals	Alphakids Plus	Gardner	Early Level 8	3
Mammals	Go Facts	A&C Black	Animals	9
Man in the Moon, The	Kingscourt Reading, Extension	Kingscourt	Set 5	6
Man Who Rode the Tiger, The	PM Plus	Nelson Thornes	Silver Level	10
Man-Eating Snails	Story Street	Pearson	Step 8	9
Mango Tree, The	Storyworlds	Heinemann	Stage 5 Our World	4
Mantu the Elephant	Rigby Star	Rigby	Gold Level	9
Maps	Discovery World	Heinemann	Stage E	7
Marble Patch, The	PM Storybooks	Nelson Thornes	Purple Set C	8
Market, The	Sails Foundation	Heinemann	Pink C – Come	1A
Marty's Birthday	Skyrider LM Chapters	Gardner	Set 2	8
Mary, Mary, Fried Canary	Crunchies	Orchard	Seriously Silly Rhymes	9
Mary-Anne and the Cat Baby	Oxford Reading Tree	OUP	More Allstars Pack 3a	10
Masterpiece, The	Kingscourt Reading, Extension	Kingscourt	Set 10	10
Materials	Discovery World	Heinemann	Stage C	3
Matsumura's Ice Sculpture	Four Corners	Pearson	Year 1	4
Matthew and Emma	PM Gems	Nelson Thornes	Magenta 2/3	2
Matt's Big Day	Spotty Zebra	Nelson Thornes	Red – Change	3
Matt's Good Idea	PM Gems	Nelson Thornes	Green 14	5
Matt's Socks	Spotty Zebra	Nelson Thornes	Pink A – Change	1B
Max and Jake	PM Plus	Nelson Thornes	Green Level	5
Max and the Apples	Storyworlds	Heinemann	Stage 4 Animal World	2
Max and the Bird House	PM Plus	Nelson Thornes	Blue Level	4
Max and the Cat	Storyworlds	Heinemann	Stage 4 Animal World	3
Max and the Drum	Storyworlds	Heinemann	Stage 4 Animal World	3
Max and the Little Plant	PM Plus	Nelson Thornes	Yellow Level	3
Max Comes Home	First Stories	Gardner	Emergent B	1A
Max Gets Ready	Rigby Star	Rigby	Red Level	2
Max Goes Fishing	PM Plus	Nelson Thornes	Yellow Level	3
Max Rides His Bike	PM Plus	Nelson Thornes	Yellow Level	3
Max Saves a Frog	PM Gems	Nelson Thornes	Green 12	5
Max Wants to Fly	Storyworlds	Heinemann	Stage 4 Animal World	3
Maya's Family	Oxford Reading Tree	OUP	Fireflies Stage 1+	1A
May-Ling's Party	Oxford Reading Tree	OUP	Citizenship Stories Stage 9/10	10
Maze Craze, The	Skyrider LM Chapters	Gardner	Set 2	8
Me	First Facts	Badger	Level 1	1A
Me	PM Storybook Starters	Nelson Thornes	Set 1	1A
Me and My Dog	Dragonflies	Gardner	Green	5
Me and My Dog	Lighthouse	Ginn	Pink A: 7	1A
Me, Myself and I	Kingscourt Reading, Core	Kingscourt	Level 13 Collection	5
Medal for Poppy, A	Crunchies	Orchard	Colour Crackers	9
Meerkat Chat	Kingscourt Reading, Core	Kingscourt	Level 20 Little Books	9

TITLE	SERIES	PUBLISHER	SET (OR AUTHOR)	BAND
Meet Erdene	Four Corners	Pearson	Year 2	7
Meet Me at the Water Hole	Kingscourt Reading, Extension	Kingscourt	Set 6	6
Meg Goes to Bed	PM Photo Stories	Nelson Thornes	Magenta 2/3	2
Meg's Cat	Lighthouse	Ginn	Yellow: 8	3
Meg's Messy Room	PM Photo Stories	Nelson Thornes	Magenta 2/3	1B
Meg's Tiny Red Teddy	PM Photo Stories	Nelson Thornes	Magenta 2/3	2
Merry Go Round, The	PM Storybooks	Nelson Thornes	Red Set A	2
Messy Hands	Spotty Zebra	Nelson Thornes	Pink A – Ourselves	1A
Mice	Kingscourt Reading, Core	Kingscourt	Level 15 Collection	6
Mice	Literacy Links Plus	Kingscourt	Early D	6
Mice	PM Non-fiction	Nelson Thornes	Orange Level	6
Mice	Sails Foundation	Heinemann	Pink C – Go	1A
Mice at School	Kingscourt Reading, Core	Kingscourt	Level 15 Little Books	6
Mice Have a Meeting, The	PM Plus	Nelson Thornes	Orange Level	6
Mice in School	Alphakids Plus	Gardner	Extending Level 19	7
Mice in Space	Alphakids Plus	Gardner	Transitional Level 12	4
Mice, The	Sails Foundation	Heinemann	Pink B – Went	1A
Micky the Muckiest Boy	Crunchies	Orchard	The One And Only	7
Microscope	Story Chest	Kingscourt	Get-ready Set DD	2
Middle of Nowhere, The	Rigby Star	Rigby	Star Plus	10
Midge and the Eggs	Oxford Reading Tree	OUP	Stage 3 Sparrows	4
Midge in Hospital	Oxford Reading Tree	OUP	Stage 3 Sparrows	3
Mighty Machines	Alphakids Plus	Gardner	Early Level 6	3
Mighty Machines	National Geographic	Rigby	Green Level	6
Mighty Mountains	AlphaWorld	Gardner	Level 15 (trans)	6
Mike's Parachute Jump	Sunshine Readers	Gardner	Purple Level	7
Milk Shake	Alphakids Plus	Gardner	Emergent Level 3	2
Millennium Scrapbook, A	Info Trail	Pearson	Emergent Geography	10
Minestrone Mob, The	Rockets	A&C Black	Wallace, Karen	10
Minh's New Life	PM Plus	Nelson Thornes	Silver Level	10
Minibeast Encyclopaedia	Discovery World	Heinemann	Stage C	8
Mirror Island	Oxford Reading Tree	OUP	Stage 6 & 7 More Stories B	6
Mirrors	Oxford Reading Tree	OUP	Fireflies, More – Stage 3	2
Misha Disappears	Literacy Links Plus	Kingscourt	Fluent D	8
Miss Blossom	Pathways	Collins	Year 2	6
Miss Pool Is Cool	Dragonflies	Gardner	Yellow/Blue	4
Miss Popple's Pets	Literacy Links Plus	Kingscourt	Emergent A	1A
Miss Ross is Cross	Web Fiction	OUP	Stage 9 (Variety)	7
Missing Shoes, The, Part 1	Story Street	Pearson	Step 4	4
Missing Shoes, The, Part 2	Story Street	Pearson	Step 4	4
Mitch to the Rescue	PM Storybooks	Nelson Thornes	Orange Set B	6
Mitt For Me, A	First Stories	Gardner	Emergent B	1A
Modern Day Explorer: Steve Fossett	Oxford Reading Tree	OUP	Fireflies Stage 8	10
Mojo and Weeza and the Funny Thing	Big Cat	Collins	Blue	4
Moneypenny and the Pond	Web Fiction	OUP	Stage 8 (Variety)	8
Moneypenny Goes Camping	Web Fiction	OUP	Stage 8 (Variety)	8
Moneypenny's Big Walk	Web Fiction	OUP	Stage 8 (Variety)	8
Monkey and Fire	Literacy Links Plus	Kingscourt	Early D	7
Monkey Business	Kingscourt Reading, Extension	Kingscourt	Set 10	10
Monkey on the Roof	PM Plus	Nelson Thornes	Red Level	2
Monkey Tricks	Oxford Reading Tree	OUP	Stage 2 Patterned Stories	2

TITLE	SERIES	PUBLISHER	SET (OR AUTHOR)	BAND
Monkey Tricks	PM Storybooks	Nelson Thornes	Turquoise Set A	7
Monkeys	Pathways	Collins	Year 2	10
Monkeys	Sails Foundation	Heinemann	Pink A – Am	1A
Monkeys and Apes	PM Non-fiction	Nelson Thornes	Turquoise Level	8
Monster at the Beach, The	Kingscourt Reading, Extension	Kingscourt	Set 3	3
Monster in the Cave, The	Lighthouse	Ginn	Turquoise: 7	7
Monster in the Cupboard, The	Storyworld Bridges	Heinemann	Stage 10	9
Monster is Coming! The	Rigby Star	Rigby	Gold Level	9
Monster Machines	AlphaWorld	Gardner	Level 23 (ext)	10
Monster Meal	Rigby Star	Rigby	Red Level	1A
Monster Mistake, A	Oxford Reading Tree	OUP	Stage 5 More Stories A	4
Monster on the Street, A – Part 1	Story Street	Pearson	Step 7	9
Monster on the Street, A – Part 2	Story Street	Pearson	Step 7	9
Monster Sandwich, A	Story Chest	Kingscourt	Get-ready Set B	2
Monster Town, The	Sails Foundation	Heinemann	Pink B – This	1A
Monsters	Alphakids	Gardner	Emergent Level 3	2
Monster's Baking Day	Pathways	Collins	Year 1	5
Monty and the Ghost Train	Storyworlds	Heinemann	Stage 2 Fantasy World	2
Monty at McBurgers	Storyworlds	Heinemann	Stage 2 Fantasy World	2
Monty at the Party	Storyworlds	Heinemann	Stage 2 Fantasy World	2
Monty at the Seaside	Storyworlds	Heinemann	Stage 2 Fantasy World	2
Moon Adventure	Story Street	Pearson	Step 4	5
Moon Cheese	Web Guided Reading	OUP	Stage 7 (Duck Green)	6
Moon, The	Sails Foundation	Heinemann	Pink B – See	1A
Moppet on the Run	PM Storybooks	Nelson Thornes	Purple Set A	8
More Macdonalds	Story Street	Pearson	Step 8	10
More Spaghetti!	PM Plus	Nelson Thornes	Orange Level	6
More! More! More!	Story Chest	Kingscourt	Stage 7	10
Morning Star	Literacy Links Plus	Kingscourt	Fluent A	10
Morris Mouse	Kingscourt Reading, Core	Kingscourt	Level 14 Benchmark Bk	5
Morris Plays Hide and Seek	Big Cat	Collins	Orange	5
Mosque School	Oxford Reading Tree	OUP	Stage 4 Sparrows	3
Mother Bear's Scarf	PM Gems	Nelson Thornes	Yellow 8	3
Mother Bird	PM Plus	Nelson Thornes	Red Level	2
Mother Tiger and Her Cubs	PM Plus	Nelson Thornes	Blue Level	4
Mother's Day	PM Plus	Nelson Thornes	Yellow Level	3
Mother's Day Harmony	Sunshine Readers	Gardner	Purple Level	8
Motorbike Photo, The	PM Plus	Nelson Thornes	Gold Level	9
Motorway, The	Oxford Reading Tree	OUP	Stage 7 More Stories A	7
Mountains, Hills and Cliffs	PM Plus Non-fiction	Nelson Thornes	Gold Level	9
Mouse	Story Chest	Kingscourt	Get-ready Set B	2
Mouse and the Bull, The	Genre Range	Pearson	Beginner Traditional Tales	3
Mouse Stone, The	Lighthouse	Ginn	Purple: 5	8
Mouse Train	Story Chest	Kingscourt	Get-ready Set CC	1B
Mouse-deer and the Crocodiles, The	PM Plus	Nelson Thornes	Turquoise Level	7
Mouse-deer Escapes, The	PM Plus	Nelson Thornes	Turquoise Level	7
Moving Big Trees	Alphakids Plus	Gardner	Extending Level 22	9
Moving Day	Rigby Star	Rigby	Pink Level	1B
Moving Home	AlphaWorld	Gardner	Level 21 (ext)	9
Mr Croc's Clock	Rockets	A&C Black	Rodgers, Frank	8
Mr Croc's Silly Sock	Rockets	A&C Black	Rodgers, Frank	8

TITLE	SERIES	PUBLISHER	SET (OR AUTHOR)	BAND
Mr Croc's Walk	Rockets	A&C Black	Rodgers, Frank	9
Mr Jelly's Surprise	Web Guided Reading	OUP	Stage 4 (Duck Green)	3
Mr Marvel and the Cake	Storyworlds	Heinemann	Stage 3 Fantasy World	2
Mr Marvel and the Car	Storyworlds	Heinemann	Stage 3 Fantasy World	2
Mr Marvel and the Lemonade	Storyworlds	Heinemann	Stage 3 Fantasy World	2
Mr Marvel and the Washing	Storyworlds	Heinemann	Stage 3 Fantasy World	2
Mr Smarty Loves to Party	Kingscourt Reading, Extension	Kingscourt	Set 4	4
Mr Wolf Tries Again	Alphakids	Gardner	Early Level 9	4
Mrs Barmy	Pathways	Collins	Year 1	4
Mrs Bold	Literacy Links Plus	Kingscourt	Early B	4
Mrs Mog's Cats	Rigby Star	Rigby	Blue Level	4
Mrs Pepperpot's Pet	Literacy Links Plus	Kingscourt	Fluent B	8
Mrs Spider's Beautiful Web	PM Storybooks	Nelson Thornes	Green Set A	5
Mrs Wishy-Washy's Tub	Story Chest	Kingscourt	Get-ready Set BB	1A
Muddled Monsters, The	Rockets	A&C Black	Anderson, Scoular	8
Muffin is Trapped	PM Storybooks	Nelson Thornes	Purple Set B	8
Mum	PM Storybook Starters	Nelson Thornes	Set 1	1A
Mum to the Rescue	Oxford Reading Tree	OUP	Stage 5 More Stories B	5
Mumps	PM Storybooks	Nelson Thornes	Yellow Set A	3
Mums and Dads	PM Storybook Starters	Nelson Thornes	Set 1	1A
Mum's New Car	Oxford Reading Tree	OUP	Robins Pack 1	9
Mum's Photo Album	Spotty Zebra	Nelson Thornes	Red – Change	2
Munching Monster	Kingscourt Reading, Extension	Kingscourt	Set 5 (play)	5
Mushrooms and Toadstools	AlphaWorld	Gardner	Level 14 (trans)	7
Mushrooms for Dinner	PM Storybooks	Nelson Thornes	Blue Set A	4
Musician: Vanessa Mae	Oxford Reading Tree	OUP	Fireflies Stage 8	10
My Accident	PM Storybook Starters	Nelson Thornes	Set 2	1B
My Baby	Kingscourt Reading, Extension	Kingscourt	Set 2	2
My Baby Sister	Alphakids	Gardner	Emergent Level 2	1B
My Balloon Man	First Stories	Gardner	Emergent E	1A
My Bean Diary	Discovery World	Heinemann	Stage C	4
My Bed is Soft	National Geographic	Rigby	Red Level	1B
My Best Bear	Dragonflies	Gardner	Pink	1A
My Big Brother	PM Non-fiction	Nelson Thornes	Yellow Level	4
My Bike	Kingscourt Reading, Extension	Kingscourt	Set 2	2
My Book	PM Plus	Nelson Thornes	Red Level	2
My Breakfast	Lighthouse	Ginn	Red: 2	2
My Brother	Dragonflies	Gardner	Blue	4
My Brother, the Bridesmaid	Lighthouse	Ginn	White 4	10
My Brother's Birthday	Alphakids Plus	Gardner	Early Level 7	3
My Brown Cow	Story Chest	Kingscourt	Ready-set-go Set BB	2
My Camera	Rigby Star	Rigby	Red Level	2
My Cat	First Stories	Gardner	Emergent B	1A
My Cat	Lighthouse	Ginn	Pink A: 3	1A
My Cat Has Had Kittens	I Love Reading	Ticktock	Blue Level	4
My Chinese New Year	Rigby Star Non-fiction	Rigby	Red Level	3
My Clothes	PM Plus	Nelson Thornes	Starters Two	1B
My Dad	PM Non-fiction	Nelson Thornes	Yellow Level	4
My Diary	Genre Range	Pearson	Emergent Letters	5
My Diary by Fairy Godmother	Alphakids	Gardner	Extending Level 20	8
My Diary of an Oak Tree	Web Weavers Non-fiction	OUP	First Non-fiction: Pack B	4

TITLE	SERIES	PUBLISHER	SET (OR AUTHOR)	BAND
My Dinner	Alphakids Plus	Gardner	Emergent Level 2	1A
My Dog	Alphakids Plus	Gardner	Emergent Level 3	2
My Dog	Kingscourt Reading, Core	Kingscourt	Level 17 Collection	7
My Dog Has Had Puppies	I Love Reading	Ticktock	Blue Level	4
My Face	First Facts	Badger	Level 1	2
My Family	First Stories	Gardner	Emergent B	1A
My Family Tree	First Facts	Badger	Level 2	3
My Farm	Alphakids Plus	Gardner	Early Level 6	3
My First Cat	Badger NF Guided Reading	Chrysalis	Veronica Watts	7
My Fish Bowl	Alphakids Plus	Gardner	Emergent Level 2	1B
My Five Senses	First Facts	Badger	Level 1	1B
My Friend	First Stories	Gardner	Emergent C	1A
My Gran and Grandad	PM Non-fiction	Nelson Thornes	Yellow Level	4
My Grandpa Plants the Rainforest	Alphakids Plus	Gardner	Transitional Level 17	7
My Hat	Sails Foundation	Heinemann	Pink B – On	1A
My Hats	Alphakids Plus	Gardner	Emergent Level 2	1B
My History	Discovery World	Heinemann	Stage B	1B
My Home	Story Chest	Kingscourt	Ready-set-go Set B	2
My House	Literacy Links Plus	Kingscourt	Early D	5
My Journey Around the World	Web Weavers Non-fiction	OUP	Non-fiction – Toys	9
My Little Cat	PM Plus	Nelson Thornes	Starters Two	1B
My Little Dog	PM Storybook Starters	Nelson Thornes	Set 2	1B
My Little Sister	First Stories	Gardner	Emergent B	1B
My Little Sister	PM Non-fiction	Nelson Thornes	Yellow Level	4
My Monster Friends	Literacy Links Plus	Kingscourt	Early B	5
My Mum and Dad	Story Chest	Kingscourt	Ready-set-go Set CC	3
My Name is Shoshana	Dragonflies	Gardner	Orange	6
My New Bike	Pathways	Collins	Year 1	3
My New Truck	First Stories	Gardner	Emergent D	1B
My Painting	First Stories	Gardner	Emergent A	1A
My Pet	Web Weavers Non-fiction	OUP	Stage 2 First Words NF	3
My Pet Lamb	Alphakids Plus	Gardner	Transitional Level 12	5
My Place	Kingscourt Reading, Core	Kingscourt	Level 1 Benchmark Bk	1A
My Sad Skeleton	Sunshine Readers	Gardner	Light Blue Level	7
My Sandcastle	PM Plus	Nelson Thornes	Starters Two	1B
My School	First Facts	Badger	Level 3	4
My School Bag	First Stories	Gardner	Emergent F	1A
My Scrapbook	Kingscourt Reading, Extension	Kingscourt	Set 5	5
My Shells	Alphakids	Gardner	Transitional Level 16	6
My Sister	Dragonflies	Gardner	Yellow/Blue	3
My Snowman	First Stories	Gardner	Emergent E	1B
My Special Book	Kingscourt Reading, Extension	Kingscourt	Set 1	1B
My Street	Alphakids	Gardner	Transitional Level 16	6
My Tower	PM Plus	Nelson Thornes	Red Level	2
My Toys	AlphaWorld	Gardner	Band 1A: Pink	1A
My Toys	First Facts	Badger	Level 2	2
My Toys, Gran's Toys	Web Weavers Non-fiction	OUP	Non-fiction – Toys	6
My Trip	Alphakids Plus	Gardner	Early Level 10	5
My Trip	Sails Foundation	Heinemann	Pink B – Was	1A
My Two Families	PM Storybooks	Nelson Thornes	Silver Set A	10
My Week	Oxford Reading Tree	OUP	Fireflies Stage 3	3

TITLE	SERIES	PUBLISHER	SET (OR AUTHOR)	BAND
Mystery Man, The	Rigby Star	Rigby	Star Plus	10
Mystery of Mrs Kim, The	Rigby Star	Rigby	Star Plus	10

N

TITLE	SERIES	PUBLISHER	SET (OR AUTHOR)	BAND
Nama's Hats	Web Fiction	OUP	Stage 1 (Variety)	2
Natalie Du Toit	Lighthouse	Ginn	Gold: 8	10
Natural Disasters	Alphakids	Gardner	Extending Level 19	8
Nature Trail	Rigby Star	Rigby	Red Level	2
Naughty Ann, The	PM Storybooks	Nelson Thornes	Green Set A	5
Naughty Children	Oxford Reading Tree	OUP	Stage 2 Patterned Stories	2
Naughty Joe	Storyworlds	Heinemann	Stage 2 Our World	2
Naughty Monkey	Sails Foundation	Heinemann	Pink C – Said	1A
Ned the Fighting Donkey	Web Fiction	OUP	Stage 4 (Variety)	3
Ned's Noise Machine	Rigby Star	Rigby	Pink Level	1A
Nelly Paints a Monster	Web Fiction	OUP	Stage 1 (Variety)	2
Nelly the Monster-sitter	Oxford Reading Tree	OUP	More Allstars Pack 2a	10
Nelson Gets a Fright	PM Storybooks	Nelson Thornes	Purple Set A	8
Nelson is Kidnapped	PM Storybooks	Nelson Thornes	Silver Set A	10
Nelson, the Baby Elephant	PM Storybooks	Nelson Thornes	Turquoise Set A	7
Nest on the Beach, The	PM Plus	Nelson Thornes	Green Level	5
Nest, The	Kingscourt Reading, Extension	Kingscourt	Set 1	1B
Nest, The	Story Chest	Kingscourt	Get-ready Set CC	2
Nesting Place, The	PM Storybooks	Nelson Thornes	Turquoise Set C	7
Nests and Shelters	First Explorers	Kingscourt	Level 1	8
New Baby, The	Oxford Reading Tree	OUP	Stage 5 More Stories B	5
New Baby, The	PM Storybooks	Nelson Thornes	Yellow Set A	3
New Boots	PM Plus	Nelson Thornes	Yellow Level	3
New Boy, The	Storyworlds	Heinemann	Stage 7 Our World	6
New Classroom, A	Oxford Reading Tree	OUP	Stage 5 More Stories B	5
New Clothes	National Geographic	Rigby	Yellow Level	3
New Dog, A	Oxford Reading Tree	OUP	Stage 2 Storybooks	2
New Girl, The	Skyrider LM Chapters	Gardner	Set 2	9
New Glasses for Max	PM Plus	Nelson Thornes	Green Level	5
New Hat, The	Rigby Star	Rigby	Red Level	1B
New House, The	Oxford Reading Tree	OUP	Stage 4 Storybooks	4
New House, The	Sails Foundation	Heinemann	Pink B – For	1A
New Kite, The	Big Cat	Collins	Yellow	3
New Pants	Story Chest	Kingscourt	Get-ready Set AA	2
New Pet, The	Rigby Star	Rigby	Pink Level	1A
New School for Megan, A	PM Storybooks	Nelson Thornes	Purple Set B	8
New School, A	Story Street	Pearson	Step 8	9
New Tie, The	New Way	Nelson Thornes	Green Easy Start Set B	4
New Trees	Oxford Reading Tree	OUP	Stage 2 More Patterned Stories	2
News on Shoes	Kingscourt Reading, Extension	Kingscourt	Set 9	9
Next Door Neighbour, The	Storyworlds	Heinemann	Stage 7 Our World	6
Next Door Pets	Rigby Star	Rigby	Red Level	1A
Nick Butterworth: Making Books	Big Cat	Collins	Green	6
Night Animals	Oxford Reading Tree	OUP	Fireflies Stage 4	4
Night Noises	Kingscourt Reading, Extension	Kingscourt	Set 4	4

TITLE	SERIES	PUBLISHER	SET (OR AUTHOR)	BAND
Night of Light	Spotty Zebra	Nelson Thornes	Pink B – Ourselves	3
Night Sky, The	National Geographic	Rigby	Blue Level	4
Night Train, The	Story Chest	Kingscourt	Ready-set-go Set C	2
Night Walk, The	PM Storybooks	Nelson Thornes	Gold Set C	9
Night-time	Story Chest	Kingscourt	Get-ready Set B	2
Nine Children at the Pool	PM Maths	Nelson Thornes	Stage B	3
No Ball Games!	Rigby Star	Rigby	Orange Level	5
No Extras	Literacy Links Plus	Kingscourt	Early C	5
No Running!	Lighthouse	Ginn	Blue: 7	4
No Space to Waste	Kingscourt Reading, Extension	Kingscourt	Set 9	9
No, No	Story Chest	Kingscourt	Ready-set-go Set D	2
Noah's Ark Adventure	Oxford Reading Tree	OUP	Stage 5 More Stories B	5
Nobody Got Wet	Oxford Reading Tree	OUP	Stage 4 More Stories A	4
Nobody Wanted to Play	Oxford Reading Tree	OUP	Stage 3 Storybooks	2
Noodle Race, The	PM Photo Stories	Nelson Thornes	Green 13	5
Noses	Literacy Links Plus	Kingscourt	Emergent D	4
Not Now, Bernard	Pelican Big Bks	Pearson	McKee, David	5
Not Too Young & other stories	New Way	Nelson Thornes	Yellow Platform Books	8
Nothing to be Scared About	Sunshine Readers	Gardner	Purple Level Supplementary	9
Now and Then	National Geographic	Rigby	Yellow Level	3
Now I Am Eight	AlphaWorld	Gardner	Level 19 (ext)	8
Number Plates	PM Storybooks	Nelson Thornes	Turquoise Set B	7
Nursery and Action Rhymes	Genre Range	Pearson	Beginner Poetry	5
Nuts	Genre Range	Pearson	Beginner Comics	3

O

TITLE	SERIES	PUBLISHER	SET (OR AUTHOR)	BAND
Ocean Adventure!	Oxford Reading Tree	OUP	Stage 9 True Stories	10
Oceans, Seas and Coasts	PM Plus Non-fiction	Nelson Thornes	Gold Level	9
Octopus's Legs	Web Fiction	OUP	Stage 3 (Variety)	3
Odd Eggs	Oxford Reading Tree	OUP	Fireflies Stage 10	10
Odd Socks	Literacy Links Plus	Kingscourt	Early B	5
Off Goes the Hose!	Dragonflies	Gardner	Pink	1B
Off to School	Kingscourt Reading, Core	Kingscourt	Level 2 Little Books	1B
Off to the Shop	Kingscourt Reading, Extension	Kingscourt	Set 6	6
Off Went the Light	Dragonflies	Gardner	Yellow/Blue	3
Oh No, Jo, No!	Web Guided Reading	OUP	Stage 1 (Duck Green)	2
Oh, Columbus!	Literacy Links Plus	Kingscourt	Fluent B	8
Oh, Jump in a Sack	Story Chest	Kingscourt	Ready-set-go Set D	3
Old King Cole Played in Goal	Crunchies	Orchard	Seriously Silly Rhymes	7
Old Vase, The	Oxford Reading Tree	OUP	Robins Pack 1	8
Old Woman and the Hen, The	Storyworlds	Heinemann	Stage 2 Once Upon a Time	2
Old Woman Who Lived in a Vinegar Bottle, The	Storyworlds	Heinemann	Stage 6 Once Upon a Time	5
Olly the Octopus	Storyworlds	Heinemann	Stage 6 Fantasy World	6
Olympics, The	National Geographic	Rigby	Gold Level	10
On and Off	PM Plus Non-fiction	Nelson Thornes	Starters Two	1B
On Safari	National Geographic	Rigby	Gold Level	10
On the Ball	Skyrider LM Chapters	Gardner	Set 2	9
On The Beach	Oxford Reading Tree	OUP	Fireflies, More – Stage 1+	1A
On the Farm	Four Corners	Pearson	Year 2	8

TITLE	SERIES	PUBLISHER	SET (OR AUTHOR)	BAND
On the Move	First Explorers	Kingscourt	Level 1	8
On the Sand	Oxford Reading Tree	OUP	Stage 3 Storybooks	3
Once Upon a Rhyme	Skyrider LM Chapters	Gardner	Set 1	9
One Picture	PM Maths	Nelson Thornes	Stage A	1B
One Step, Two Steps	AlphaWorld	Gardner	Band 3: Yellow	3
One, One is the Sun	Story Chest	Kingscourt	Get-ready Set C	2
One, Two, Three ... Off to the Sea!	Pelican Big Bks	Pearson	Body, Wendy	4
Only an Octopus	Literacy Links Plus	Kingscourt	Early C	6
Oogly Gum Chasing Gum, The	Literacy Links Plus	Kingscourt	Fluent B	9
Open Wide, Wilbur!	Crunchies	Orchard	Colour Crackers	9
Optometrist, The	PM Non-fiction	Nelson Thornes	Blue Level	5
Orang-utan Baby	I Love Reading	Ticktock	Blue Level	4
Orang-utan Baby	I Love Reading	Ticktock	Orange Level	6
Orang-utan Baby	I Love Reading	Ticktock	Purple Level	8
Oscar's Day	Four Corners	Pearson	Year 1	4
Our Baby	PM Non-fiction	Nelson Thornes	Yellow Level	4
Our Bodies	PM Plus Non-fiction	Nelson Thornes	Orange Level	6
Our Camping Trip	Lighthouse	Ginn	Yellow: 5	3
Our Chore Chart	Kingscourt Reading, Extension	Kingscourt	Set 2	2
Our Class	Oxford Reading Tree	OUP	Fireflies Stage 2	3
Our Classroom Pet	Alphakids Plus	Gardner	Transitional Level 14	5
Our Clothes	PM Plus Non-fiction	Nelson Thornes	Orange Level	6
Our Day	Sails Foundation	Heinemann	Pink B – Went	1A
Our Dog Sam	Literacy Links Plus	Kingscourt	Emergent C	2
Our Favourite Food	AlphaWorld	Gardner	Band 4: Blue	3
Our Feelings	Rigby Star Non-fiction	Rigby	White Level	8
Our Five Senses	Rigby Star Non-fiction	Rigby	Pink Level	1B
Our House is a Safe House	PM Plus Non-fiction	Nelson Thornes	Blue Level	4
Our Market	AlphaWorld	Gardner	Band 4: Blue	4
Our Mum	PM Non-fiction	Nelson Thornes	Yellow Level	4
Our New House	PM Plus Non-fiction	Nelson Thornes	Blue Level	4
Our New Puppy	National Geographic	Rigby	Red Level	1B
Our New Year Dragon	Alphakids Plus	Gardner	Extending Level 19	8
Our Old Friend Bear	PM Storybooks	Nelson Thornes	Silver Set C	10
Our Parents	PM Non-fiction	Nelson Thornes	Blue Level	5
Our Place	Pathways	Collins	Year 1	5
Our School Week	First Facts	Badger	Level 3	4
Our Week	Kingscourt Reading, Extension	Kingscourt	Set 1	1B
Out in the Weather	PM Storybook Starters	Nelson Thornes	Set 2	1B
Out of Milk	Spotty Zebra	Nelson Thornes	Pink A – Ourselves	1B
Outing, The	Oxford Reading Tree	OUP	Stage 6 & 7 Stories	7
Over and Under	Oxford Reading Tree	OUP	Fireflies Stage 2	2
Over the Stile and Into the Sack	Crunchies	Orchard	Twice Upon a Time	8
Owl	Pathways	Collins	Year 2	7
Owls	Kingscourt Reading, Core	Kingscourt	Level 10 Little Books	4
Owls	PM Non-fiction	Nelson Thornes	Gold Level	9
Owls in the Garden	PM Storybooks	Nelson Thornes	Gold Set A	9
Owl's Party	Pathways	Collins	Year 1	6
Oxford First Science Dictionary	Badger NF Guided Reading	OUP	Graham Peacock	9
Ozlo's Beard	Lighthouse	Ginn	Purple: 1	8

TITLE	SERIES	PUBLISHER	SET (OR AUTHOR)	BAND
				P
Pacific Island Scrapbook	Big Cat	Collins	Purple	8
Pack it Up, Ben	Pathways	Collins	Year 1	5
Packing for a Holiday	Spotlight on Fact	Collins	Y2 The Seaside	7
Packing My Bag	PM Storybook Starters	Nelson Thornes	Set 2	1B
Paint My Room	Alphakids	Gardner	Transitional Level 14	5
Painting	Alphakids Plus	Gardner	Emergent Level 2	1B
Painting Lesson, The	Skyrider LM Chapters	Gardner	Set 1	8
Pancake, The	Oxford Reading Tree	OUP	Stage 1 First Words	1A
Pandas in the Mountains	PM Storybooks	Nelson Thornes	Gold Set C	9
Pandora's Box	Kingscourt Reading, Extension	Kingscourt	Set 8	8
Papa's Spaghetti	Literacy Links Plus	Kingscourt	Early D	5
Paper Boy & other stories, The	New Way	Nelson Thornes	Green Platform Books	6
Parachutes	Kingscourt Reading, Extension	Kingscourt	Set 7	7
Parade, The	PM Plus	Nelson Thornes	Starters Two	1B
Parcel, The	Alphakids	Gardner	Emergent Level 3	2
Park, The	National Geographic	Rigby	Blue Level	4
Party Animals	Kingscourt Reading, Core	Kingscourt	Level 14 Little Books	5
Party Clown, The	PM Photo Stories	Nelson Thornes	Blue 11	4
Party for Brown Mouse, The	PM Plus	Nelson Thornes	Yellow Level	3
Party Hats	PM Plus	Nelson Thornes	Starters Two	1B
Party, The	Alphakids	Gardner	Emergent Level 3	2
Party, The	First Stories	Gardner	Emergent E	1A
Party, The	Sails Foundation	Heinemann	Pink A – Is	1A
Pass the Pasta, Please	Kingscourt Reading, Extension	Kingscourt	Set 2	2
Pass the Present	Kingscourt Reading, Extension	Kingscourt	Set 2	2
Pasta Party	Alphakids Plus	Gardner	Early Level 6	3
Patrick and the Leprechaun	PM Storybooks	Nelson Thornes	Gold Set B	9
Patterns	Kingscourt Reading, Core	Kingscourt	Level 1 Little Books	1A
Patterns	Oxford Reading Tree	OUP	Fireflies, More – Stage 3	4
Patterns are Fun!	Kingscourt Reading, Core	Kingscourt	Level 2 Little Books	1B
Paws and Claws	Kingscourt Reading, Core	Kingscourt	Level 3 Collection	2
Peanut Prankster, The	Rockets	A&C Black	Wallace, Karen	10
Peanuts	Rigby Star Non-fiction	Rigby	Purple Level	7
Pedal Power	Rigby Star Non-fiction	Rigby	Purple Level	8
Pedlar's Caps, The	PM Storybooks	Nelson Thornes	Purple Set A	8
Pencil, The	PM Storybook Starters	Nelson Thornes	Set 2	1B
Penguin Rescue	First Facts	Badger	Level 4	8
Penguin Rescue	PM Plus	Nelson Thornes	Silver Level	10
Penguins	Alphakids Plus	Gardner	Extending Level 19	8
People and Places	First Explorers	Kingscourt	Level 2	8
People Live in the Desert	National Geographic	Rigby	Green Level	6
People Who Help Us	First Facts	Badger	Level 4	8
Pepper's Adventure	PM Storybooks	Nelson Thornes	Green Set A	5
Percy and the Badger	Big Cat	Collins	Blue	4
Percy and the Rabbit	Big Cat	Collins	Yellow	3
Percy the Pink	Walker Starters	Walker	West, Colin	8
Perfect Paper Planes	PM Plus	Nelson Thornes	Gold Level	9

TITLE	SERIES	PUBLISHER	SET (OR AUTHOR)	BAND
Perfect Pizza, The	Rigby Star	Rigby	Turquoise Level	7
Perfect Pizza, The	Rockets	A&C Black	Anderson, Scoular	8
Perfect Present, The	Lighthouse	Ginn	White 2	10
Pet Day at School	Kingscourt Reading, Core	Kingscourt	Level 7 Little Books	3
Pet Detectives: The Ball Burglary	Big Cat	Collins	Gold	9
Pet Detectives: Tortoise Trouble	Big Cat	Collins	Purple	8
Pet for Me, A	Alphakids	Gardner	Early Level 8	3
Pet for Sam, A	Story Street	Pearson	Step 2	2
Pet Shop	Story Chest	Kingscourt	Ready-set-go Set CC	3
Pet Shop, The	Oxford Reading Tree	OUP	Stage 1+ Patterned Stories	1A
Pet Tarantula, The	Kingscourt Reading, Extension	Kingscourt	Set 9	9
Pet Vet	Skyrider LM Chapters	Gardner	Set 1	7
Pete Little	PM Storybooks	Nelson Thornes	Green Set A	5
Pete Paints a Picture	Kingscourt Reading, Core	Kingscourt	Level 6 Benchmark Bk	3
Peter and the Wolf	PM Plus	Nelson Thornes	Gold Level	9
Peter and the Wolf & other stories	New Way	Nelson Thornes	Blue Parallel Books	7
Pete's New Shoes	Literacy Links Plus	Kingscourt	Early B	5
Pets	AlphaWorld	Gardner	Band 3: Yellow	2
Pets	First Facts	Badger	Level 1	1A
Pets	PM Storybook Starters	Nelson Thornes	Set 1	1A
Pets	Web Guided Reading	OUP	Stage 3 (Duck Green)	2
Pets With Fur	First Facts	Badger	Level 1	1B
Pets, The	Sails Foundation	Heinemann	Pink B – Look	1A
Phew, Sidney!	Crunchies	Orchard	Colour Crackers	9
Philippa and the Dragon	Literacy Links Plus	Kingscourt	Early C	6
Photo Book, The	PM Storybooks	Nelson Thornes	Red Set A	2
Photo Time	PM Plus	Nelson Thornes	Red Level	2
Photograph, The	Oxford Reading Tree	OUP	Robins Pack 2	9
Pick Up That Crisp Packet!	Info Trail	Pearson	Beginner Geography	4
Picked for the Team	PM Storybooks	Nelson Thornes	Gold Set C	9
Picky Prince, The	Rigby Star	Rigby	White Level	10
Picnic Boat, The	PM Plus	Nelson Thornes	Green Level	5
Picnic For Two	PM Maths	Nelson Thornes	Stage A	1B
Picnic Tree, The	PM Photo Stories	Nelson Thornes	Green 14	5
Picnic, The	Alphakids Plus	Gardner	Early Level 11	3
Picnic, The	First Stories	Gardner	Emergent C	1A
Picture, A	Kingscourt Reading, Extension	Kingscourt	Set 2	2
Picture-Book People	Kingscourt Reading, Core	Kingscourt	Level 14 Little Books	5
Pie Thief, The	Story Chest	Kingscourt	Stage 6	9
Pied Piper of Hamelin, The	Oxford Reading Tree	OUP	Traditional Tales 5–7	8
Pied Piper, The	Storyworlds	Heinemann	Stage 7 Once Upon a Time	6
Pigeon Patrol, The	Info Trail	Pearson	Emergent Geography	4
Pigs	PM Non-fiction	Nelson Thornes	Purple Level	9
Pig's Skin	Alphakids	Gardner	Extending Level 22	9
Pioneer Girl	Oxford Reading Tree	OUP	Stage 10 True Stories	10
Pip and the Little Monkey	Oxford Reading Tree	OUP	Stage 3 Sparrows	4
Pip at the Zoo	Oxford Reading Tree	OUP	Stage 3 Sparrows	4
Pipe Down, Prudle!	Crunchies	Orchard	Colour Crackers	8
Pip's Thank-You Letter	Genre Range	Pearson	Beginner Letters	2
Pirate Adventure	Oxford Reading Tree	OUP	Stage 5 Storybooks	5
Pirate Gold	Web Fiction	OUP	Stage 9 (Variety)	10

TITLE	SERIES	PUBLISHER	SET (OR AUTHOR)	BAND
Pirate Party	Big Cat	Collins	Gold	8
Pirate Pete and the Monster	Storyworlds	Heinemann	Stage 4 Fantasy World	3
Pirate Pete and the Treasure Island	Storyworlds	Heinemann	Stage 4 Fantasy World	3
Pirate Pete Keeps Fit	Storyworlds	Heinemann	Stage 4 Fantasy World	3
Pirate Pete Loses His Hat	Storyworlds	Heinemann	Stage 4 Fantasy World	3
Pirates	Big Cat	Collins	Red B	1B
Pirates Ahoy!	Story Street	Pearson	Step 5	6
Pirates, The	Story Chest	Kingscourt	Stage 2	6
Pizza For Dinner	Literacy Links Plus	Kingscourt	Early C	6
Places to Visit	Spotlight on Fact	Collins	Y2 The Seaside	9
Planets, The	First Facts	Badger	Level 4	8
Plants	Alphakids	Gardner	Emergent Level 5	2
Plants	Go Facts	A&C Black	Plants	10
Plants All Round	First Explorers	Kingscourt	Level 1	8
Plants as Food	Go Facts	A&C Black	Plants	10
Plants Have Leaves	First Facts	Badger	Level 1	1B
Play, The	First Stories	Gardner	Emergent C	1A
Play, The	Oxford Reading Tree	OUP	Stage 4 Storybooks	4
Play, The	PM Plus	Nelson Thornes	Starters One	1A
Play, The	Rigby Star	Rigby	Pink Level	1B
Playing	Alphakids	Gardner	Emergent Level 1	1A
Playing	First Stories	Gardner	Emergent E	1B
Playing	PM Storybook Starters	Nelson Thornes	Set 1	1A
Playing Outside	AlphaWorld	Gardner	Band 1A: Pink	1A
Playing Outside	PM Plus	Nelson Thornes	Starters Two	1B
Playing Skittles	PM Gems	Nelson Thornes	Blue 9	4
Playing Together	Spotty Zebra	Nelson Thornes	Pink B – Ourselves	2
Playing with Dough	PM Plus Non-fiction	Nelson Thornes	Red Level	2
Playing with Milly	PM Gems	Nelson Thornes	Blue 9	4
Please Do Not Drop Your Jelly Beans	Kingscourt Reading, Extension	Kingscourt	Set 7	7
Please Don't Sneeze!	Kingscourt Reading, Extension	Kingscourt	Set 6	7
Please Mum!	Lighthouse	Ginn	Red: 9	2
Plop!	Story Chest	Kingscourt	Ready-set-go Set B	2
Pocket Money	Oxford Reading Tree	OUP	Stage 8 More Stories A	8
Pol and Pax	New Way	Nelson Thornes	Blue Parallel Books	7
Pol and Pax in the Salty Red Sea	New Way	Nelson Thornes	Orange Parallel Books	10
Pol and Pax on Earth	New Way	Nelson Thornes	Violet Parallel Books	9
Pol and Pax on the Third Moon	New Way	Nelson Thornes	Yellow Platform Books	8
Polar Bears	First Facts	Badger	Level 4	7
Polar Bears	Kingscourt Reading, Core	Kingscourt	Level 8 Little Books	4
Polar Bears	PM Non-fiction	Nelson Thornes	Silver Level	10
Poles Apart	Rigby Star	Rigby	Purple Level	8
Pollution	Alphakids	Gardner	Extending Level 21	9
Polly the Most Poetic Person	Crunchies	Orchard	The One And Only	8
Pond Where Harriet Lives, The	Kingscourt Reading, Extension	Kingscourt	Set 4	4
Pond, The	Alphakids Plus	Gardner	Emergent Level 5	2
Pond, The	Big Cat	Collins	Pink B	1A
Ponds and Rivers	First Explorers	Kingscourt	Level 1	8
Pony Club, The	PM Photo Stories	Nelson Thornes	Green 14	5
Poor Old Mum!	Oxford Reading Tree	OUP	Stage 4 More Stories A	3
Poor Puppy!	First Stories	Gardner	Emergent F	1B

TITLE	SERIES	PUBLISHER	SET (OR AUTHOR)	BAND
Poor Sam	Genre Range	Pearson	Beginner Plays	4
Pop! A Play	Rigby Star	Rigby	Yellow Level	3
Pop! Pop! Pop!	Dragonflies	Gardner	Orange	6
Popcorn Fun	PM Plus	Nelson Thornes	Green Level	5
Poppy's Puppets	Web Guided Reading	OUP	Stage 2 (Duck Green)	3
Port, The	AlphaWorld	Gardner	Level 20 (ext)	8
Posh Party, The	Rockets	A&C Black	Anderson, Scoular	9
Postcard, The	New Way	Nelson Thornes	Green Easy Start Set A	4
Postcards	Genre Range	Pearson	Beginner Letters	4
Pot of Gold, A	Skyrider LM Chapters	Gardner	Set 2	8
Potty Panto, The	Rockets	A&C Black	Anderson, Scoular	9
Power Cut, The	Oxford Reading Tree	OUP	Stage 7 More Stories C	6
Precious Potter	Crunchies	Orchard	Colour Crackers	8
Predators	Alphakids	Gardner	Transitional Level 16	7
Present for Dad, A	Alphakids	Gardner	Extending Level 22	9
Present for Jojo, A	Story Street	Pearson	Step 6	7
Present For Karl, A	PM Photo Stories	Nelson Thornes	Red 4	2
Present For Our Teacher, A	AlphaWorld	Gardner	Band 6: Orange	6
Present, The	First Stories	Gardner	Emergent A	1A
Presents	Kingscourt Reading, Extension	Kingscourt	Set 2	2
Presents	Storyworlds	Heinemann	Stage 5 Our World	4
Presents for Jack and Billy	PM Gems	Nelson Thornes	Red 5	2
Presents, The	Sails Foundation	Heinemann	Pink B – For	1A
Prickles the Porcupine	PM Plus	Nelson Thornes	Purple Level	8
Princess and the Pea, The	Storyworlds	Heinemann	Stage 6 Once Upon a Time	5
Princess Jo	Alphakids Plus	Gardner	Transitional Level 17	6
Printing Machine, The	Literacy Links Plus	Kingscourt	Early B	4
Prize Day	PM Gems	Nelson Thornes	Green 12	5
Proper Bike, A	Oxford Reading Tree	OUP	Robins Pack 1	8
Psid and Bolter	Oxford Reading Tree	OUP	All Stars Pack 3	10
Pterosaur's Long Flight	PM Storybooks	Nelson Thornes	Orange Set B	6
Public Art	Oxford Reading Tree	OUP	Fireflies Stage 5	7
Pumpkin House, The	Literacy Links Plus	Kingscourt	Fluent B	7
Pumpkin Mountain & The Nightingale	New Way	Nelson Thornes	Yellow Platform Books	9
Pumpkin, The	Story Chest	Kingscourt	Ready-set-go Set C	3
Puppet Play, A	Kingscourt Reading, Extension	Kingscourt	Set 2	2
Puppy at the Door	PM Plus	Nelson Thornes	Turquoise Level	7
Puppy, The	First Stories	Gardner	Emergent A	1A
Purr-fect!	Dragonflies	Gardner	Yellow/Blue	4
Push and Pull	Oxford Reading Tree	OUP	Fireflies, More – Stage 2	2
Pushing and Pulling	AlphaWorld	Gardner	Level 13 (trans)	5
Puss-in-Boots	Literacy Links Plus	Kingscourt	Traditional Tale	8
Puss-in-Boots	PM Traditional Tales	Nelson Thornes	Purple Level	8
Pussy and the Birds	PM Storybooks	Nelson Thornes	Red Set A	2
Put On a Clown Face	Oxford Reading Tree	OUP	Fireflies, More – Stage 1+	1B
Puzzle for Scruffy, A	PM Photo Stories	Nelson Thornes	Red 5	2
Puzzle, The	Kingscourt Reading, Extension	Kingscourt	Set 1	1B

TITLE	SERIES	PUBLISHER	SET (OR AUTHOR)	BAND
				Q
Quarrel, The	Oxford Reading Tree	OUP	Citizenship Stories Stage 9/10	9
Queen's Parrot, The	Literacy Links Plus	Kingscourt	Early D	6
Quest, The	Oxford Reading Tree	OUP	Stage 9 Stories	9
Quiet Morning for Mum, A	Lighthouse	Ginn	Blue: 2	4
Quilt With a Difference, A	Skyrider LM Chapters	Gardner	Set 1	9
				R
Rabbit Dance, The	Kingscourt Reading, Core	Kingscourt	Gold	9
Rabbit Rescue	Kingscourt Reading, Core	Kingscourt	Gold	7
Rabbits' Ears	PM Plus	Nelson Thornes	Blue Level	4
Rabbit's Surprise Birthday	Rigby Star	Rigby	Purple Level	8
Rabbit's Trick	Web Fiction	OUP	Stage 4 (Variety)	3
Raccoon Wakes Up	PM Gems	Nelson Thornes	Red 3	2
Race to Green End, The	PM Storybooks	Nelson Thornes	Turquoise Set C	7
Race to the Pole	National Geographic	Rigby	White Level	10
Racoons	PM Non-fiction	Nelson Thornes	Gold Level	9
Rain	Alphakids	Gardner	Emergent Level 4	2
Rain Arrow, The	Pathways	Collins	Year 2	7
Rain Forest, The	National Geographic	Rigby	Purple Level	9
Rain in the Park	Spotty Zebra	Nelson Thornes	Pink B – Change	2
Rain is Water	PM Plus Non-fiction	Nelson Thornes	Yellow Level	3
Rainbow Adventure, The	Oxford Reading Tree	OUP	Stage 8 Stories	8
Rainbow Fish, The	Sunshine Readers	Gardner	Orange Level Supplementary	6
Rainbow Town	Sails Foundation	Heinemann	Pink B – And	1A
Rainforest Birds	Alphakids Plus	Gardner	Extending Level 24	9
Rainforest Life	First Explorers	Kingscourt	Level 2	9
Rainforest Plants	Alphakids	Gardner	Early Level 10	4
Rally Car Race	PM Plus	Nelson Thornes	Purple Level	8
Rally Car, The	Sails Foundation	Heinemann	Pink B – On	1A
Rani Comes to Stay	PM Photo Stories	Nelson Thornes	Yellow 8	3
Rapunzel	Literacy Links Plus	Kingscourt	Fluent D	8
Rare Bird, The	Alphakids Plus	Gardner	Extending Level 23	9
Rat for Mouse, A	Story Street	Pearson	Step 7	8
Rat-a-tat-tat	Big Cat	Collins	Yellow	3
Rather Small Turnip, The	Crunchies	Orchard	Seriously Silly Stories	10
Rat's Funny Story	Story Chest	Kingscourt	Get-ready Set BB	2
Ready, Set, Go!	Skyrider LM Chapters	Gardner	Set 1	8
Real Princess, The	Alphakids	Gardner	Extending Level 19	8
Rebecca and the Concert	PM Storybooks	Nelson Thornes	Orange Set C	6
Rebecca at the Funfair	Big Cat	Collins	Yellow	3
Recycle Michael	Kingscourt Reading, Extension	Kingscourt	Set 4	4
Red and Blue and Yellow	PM Non-fiction	Nelson Thornes	Red Level	3
Red Bird	Pathways	Collins	Year 1	4
Red Block, Blue Block	PM Maths	Nelson Thornes	Stage A	2
Red Doll & other stories, The	New Way	Nelson Thornes	Green Platform Books	5

TITLE	SERIES	PUBLISHER	SET (OR AUTHOR)	BAND
Red Planet	Oxford Reading Tree	OUP	Stage 6 & 7 Stories	7
Red Puppy	PM Plus	Nelson Thornes	Red Level	2
Red Riding Hood	Pelican Big Bks	Pearson	Cullimore, Stan	5
Red Riding Hood (play)	Pathways	Collins	Year 2	6
Red Squirrel Adventure	PM Plus	Nelson Thornes	Green Level	5
Red Squirrel Hides Some Nuts	PM Plus	Nelson Thornes	Yellow Level	3
Red Ted at the Beach	Storyworlds	Heinemann	Stage 4 Our World	3
Red Ted Goes to School	Storyworlds	Heinemann	Stage 4 Our World	3
Reds and Blues	Oxford Reading Tree	OUP	Stage 1+ First Sentences	2
Relay Race, The	PM Gems	Nelson Thornes	Green 13	5
Reptiles	Alphakids Plus	Gardner	Early Level 10	4
Reptiles	Badger NF Guided Reading	Chrysalis	Living Nature	8
Reptiles	Go Facts	A&C Black	Animals	9
Rescue at Sea	Storyworlds	Heinemann	Stage 8 Our World	7
Rescue!	Lighthouse	Ginn	Purple: 6	8
Rescue!	Oxford Reading Tree	OUP	Stage 9 More Stories A	8
Rescue!	Sunshine Readers	Gardner	Light Blue Level Supplementary	5
Rescue, The	PM Storybooks	Nelson Thornes	Green Set B	5
Rescue, The	Web Guided Reading	OUP	Stage 6 (Duck Green)	6
Rescuing Nelson	PM Storybooks	Nelson Thornes	Turquoise Set B	7
Revenge of the Three Little Pigs	Alphakids	Gardner	Early Level 10	4
Rex Plays Fetch	PM Plus	Nelson Thornes	Purple Level	8
Rhode Island Roy	Crunchies	Orchard	Colour Crackers	9
Rhyme Game, The	Kingscourt Reading, Extension	Kingscourt	Set 3	3
Rhyming Poems	Genre Range	Pearson	Beginner Poetry	9
Rhyming Princess, The	Kingscourt Reading, Extension	Kingscourt	Set 8	8
Rhythm and Shoes	Skyrider LM Chapters	Gardner	Set 1	8
Rice	National Geographic	Rigby	Gold Level	9
Rice Cakes	Literacy Links Plus	Kingscourt	Early D	6
Riddle Stone, The; Part 1	Oxford Reading Tree	OUP	Stage 7 More Stories C	7
Riddle Stone, The; Part 2	Oxford Reading Tree	OUP	Stage 7 More Stories C	7
Rides, The	Sails Foundation	Heinemann	Pink C – Get	1A
Riding High	PM Storybooks	Nelson Thornes	Purple Set C	8
Riding My Bike	Alphakids Plus	Gardner	Emergent Level 5	3
Riding the Skateboard Ramps	PM Plus	Nelson Thornes	Silver Level	10
Riding to Craggy Rock	PM Storybooks	Nelson Thornes	Turquoise Set C	7
Right Place for Jupiter, The	PM Storybooks	Nelson Thornes	Silver Set C	10
River Rafting Fun	PM Plus	Nelson Thornes	Gold Level	9
River, The	AlphaWorld	Gardner	Level 14 (trans)	5
Rivers, Streams and Lakes	PM Plus Non-fiction	Nelson Thornes	Gold Level	9
Road Safety	Discovery World Links	Heinemann	Stage D	7
Roads and Bridges	Alphakids	Gardner	Early Level 11	5
Roar Like a Tiger	PM Plus	Nelson Thornes	Yellow Level	3
Rob Goes to Hospital ...	New Way	Nelson Thornes	Green Easy Start Set A	4
Robby in the River	Lighthouse	Ginn	Green: 4	5
Roberto's Smile	Story Chest	Kingscourt	Ready-set-go Set BB	3
Robin Hood	Oxford Reading Tree	OUP	Stage 6 & 7 Stories	6
Robin Hood and the Silver Trophy	PM Traditional Tales	Nelson Thornes	Silver Level	10
Robin Hood Meets Little John	PM Plus	Nelson Thornes	Silver Level	10
Robin Hood Raps	Crunchies	Orchard	Raps	10
Robot Crash	Kingscourt Reading, Extension	Kingscourt	Set 4	4

TITLE	SERIES	PUBLISHER	SET (OR AUTHOR)	BAND
Robot, The	Big Cat	Collins	Pink B	1B
Robot, The	Sails Foundation	Heinemann	Pink C – Said	1A
Robots	AlphaWorld	Gardner	Level 22 (ext)	10
Robots	Big Cat	Collins	Blue	4
Robots	Oxford Reading Tree	OUP	Fireflies Stage 9	9
Robot's Special Day	Oxford Reading Tree	OUP	More Allstars Pack 1a	9
Robots, The	Storyworlds	Heinemann	Stage 3 Our World	2
Rock Climbing	Alphakids Plus	Gardner	Extending Level 21	9
Rock Pools, The	PM Storybook Starters	Nelson Thornes	Set 2	1B
Rocket Ship, The	PM Plus	Nelson Thornes	Orange Level	6
Rohan Goes to Big School	Web Fiction	OUP	Stage 7 (Variety)	8
Roll Over	Literacy Links Plus	Kingscourt	Early B	3
Roller Blade Run, The	PM Storybooks	Nelson Thornes	Purple Set A	8
Roller Blades for Luke	PM Storybooks	Nelson Thornes	Orange Set C	6
Rollercoaster	Rigby Star	Rigby	Gold Level	9
Roller-Coaster Ride	PM Plus	Nelson Thornes	Purple Level	8
Roly-Poly	Story Chest	Kingscourt	Stage 2	6
Roman Adventure	Oxford Reading Tree	OUP	Stage 7 More Stories A	7
Romans	Oxford Reading Tree	OUP	Fireflies Stage 10	10
Ronald the Tough Sheep	Oxford Reading Tree	OUP	All Stars Pack 3	9
Roof and a Door, A	PM Non-fiction	Nelson Thornes	Red Level	3
Room Full of Light, A	Pathways	Collins	Year 1	4
Rope Swing, The	Oxford Reading Tree	OUP	Stage 3 Storybooks	3
Rope That Cow!	Story Street	Pearson	Step 4	5
Rory's Big Chance	PM Plus	Nelson Thornes	Silver Level	10
Rose Rest-home, The	Sunshine Readers	Gardner	Light Blue Level Supplementary	6
Rosie Moon	Alphakids	Gardner	Extending Level 18	6
Rotten Apples	Oxford Reading Tree	OUP	Stage 6 More Stories A	6
Rough and Smooth	AlphaWorld	Gardner	Band 5: Green	5
Round and Round	PM Plus Non-fiction	Nelson Thornes	Starters Two	1B
Round and Round	Spotty Zebra	Nelson Thornes	Red – Ourselves	3
Rover Goes to School	Rockets	A&C Black	Powling, Chris	9
Rover Shows Off	Rockets	A&C Black	Powling, Chris	9
Rover the Champion	Rockets	A&C Black	Powling, Chris	9
Rover's Birthday	Rockets	A&C Black	Powling, Chris	9
Roy and the Budgie	Oxford Reading Tree	OUP	Stage 3 Sparrows	3
Roy G. Biv	Story Chest	Kingscourt	Ready-set-go Set CC	3
Royal Dinner, The	Literacy Links Plus	Kingscourt	Contemporary Stories	4
Royal Raps	Crunchies	Orchard	Raps	9
Royal Roar, The	Rockets	A&C Black	Rodgers, Frank	9
Rubbish Monster, The	Story Street	Pearson	Step 6	6
Ruby the Rudest Girl	Crunchies	Orchard	The One And Only	7
Ruff and Me	First Stories	Gardner	Emergent C	1B
Rumpelstiltskin	Literacy Links Plus	Kingscourt	Traditional Tale	7
Rumpelstiltskin	PM Traditional Tales	Nelson Thornes	Gold Level	9
Run, Rabbit, Run!	Alphakids Plus	Gardner	Early Level 6	2
Run, Rabbit, Run!	PM Plus	Nelson Thornes	Red Level	2
Runaround Rowdy	PM Plus	Nelson Thornes	Silver Level	10
Runaway Cakes and Skipalong Pots	Crunchies	Orchard	Twice Upon a Time	7
Runaway Engine	Kingscourt Reading, Core	Kingscourt	Level 11 Collection	4
Runaway Nose, The	Alphakids Plus	Gardner	Extending Level 23	9

TITLE	SERIES	PUBLISHER	SET (OR AUTHOR)	BAND
Running Shoes, The	PM Plus	Nelson Thornes	Purple Level	8
Rupert Goes to School	Kingscourt Reading, Extension	Kingscourt	Set 9	9
Rush Hour	Rigby Star	Rigby	Yellow Level	3

S

Safari Adventure	Oxford Reading Tree	OUP	Stage 5 More Stories C	5
Sailing to a New Land	PM Plus	Nelson Thornes	Gold Level	9
Sailors	Sails Foundation	Heinemann	Pink A – Am	1A
Salad	Story Chest	Kingscourt	Get-ready Set BB	1A
Sally and the Daisy	PM Storybooks	Nelson Thornes	Red Set A	2
Sally and the Elephants	PM Gems	Nelson Thornes	Magenta 2/3	2
Sally and the Leaves	PM Gems	Nelson Thornes	Magenta 2/3	2
Sally and the Sparrows	PM Storybooks	Nelson Thornes	Yellow Set B	3
Sally's Beans	PM Storybooks	Nelson Thornes	Yellow Set A	3
Sally's Friends	PM Storybooks	Nelson Thornes	Blue Set A	4
Sally's New Shoes	PM Storybook Starters	Nelson Thornes	Set 2	1B
Sally's Picture	Literacy Links Plus	Kingscourt	Early A	5
Sally's Red Bucket	PM Storybooks	Nelson Thornes	Red Set A	4
Sally's Snowman	PM Gems	Nelson Thornes	Red 3	2
Salmon's Journey, The	Web Weavers Non-fiction	OUP	Non-fiction – Animals	8
Sam and Bingo	PM Plus	Nelson Thornes	Red Level	2
Sam and Kim	Skyrider LM Chapters	Gardner	Set 1	8
Sam and the Waves	PM Plus	Nelson Thornes	Yellow Level	3
Sam Goes to School	PM Plus	Nelson Thornes	Yellow Level	3
Sam Hides Red Ted	Storyworlds	Heinemann	Stage 4 Our World	3
Sam Plays Paddle Ball	PM Plus	Nelson Thornes	Blue Level	4
Sam Runs Away	Story Street	Pearson	Step 8	9
Sam, Sam	Kingscourt Reading, Core	Kingscourt	Level 8 Collection	3
Sam, the Big, Bad Cat	Big Cat	Collins	Yellow	3
Sam's Balloon	PM Plus	Nelson Thornes	Red Level	2
Sam's Bus	Pathways	Collins	Year 1	4
Sam's Dad	Kingscourt Reading, Extension	Kingscourt	Set 9	9
Sam's Haircut	PM Plus	Nelson Thornes	Green Level	5
Sam's Painting	PM Plus	Nelson Thornes	Blue Level	4
Sam's Picnic	PM Plus	Nelson Thornes	Red Level	2
Sam's Race	PM Plus	Nelson Thornes	Red Level	2
Sam's Zoo	Story Street	Pearson	Step 3	3
Sand Witch, The	Oxford Reading Tree	OUP	All Stars Pack 1	9
Sandcastle, The	First Stories	Gardner	Emergent A	1A
Sandwich Scam, The	Rockets	A&C Black	Wallace, Karen	9
Sandwiches	Alphakids	Gardner	Emergent Level 2	2
Sandy	New Way	Nelson Thornes	Yellow Platform Books	9
Sandy Gets a Lead	PM Gems	Nelson Thornes	Yellow 6	3
Sandy Goes to the Vet	PM Gems	Nelson Thornes	Blue 11	4
Sarah and the Barking Dog	PM Storybooks	Nelson Thornes	Orange Set B	6
Sarah and Will	Alphakids	Gardner	Early Level 10	4
Sarah's Pet	Kingscourt Reading, Extension	Kingscourt	Set 7	7
Sausage	Oxford Reading Tree	OUP	All Stars Pack 2	10
Sausage and the Little Visitor	Rockets	A&C Black	Morgan, Michaela	7

TITLE	SERIES	PUBLISHER	SET (OR AUTHOR)	BAND
Sausage and the Spooks	Rockets	A&C Black	Morgan, Michaela	7
Sausage in Trouble	Rockets	A&C Black	Morgan, Michaela	7
Sausages	PM Storybooks	Nelson Thornes	Red Set A	2
Save Floppy!	Oxford Reading Tree	OUP	Stage 8 More Stories A	8
Save Our Baby!	Story Street	Pearson	Step 2	2
Saving Hoppo	PM Plus	Nelson Thornes	Orange Level	6
Saving the Oceans	AlphaWorld	Gardner	Level 21 (ext)	10
Saving The Rainforests	AlphaWorld	Gardner	Level 20 (ext)	8
Saving Up	AlphaWorld	Gardner	Band 6: Orange	6
Say Cheese!	Kingscourt Reading, Extension	Kingscourt	Set 3	3
Scab on the Knee, A	Info Trail	Pearson	Beginner Science	5
Scare and Dare	Alphakids	Gardner	Early Level 9	4
Scarecrow, The	Skyrider LM Chapters	Gardner	Set 2	9
Scarecrows	Oxford Reading Tree	OUP	Stage 5 More Stories B	5
Scaredy Cat	Rigby Star	Rigby	Pink Level	1B
Scare-kid	Literacy Links Plus	Kingscourt	Fluent A	9
Scarf, The	Oxford Reading Tree	OUP	Stage 4 More Stories B	4
Scary Masks, The	PM Photo Stories	Nelson Thornes	Blue 9	4
Scary Snakes	I Love Reading	Ticktock	Blue Level	4
Scary Snakes	I Love Reading	Ticktock	Orange Level	6
Scary Snakes	I Love Reading	Ticktock	Purple Level	8
School Band, The	Dragonflies	Gardner	Green	5
School Band, The	Oxford Reading Tree	OUP	Fireflies, More – Stage 3	3
School Concert, The	Rigby Star	Rigby	Star Plus	10
School Days, Cool Days	Kingscourt Reading, Extension	Kingscourt	Set 8	8
School Fair, The	PM Plus	Nelson Thornes	Turquoise Level	7
School Fair, The	Storyworlds	Heinemann	Stage 6 Our World	6
School for Sausage	Rockets	A&C Black	Morgan, Michaela	7
School News, The	Alphakids	Gardner	Transitional Level 16	6
School Rules	First Facts	Badger	Level 3	4
Science Dictionary	Discovery World	Heinemann	Stage F	9
Scissors	Kingscourt Reading, Extension	Kingscourt	Set 2	2
Scrapbook of Me	Kingscourt Reading, Core	Kingscourt	Level 13 Little Books	5
Scruffy Runs Away	PM Photo Stories	Nelson Thornes	Blue 10	4
Sculpture	Kingscourt Reading, Extension	Kingscourt	Set 9	9
Sea Giants	Alphakids Plus	Gardner	Extending Level 20	8
Sea Mystery, A	Oxford Reading Tree	OUP	Stage 7 More Stories C	6
Sea Otter Goes Hunting	PM Plus	Nelson Thornes	Purple Level	8
Sea Otters	Kingscourt Reading, Extension	Kingscourt	Set 10	10
Sea Stars	Alphakids	Gardner	Transitional Level 17	6
Seagull is Clever	PM Storybooks	Nelson Thornes	Yellow Set A	3
Seagull, The	Kingscourt Reading, Core	Kingscourt	Level 3 Benchmark Bk	2
Seahorses	Alphakids Plus	Gardner	Transitional Level 14	6
Seashore Plants	Alphakids Plus	Gardner	Transitional Level 16	7
Seaside, The	Badger NF Guided Reading	Franklin Watts	Changing Times	8
Seaside, The	Oxford Reading Tree	OUP	Cross-curricular Jackdaws	9
Seaside, Then and Now, The	Oxford Reading Tree	OUP	Fireflies, More – Stage 5	6
Seasons	Badger NF Guided Reading	Badger	First Facts	5
Seasons	Discovery World	Heinemann	Stage A	1B
Seasons	First Facts	Badger	Level 3	5
Seasons and Weather	PM Plus Non-fiction	Nelson Thornes	Purple Level	8

TITLE	SERIES	PUBLISHER	SET (OR AUTHOR)	BAND
Seat Belt Song, The	PM Storybooks	Nelson Thornes	Turquoise Set B	7
Sebastian	Alphakids	Gardner	Early Level 9	4
Sebastian Gets the Hiccups	Alphakids	Gardner	Transitional Level 13	5
Sebastian Learns to Fly	Alphakids Plus	Gardner	Emergent Level 5	2
Sebastian Tidies Up	Alphakids	Gardner	Extending Level 18	7
Sebastian's New Sister	Alphakids Plus	Gardner	Early Level 10	4
Sebastian's Special Present	Alphakids	Gardner	Transitional Level 15	7
Secret & The Birthday Surprise, The	New Way	Nelson Thornes	Green Easy Start Set B	5
Secret Cave, The	PM Plus	Nelson Thornes	Orange Level	6
Secret Hideaway, The	PM Storybooks	Nelson Thornes	Gold Set A	9
Secret Lives of Mr & Mrs Smith, The	Sunshine Readers	Gardner	Purple Level Supplementary	10
Secret Plans, The	Oxford Reading Tree	OUP	Robins Pack 2	8
Secret Room, The	Oxford Reading Tree	OUP	Stage 4 Storybooks	4
Secret Room, The, Part 1	Story Street	Pearson	Step 2	2
Secret Room, The, Part 2	Story Street	Pearson	Step 2	2
Secret Song, The	Kingscourt Reading, Core	Kingscourt	Level 12 Collection	5
Secret, The	Rigby Star	Rigby	Star Plus	10
Seeds	Badger NF Guided Reading	Raintree	Read and Learn	5
Seeds on the Move	AlphaWorld	Gardner	Band 7: Turquoise	6
See-saw, The	Big Cat	Collins	Pink B	1A
See-saw, The	Storyworlds	Heinemann	Stage 3 Our World	2
Selfish Dog, The	Storyworlds	Heinemann	Stage 3 Once Upon a Time	2
Sending Messages	Alphakids	Gardner	Extending Level 23	10
Sense This	First Explorers	Kingscourt	Level 1	8
Separate Ways	PM Plus	Nelson Thornes	Silver Level	10
Serve Me, Stefan	Web Fiction	OUP	Stage 9 (Variety)	10
Seven Continents, The	Rigby Star Non-fiction	Rigby	Star Plus Level	10
Seven Foolish Fishermen	PM Traditional Tales	Nelson Thornes	Gold Level	9
Seven in a Line	PM Maths	Nelson Thornes	Stage B	3
Shadow Puppets	Alphakids	Gardner	Early Level 7	3
Shadows and Shade	AlphaWorld	Gardner	Level 12 (trans)	5
Shampoozal	Crunchies	Orchard	Seriously Silly Stories	10
Shapes on the Seashore	Big Cat	Collins	Red A	2
Shapes with a Rope	PM Maths	Nelson Thornes	Stage B	3
Shark Attack!	AlphaWorld	Gardner	Level 16 (trans)	6
Shark With No Teeth, The	Storyworlds	Heinemann	Stage 8 Animal World	6
Sharks	Alphakids Plus	Gardner	Transitional Level 17	7
Sharks	Oxford Reading Tree	OUP	Fireflies, More – Stage 5	6
Shark's Tooth	Web Fiction	OUP	Stage 3 (Variety)	3
Sheep	PM Non-fiction	Nelson Thornes	Purple Level	9
Sheepless Night, A	Web Fiction	OUP	Stage 6 (Variety)	8
Shells	Oxford Reading Tree	OUP	Fireflies Stage 4	4
Shimbir	Dragonflies	Gardner	Orange	6
Shingo's Grandfather	Sunshine Readers	Gardner	Purple Level Supplementary	9
Shiny Key, The	Oxford Reading Tree	OUP	Stage 6 More Stories A	6
Shoe Grabber, The	Kingscourt Reading, Core	Kingscourt	Level 15 Benchmark Bk	6
Shoe, A	Sails Foundation	Heinemann	Pink B – This	1A
Shoo, Fly!	Kingscourt Reading, Extension	Kingscourt	Set 6	6
Shoo, Fly!	Story Chest	Kingscourt	Get-ready Set AA	1B
Shoo, Shoo, Shoo!	Kingscourt Reading, Core	Kingscourt	Level 7 Collection	3
Shooter Shrinker, The	Alphakids	Gardner	Extending Level 23	10

TITLE	SERIES	PUBLISHER	SET (OR AUTHOR)	BAND
Shooting Star, The	PM Storybooks	Nelson Thornes	Gold Set C	9
Shopping	Kingscourt Reading, Extension	Kingscourt	Set 2	2
Shopping	Oxford Reading Tree	OUP	Stage 1+ More Patterned Stories	2
Shopping	Rigby Star	Rigby	Red Level	2
Shopping	Sails Foundation	Heinemann	Pink B – Look	1A
Shopping	Story Street	Pearson	Step 2	2
Shopping for a Party	Oxford Reading Tree	OUP	Fireflies Stage 2	2
Shopping List, The	Kingscourt Reading, Extension	Kingscourt	Set 6	6
Shopping Mall, The	PM Storybook Starters	Nelson Thornes	Set 1	1A
Shopping with Grandma	PM Photo Stories	Nelson Thornes	Blue 10	4
Show and Tell	Alphakids	Gardner	Early Level 8	3
Show, The	Sails Foundation	Heinemann	Pink A – Is	1A
Shut in the Barn	Alphakids Plus	Gardner	Transitional Level 15	6
Shut the Gate!	Alphakids Plus	Gardner	Emergent Level 5	2
Side By Side	AlphaWorld	Gardner	Level 24 (ext)	10
Signs	Alphakids Plus	Gardner	Emergent Level 5	2
Silkworms	AlphaWorld	Gardner	Level 17 (trans)	6
Silly Old Possum	Story Chest	Kingscourt	Get-ready Set C	2
Silly Sons and Dozy Daughters	Crunchies	Orchard	Twice Upon a Time	9
Silly Tricks	Sails Foundation	Heinemann	Pink C – Are	1A
Silva the Seal	Alphakids Plus	Gardner	Transitional Level 15	6
Silver and Prince	PM Storybooks	Nelson Thornes	Silver Set C	10
Simple Rhyming Dictionary, A	Pelican Big Bks	Pearson	Palmer, Sue	6
Singing Giant, The (play)	Rigby Star	Rigby	Green Level	5
Singing Giant, The (story)	Rigby Star	Rigby	Green Level	5
Singing Princess, The	Rigby Star	Rigby	White Level	10
Sinking Feeling, A	Oxford Reading Tree	OUP	Stage 2 Patterned Stories	2
Sir Andrew the Brave	Alphakids	Gardner	Extending Level 21	8
Sir Ben and the Dragon	Web Fiction	OUP	Stage 5 (Variety)	4
Sir Ben and the Monster	Web Fiction	OUP	Stage 5 (Variety)	5
Sir Ben and the Robbers	Web Fiction	OUP	Stage 5 (Variety)	5
Six in a Bed	Oxford Reading Tree	OUP	Stage 1 First Words	1B
Six Under the Sea	PM Maths	Nelson Thornes	Stage B	3
Skate Rider	Alphakids Plus	Gardner	Transitional Level 16	7
Skateboarding	Oxford Reading Tree	OUP	Fireflies Stage 6	9
Skating	Story Chest	Kingscourt	Ready-set-go Set AA	2
Skating at Rainbow Lake	PM Storybooks	Nelson Thornes	Silver Set B	10
Skeleton on the Bus, The	Literacy Links Plus	Kingscourt	Fluent B	8
Skeletons	Kingscourt Reading, Extension	Kingscourt	Set 3	3
Skeletons	Oxford Reading Tree	OUP	Fireflies Stage 10	10
Ski Lesson, The	Kingscourt Reading, Extension	Kingscourt	Set 6	6
Skier, The	PM Storybook Starters	Nelson Thornes	Set 1	1A
Skin	Literacy Links Plus	Kingscourt	Early B	4
Skipper McFlea	Sunshine Readers	Gardner	Light Blue Level	6
Skipper's Happy Tail	Dragonflies	Gardner	Green	5
Skipping Rope, The	PM Plus	Nelson Thornes	Green Level	5
Skunks	PM Non-fiction	Nelson Thornes	Gold Level	9
Sky Changes	PM Plus Non-fiction	Nelson Thornes	Purple Level	8
Sky is Falling, The	Kingscourt Reading, Extension	Kingscourt	Set 4 (play)	4
Sleeping Animals	Alphakids	Gardner	Early Level 6	3
Sleeping Beauty	Genre Range	Pearson	Emergent Traditional Tales	7

TITLE	SERIES	PUBLISHER	SET (OR AUTHOR)	BAND
Sleeping Beauty	Oxford Reading Tree	OUP	Stage 5 More Stories C	5
Sleeping Beauty, The	PM Traditional Tales	Nelson Thornes	Silver Level	10
Sleeping Out	Story Chest	Kingscourt	Ready-set-go Set C	3
Sleepy Bear	Literacy Links Plus	Kingscourt	Early A	4
Sleepy Sammy	Crunchies	Orchard	Colour Crackers	8
Slug, the Sea Monster	Storyworlds	Heinemann	Stage 6 Fantasy World	5
Sly Fox and Little Red Hen	PM Traditional Tales	Nelson Thornes	Purple Level	8
Small and Large	Four Corners	Pearson	Year 1	1B
Smallest Horses, The	PM Plus	Nelson Thornes	Turquoise Level	7
Smallest Tree, The	Literacy Links Plus	Kingscourt	Fluent D	7
Smudger and the Smelly Fish	Rockets	A&C Black	Ryan, Margaret	10
Snail	Stopwatch	A&C Black		9
Snails	Alphakids	Gardner	Transitional Level 13	6
Snails	First Stories	Gardner	Emergent A	1A
Snake is Going Away!	Rigby Star	Rigby	Red Level	2
Snake That Couldn't Hiss, The	Storyworlds	Heinemann	Stage 8 Animal World	6
Snake, The	Sails Foundation	Heinemann	Pink B – Was	1A
Snakes	Alphakids Plus	Gardner	Extending Level 24	9
Snake's Dinner	Alphakids	Gardner	Early Level 7	3
Snake's Reward	Kingscourt Reading, Core	Kingscourt	Level 14 Little Books	5
Snake's Sore Head	Kingscourt Reading, Extension	Kingscourt	Set 3	3
Sneaky Deals and Tricky Tricks	Crunchies	Orchard	Twice Upon a Time	8
Sniffs	Alphakids Plus	Gardner	Emergent Level 3	2
Snip! Snap!	Alphakids Plus	Gardner	Transitional Level 14	5
Snow Games	Story Street	Pearson	Step 6	7
Snow on the Hill	PM Storybooks	Nelson Thornes	Green Set B	5
Snow Queen, The	New Way	Nelson Thornes	Orange Parallel Books	10
Snow Surprise	Web Guided Reading	OUP	Stage 5 (Duck Green)	4
Snow Troll	Oxford Reading Tree	OUP	More Allstars Pack 1a	9
Snow White and the Seven Dwarfs	PM Traditional Tales	Nelson Thornes	Gold Level	9
Snow, The	Sails Foundation	Heinemann	Pink C – Me	1A
Snowball, the White Mouse	PM Plus	Nelson Thornes	Green Level	5
Snowman	Story Chest	Kingscourt	Get-ready Set AA	1B
Snowman Day	First Stories	Gardner	Emergent D	1B
Snowman, The	Kingscourt Reading, Core	Kingscourt	Level 2 Benchmark Bk	1B
Snowman, The	Oxford Reading Tree	OUP	Stage 3 More Stories A	3
Snowman, The	Sails Foundation	Heinemann	Pink B – On	1A
Snowy Gets a Wash	PM Storybooks	Nelson Thornes	Yellow Set B	3
Social Insects	Alphakids Plus	Gardner	Extending Level 22	9
Socks Off!	Alphakids	Gardner	Early Level 10	4
Soft and Hard	AlphaWorld	Gardner	Band 1B: Pink	1B
Solo Flyer	PM Storybooks	Nelson Thornes	Gold Set A	9
Solve This!	Kingscourt Reading, Extension	Kingscourt	Set 8	8
Some Things Keep Changing	AlphaWorld	Gardner	Level 24 (ext)	10
Something is There	Kingscourt Reading, Core	Kingscourt	Level 16 Collection	6
Songbird, The	Web Guided Reading	OUP	Stage 6 (Duck Green)	7
Songs and Riddles	Genre Range	Pearson	Beginner Poetry	5
Songs, Alphabet & Playground Rhymes	Genre Range	Pearson	Emergent Poetry	9
Sooty	Alphakids	Gardner	Transitional Level 12	5
Sorting	Oxford Reading Tree	OUP	Fireflies, More – Stage 2	2
Sorting Leaves	PM Maths	Nelson Thornes	Stage A	2

TITLE	SERIES	PUBLISHER	SET (OR AUTHOR)	BAND
Sounds	Big Cat	Collins	Blue	4
Sounds	Lighthouse	Ginn	Gold: 2	9
Sounds All Round	First Explorers	Kingscourt	Level 2	10
Sour Grapes	Alphakids	Gardner	Extending Level 21	9
Souvenirs	Literacy Links Plus	Kingscourt	Fluent A	7
Space Ant	Rigby Star	Rigby	Blue Level	4
Space Football	Rockets	A&C Black	Smith, Wendy	10
Space Travel	Alphakids	Gardner	Transitional Level 15	7
Spanish Omelet	PM Storybooks	Nelson Thornes	Silver Set C	10
Special Places at School	AlphaWorld	Gardner	Level 15 (trans)	6
Special Ride, The	PM Storybooks	Nelson Thornes	Gold Set B	9
Special Table, The	Kingscourt Reading, Core	Kingscourt	White	8
Speedy Bee	PM Plus	Nelson Thornes	Yellow Level	3
Speedy Bee's Dance	PM Gems	Nelson Thornes	Yellow 8	3
Spider	Literacy Links Plus	Kingscourt	Fluent C	9
Spider Bank, The	Kingscourt Reading, Core	Kingscourt	Level 19 Little Books	8
Spider in My Bedroom, A	PM Plus	Nelson Thornes	Purple Level	8
Spider, The	Sails Foundation	Heinemann	Pink C – Me	1A
Spiders	Alphakids Plus	Gardner	Early Level 10	5
Spiders	First Facts	Badger	Level 2	3
Spiders	Spotty Zebra	Nelson Thornes	Red – Change	2
Spiders Are Amazing	Web Weavers Non-fiction	OUP	Non-fiction – Animals	8
Spiders Spin Silk	National Geographic	Rigby	Turquoise Level	9
Spies, The	Sails Foundation	Heinemann	Pink C – Are	1A
Spines, Stings and Teeth	Big Cat	Collins	Green	5
Spinning Tops	PM Photo Stories	Nelson Thornes	Green 12	5
Spock the Donkey	Story Street	Pearson	Step 4	5
Spooky Eyes, The	Web Guided Reading	OUP	Stage 8 (Duck Green)	8
Sport Then and Now	Oxford Reading Tree	OUP	Fireflies Stage 7	10
Sports Day	Web Guided Reading	OUP	Stage 6 (Duck Green)	7
Sports Dictionary	Lighthouse	Ginn	Blue: 8	4
Spots	Oxford Reading Tree	OUP	Stage 2 More Stories A	3
Springs	Alphakids	Gardner	Early Level 6	3
Spy on Spiders	First Explorers	Kingscourt	Level 2	10
Spy, The	Sails Foundation	Heinemann	Pink B – On	1A
Squirrel	Oxford Reading Tree	OUP	More Allstars Pack 1a	9
Squirrels	Kingscourt Reading, Extension	Kingscourt	Set 9	9
Star and Patches	PM Plus	Nelson Thornes	Purple Level	8
Star Boy's Surprise	Big Cat	Collins	Purple	8
Star Gazing	AlphaWorld	Gardner	Level 18 (ext)	7
Star is Born, A	Rockets	A&C Black	Smith, Wendy	9
Stay Away!	AlphaWorld	Gardner	Band 4: Blue	3
Staying Alive	Alphakids	Gardner	Transitional Level 17	8
Staying at Nan's	Spotty Zebra	Nelson Thornes	Red – Ourselves	3
Stella	Kingscourt Reading, Extension	Kingscourt	Set 3	3
Stella's Staying Put	Crunchies	Orchard	Colour Crackers	8
Stew for Dinner	First Stories	Gardner	Emergent F	1A
Stone Cutter, The	Big Cat	Collins	Turquoise	6
Stone Soup	PM Traditional Tales	Nelson Thornes	Turquoise Level	7
Stone Soup	Rigby Star	Rigby	Green Level	5
Stone Soup & other stories	New Way	Nelson Thornes	Yellow Platform Books	7

TITLE	SERIES	PUBLISHER	SET (OR AUTHOR)	BAND
Stop That Dog!	Alphakids Plus	Gardner	Transitional Level 16	5
Stop the Car!	Lighthouse	Ginn	Blue: 3	4
Stop Thief!	Lighthouse	Ginn	Purple: 7	8
Stop Thief!	Story Street	Pearson	Step 6	8
Stop!	Kingscourt Reading, Core	Kingscourt	Level 5 Collection	2
Stop!	PM Storybook Starters	Nelson Thornes	Set 2	1B
Stop!	Story Chest	Kingscourt	Ready-set-go Set D	3
Stop, Look and Listen	Lighthouse	Ginn	Red: 1	2
Storm Castle	Oxford Reading Tree	OUP	Stage 9 Stories	7
Storm Is Coming, A	AlphaWorld	Gardner	Band 6: Orange	6
Storm, The	Oxford Reading Tree	OUP	Stage 4 Storybooks	4
Storms	PM Plus Non-fiction	Nelson Thornes	Silver Level	10
Stormy Weather	First Facts	Badger	Level 3	5
Story of Jeans, The	Discovery World Links	Heinemann	Stage E	9
Story of William Tell, The	PM Storybooks	Nelson Thornes	Silver Set C	10
Story of Zadig, The	Alphakids Plus	Gardner	Extending Level 24	9
Story Poems	Genre Range	Pearson	Emergent Poetry	9
Story Time with Mick	Story Street	Pearson	Step 4	5
Storytellers	Kingscourt Reading, Extension	Kingscourt	Set 10	10
Strange Dream, The	Web Fiction	OUP	Stage 7 (Variety)	7
Strange Plants	National Geographic	Rigby	Gold Level	10
Strange Shoe, The	PM Traditional Tales	Nelson Thornes	Silver Level	10
Strange Street Again	Story Street	Pearson	Step 3	4
Straw House, The	Storyworlds	Heinemann	Stage 5 Once Upon a Time	5
Strawberry Jam	Oxford Reading Tree	OUP	Stage 3 More Stories A	3
Strike	Skyrider LM Chapters	Gardner	Set 1	8
Strings	Kingscourt Reading, Extension	Kingscourt	Set 2	2
String's the Thing	Web Guided Reading	OUP	Stage 3 (Duck Green)	2
Stripes	AlphaWorld	Gardner	Band 1A: Pink	2
Stubborn Goat, The	Alphakids	Gardner	Early Level 11	5
Stuck in the Mud	Lighthouse	Ginn	Red: 8	2
Stuck in the Mud	Oxford Reading Tree	OUP	Stage 4 More Stories C	3
Stuck on an Island	Sunshine Readers	Gardner	Light Blue Level Supplementary	6
Stuff-it-in Specials, The	Rockets	A&C Black	Wallace, Karen	9
Stupid Ogre, The	Web Fiction	OUP	Stage 5 (Variety)	4
Submarine Adventure	Oxford Reading Tree	OUP	Stage 6 & 7 More Stories B	7
Sugar and Spice and All Things Nice	Kingscourt Reading, Extension	Kingscourt	Set 10	10
Summer and Winter	Kingscourt Reading, Core	Kingscourt	Level 12 Little Books	5
Summer Fair, The	Web Guided Reading	OUP	Stage 8 (Duck Green)	7
Summer in Antarctica	AlphaWorld	Gardner	Level 23 (ext)	10
Sun and the Moon, The	PM Gems	Nelson Thornes	Magenta 2/3	2
Sun and the Wind, The	Storyworlds	Heinemann	Stage 4 Once Upon a Time	3
Sun in the Sky, The	Alphakids	Gardner	Transitional Level 12	5
Sun Smile	Story Chest	Kingscourt	Stage 2	6
Sun, Sand and Space	Rockets	A&C Black	Smith, Wendy	9
Sun, The	PM Plus Non-fiction	Nelson Thornes	Silver Level	10
Sun, the Wind and the Rain, The	PM Plus Non-fiction	Nelson Thornes	Yellow Level	4
Sun's Energy, The	First Facts	Badger	Level 4	9
Sunflower Seeds	Story Chest	Kingscourt	Get-ready Set DD	3
Sunflower That Went Flop, The	Story Chest	Kingscourt	Stage 5	8
Sunita and the Wishing Well	Genre Range	Pearson	Emergent Plays	5

TITLE	SERIES	PUBLISHER	SET (OR AUTHOR)	BAND
Sunrise	Literacy Links Plus	Kingscourt	Emergent C	2
Super Sea Birds	Alphakids Plus	Gardner	Transitional Level 17	8
Super Shopping	Rigby Star	Rigby	Yellow Level	3
Superdog	Oxford Reading Tree	OUP	Stage 9 Stories	7
Surf Carnival, The	PM Storybooks	Nelson Thornes	Purple Set B	8
Surprise Dinner, The	PM Storybooks	Nelson Thornes	Gold Set B	9
Surprise for Zac, A	PM Plus	Nelson Thornes	Turquoise Level	7
Surprise Photo, The	PM Plus	Nelson Thornes	Gold Level	9
Surprise!	Kingscourt Reading, Core	Kingscourt	Level 7 Little Books	3
Surprise!	Kingscourt Reading, Core	Kingscourt	Level 14 Collection	5
Surprise, The	Oxford Reading Tree	OUP	Robins Pack 2	9
Survival	Oxford Reading Tree	OUP	Fireflies Stage 10	10
Survival Adventure	Oxford Reading Tree	OUP	Stage 9 Stories	8
Survivors in the Frozen North	PM Plus	Nelson Thornes	Silver Level	10
Swan Family, The	PM Plus	Nelson Thornes	Blue Level	4
Swan Lake	New Way	Nelson Thornes	Orange Parallel Books	10
Swap!	Oxford Reading Tree	OUP	Stage 4 More Stories B	3
Swimmer's Day, A	Spotty Zebra	Nelson Thornes	Red – Ourselves	3
Swimming Across the Pool	PM Plus	Nelson Thornes	Turquoise Level	7
Swimming Lessons	Kingscourt Reading, Extension	Kingscourt	Set 4	4
Swimming with a Dragon	PM Plus	Nelson Thornes	Green Level	5
Swimming With Dolphins	Big Cat	Collins	Gold	9
Swoop!	PM Plus	Nelson Thornes	Orange Level	6

T

TITLE	SERIES	PUBLISHER	SET (OR AUTHOR)	BAND
T J's Tree	Literacy Links Plus	Kingscourt	Early B	4
Tabby in the Tree	PM Storybooks	Nelson Thornes	Blue Set A	4
Tadpole and Frog	Stopwatch	A&C Black		7
Tadpoles	Pathways	Collins	Year 1	6
Tadpoles and Frogs	Alphakids	Gardner	Emergent Level 5	3
Tails	AlphaWorld	Gardner	Band 2: Red	2
Taking Care of Ourselves	PM Plus Non-fiction	Nelson Thornes	Orange Level	7
Taking Good Holiday Photos	Spotlight on Fact	Collins	Y2 The Seaside	9
Taking Photos	Alphakids	Gardner	Early Level 6	3
Tale of a Turban, The	Web Fiction	OUP	Stage 7 (Variety)	9
Tale of the Turnip, The	PM Traditional Tales	Nelson Thornes	Orange Level	6
Talent Quest, The	PM Storybooks	Nelson Thornes	Silver Set B	10
Talk, Talk, Talk	Big Cat	Collins	Blue	4
Tall Things	PM Non-fiction	Nelson Thornes	Red Level	3
Tarantula	Alphakids	Gardner	Early Level 11	5
Tasmanian Devils	PM Non-fiction	Nelson Thornes	Gold Level	9
Tea Party, The	Kingscourt Reading, Extension	Kingscourt	Set 2	2
Teacher, The	PM Non-fiction	Nelson Thornes	Blue Level	5
Teamwork	PM Plus	Nelson Thornes	Silver Level	10
Teasing Dad	PM Storybooks	Nelson Thornes	Blue Set B	4
Teasing Mum	PM Plus	Nelson Thornes	Green Level	5
Tec and the Cake	Big Cat	Collins	Red A	1B
Tec and the Hole	Big Cat	Collins	Red A	1B
Tec and the Litter	Big Cat	Collins	Red B	2

TITLE	SERIES	PUBLISHER	SET (OR AUTHOR)	BAND
Teddy Bears' Picnic	PM Plus	Nelson Thornes	Red Level	2
Teeth	Lighthouse	Ginn	White 3	10
Teeth	Story Chest	Kingscourt	Ready-set-go Set CC	3
Telling Prog	Spotlight on Fact	Collins	Y1 Toys and Games	4
Telling the Truth	PM Gems	Nelson Thornes	Green 14	5
Tell-tale	Story Chest	Kingscourt	Stage 6	9
Ten Apples Up On Top	Beginner Books	Collins	Le Seig, Theo	7
Ten Frogs in the Pond	PM Maths	Nelson Thornes	Stage B	4
Ten Little Caterpillars	Literacy Links Plus	Kingscourt	Early C	4
Ten Little Ducks	Kingscourt Reading, Core	Kingscourt	Level 10 Collection	4
Ten Little Garden Snails	PM Storybooks	Nelson Thornes	Green Set A	5
Terrible Tiger & other stories	New Way	Nelson Thornes	Yellow Core Book	7
Terrible Tiger, The	Rigby Star	Rigby	Blue Level	4
Terry Takes Off	Oxford Reading Tree	OUP	More Allstars Pack 1a	9
Tessa on TV	Web Fiction	OUP	Stage 9 (Variety)	9
Thanksgiving	First Stories	Gardner	Emergent C	1A
That Cat	First Stories	Gardner	Emergent E	1A
That Cat!	Web Guided Reading	OUP	Stage 4 (Duck Green)	3
That's My Boy!	Sunshine Readers	Gardner	Light Blue Level	6
That's Not My Hobby!	Rigby Star	Rigby	Turquoise Level	7
That's Not Our Dog	PM Plus	Nelson Thornes	Turquoise Level	7
That's the Life!	Kingscourt Reading, Extension	Kingscourt	Set 6	6
Then and Now	Discovery World Links	Heinemann	Stage D	9
Then and Now	Four Corners	Pearson	Year 1	2
Then and Now	Pathways	Collins	Year 2	10
There's A Boy Under the Bed	Dragonflies	Gardner	Gold	9
They All Ran Away	Lighthouse	Ginn	Red: 3	2
They Worked Together	Four Corners	Pearson	Year 2	9
Things I Like	Kingscourt Reading, Extension	Kingscourt	Set 1	1A
Things on Wheels	Badger NF Guided Reading	Aladdin/Watts	Reading About	7
Things People Make	AlphaWorld	Gardner	Level 23 (ext)	10
Things That Go	Web Weavers Non-fiction	OUP	Stage 1 First Words NF	1B
Things That Sting	Oxford Reading Tree	OUP	Fireflies Stage 7	9
Things with Wings	Kingscourt Reading, Extension	Kingscourt	Set 10	10
This House is Too Small!	Info Trail	Pearson	Beginner History	4
This is a Bad Day!	Sunshine Readers	Gardner	Orange Level	6
This is an Island	National Geographic	Rigby	Yellow Level	2
This Is for Me	Sails Foundation	Heinemann	Pink C – Me	1A
This is Me	Oxford Reading Tree	OUP	Fireflies Stage 1+	1A
Thomas Had a Temper	Alphakids	Gardner	Early Level 8	3
Those Birds!	Kingscourt Reading, Extension	Kingscourt	Set 9	9
Three Bears, The	Lighthouse	Ginn	Red: 4	2
Three Billy Goats Gruff, The	Literacy Links Plus	Kingscourt	Traditional Tale	7
Three Billy Goats Gruff, The	New Way	Nelson Thornes	Green Platform Books	5
Three Billy Goats Gruff, The	Oxford Reading Tree	OUP	Traditional Tales 5–7	4
Three Billy Goats Gruff, The	PM Traditional Tales	Nelson Thornes	Orange Level	6
Three Billy Goats, The	Storyworlds	Heinemann	Stage 3 Once Upon a Time	2
Three Goats, The	Kingscourt Reading, Extension	Kingscourt	Set 3	3
Three Kings & Kim's Star, The	New Way	Nelson Thornes	Green Easy Start Set B	5
Three Little Mice in Trouble	PM Plus	Nelson Thornes	Green Level	5
Three Little Pigs, The	Alphakids	Gardner	Early Level 8	3

TITLE	SERIES	PUBLISHER	SET (OR AUTHOR)	BAND
Three Little Pigs, The	PM Traditional Tales	Nelson Thornes	Orange Level	6
Three Magicians, The	Literacy Links Plus	Kingscourt	Fluent D	9
Three Sillies, The	Literacy Links Plus	Kingscourt	Fluent C	10
Three Wishes, The	Alphakids Plus	Gardner	Transitional Level 16	6
Three Wishes, The	Storyworlds	Heinemann	Stage 8 Once Upon a Time	7
Tickling	Alphakids	Gardner	Emergent Level 4	2
Tick-Tock	Story Chest	Kingscourt	Get-ready Set DD	1B
Tiddalik	Story Chest	Kingscourt	Stage 7	10
Tidy Your Room!	Alphakids Plus	Gardner	Early Level 8	4
Tig	Web Fiction	OUP	Stage 2 (Variety)	3
Tiger and the Jackal, The	Storyworlds	Heinemann	Stage 8 Once Upon a Time	7
Tiger Cub	I Love Reading	Ticktock	Blue Level	4
Tiger Cub	I Love Reading	Ticktock	Orange Level	6
Tiger Cub	I Love Reading	Ticktock	Purple Level	8
Tiger Hunt	Rigby Star	Rigby	Gold Level	9
Tiger Runs Away	PM Storybooks	Nelson Thornes	Blue Set B	4
Tiger, Tiger	PM Storybooks	Nelson Thornes	Red Set A	2
Tigers	Alphakids Plus	Gardner	Transitional Level 13	6
Tigers	Web Weavers Non-fiction	OUP	Non-fiction – Animals	8
Tig's Pet	Web Fiction	OUP	Stage 2 (Variety)	3
Tim and Tom & Who Will Push Me?	New Way	Nelson Thornes	Green Easy Start Set A	4
Time For Bed	Dragonflies	Gardner	Red	2
Time For Play	PM Plus Non-fiction	Nelson Thornes	Red Level	3
Time to Celebrate!	Four Corners	Pearson	Year 2	9
Time Travellers	Rockets	A&C Black	Smith, Wendy	10
Timmy	Literacy Links Plus	Kingscourt	Emergent D	3
Tim's Favourite Toy	PM Storybooks	Nelson Thornes	Blue Set B	4
Tina the Tiniest Girl	Crunchies	Orchard	The One And Only	8
Tiny and the Big Wave	PM Storybooks	Nelson Thornes	Yellow Set B	3
Tiny Dinosaurs	PM Plus	Nelson Thornes	Silver Level	10
Tiny Teddies' Picnic, The	PM Photo Stories	Nelson Thornes	Red 5	2
Tiny Tim	Crunchies	Orchard	Colour Crackers	9
To the Rescue	I Love Reading	Ticktock	Blue Level	4
Toast	First Stories	Gardner	Emergent D	1B
Toby and BJ	PM Storybooks	Nelson Thornes	Orange Set A	6
Toby and the Accident	PM Storybooks	Nelson Thornes	Turquoise Set A	7
Toby and the Big Red Van	PM Storybooks	Nelson Thornes	Orange Set B	6
Toby and the Big Tree	PM Storybooks	Nelson Thornes	Orange Set A	6
Toby at Sandy Bay	PM Storybooks	Nelson Thornes	Purple Set C	8
Toffee and Marmalade	Oxford Reading Tree	OUP	All Stars Pack 3	10
Toilets Through Time	Info Trail	Pearson	Emergent History	9
Tom is Brave	PM Storybooks	Nelson Thornes	Red Set A	2
Tom Thumb and the Football Team	Oxford Reading Tree	OUP	More Allstars Pack 2a	9
Tommy in Trouble	Web Fiction	OUP	Stage 9 (Variety)	10
Tommy's Treasure	Literacy Links Plus	Kingscourt	Fluent A	6
Tom's Birthday Treat	Storyworld Bridges	Heinemann	Stage 10	10
Tom's Handplant	Literacy Links Plus	Kingscourt	Fluent B	10
Tom's Ride	PM Plus	Nelson Thornes	Blue Level	4
Tom's Trousers	Kingscourt Reading, Extension	Kingscourt	Set 4	4
Tongue Twisters, Limericks ...	Genre Range	Pearson	Emergent Poetry	9
Tongues	Info Trail	Pearson	Emergent Science	8

TITLE	SERIES	PUBLISHER	SET (OR AUTHOR)	BAND
Tongues	Literacy Links Plus	Kingscourt	Fluent A	10
Tony and the Butterfly	Literacy Links Plus	Kingscourt	Fluent D	8
Too Big For Me	Story Chest	Kingscourt	Ready-set-go Set C	2
Too Big for Me!	First Stories	Gardner	Emergent D	1B
Too Big!	Dragonflies	Gardner	Pink	1B
Too Busy	Alphakids	Gardner	Emergent Level 3	2
Too Good to Waste	Sunshine Readers	Gardner	Orange Level	6
Too Hot!	Lighthouse	Ginn	Pink B: 7	1B
Too Many Animals	Alphakids	Gardner	Early Level 7	3
Too Many Babies	Crunchies	Orchard	Colour Crackers	8
Too Much Noise	Literacy Links Plus	Kingscourt	Early D	6
Tooth Book, The	Bright and Early Books	Collins	Le Seig, Theo	7
Top Cat	Kingscourt Reading, Core	Kingscourt	Level 20 Little Books	7
Top Dinosaurs	Big Cat	Collins	Blue	4
Top Dog	Oxford Reading Tree	OUP	Stage 1+ More First Sentences	2
Tornado, The	PM Plus	Nelson Thornes	Silver Level	10
Tour de France	Oxford Reading Tree	OUP	Fireflies Stage 6	8
Town Dog	Oxford Reading Tree	OUP	More Allstars Pack 2a	9
Town Mouse & the Country Mouse, The	Storyworlds	Heinemann	Stage 4 Once Upon a Time	3
Town Mouse and Country Mouse	Kingscourt Reading, Core	Kingscourt	Level 15 Little Books	5
Town Mouse and Country Mouse	PM Traditional Tales	Nelson Thornes	Purple Level	8
Toy Box, The	PM Plus	Nelson Thornes	Starters Two	1B
Toy Farm, The	PM Storybooks	Nelson Thornes	Orange Set A	6
Toys	Discovery World Links	Heinemann	Stage D	5
Toys and Games	Badger NF Guided Reading	Wayland	Changes	8
Toys and Games	First Facts	Badger	Level 2	3
Toys and Games Around the World	Spotlight on Fact	Collins	Y1 Toys and Games	4
Toys and Games from A to Z	Spotlight on Fact	Collins	Y1 Toys and Games	4
Toys and Games in Art	Spotlight on Fact	Collins	Y1 Toys and Games	4
Toys and Play	PM Plus Non-fiction	Nelson Thornes	Red Level	3
Toys of the Past 50 Years	Spotlight on Fact	Collins	Y1 Toys and Games	6
Toy's Party, The	Oxford Reading Tree	OUP	Stage 2 Storybooks	2
Toys' Picnic, The	First Stories	Gardner	Emergent D	1B
Toytown Bus Helps Out, The	PM Gems	Nelson Thornes	Yellow 7	3
Toytown Fire Engine, The	PM Plus	Nelson Thornes	Yellow Level	3
Toytown Helicopter, The	PM Plus	Nelson Thornes	Red Level	2
Toytown Racing Car, The	PM Plus	Nelson Thornes	Blue Level	4
Toytown Rescue, The	PM Plus	Nelson Thornes	Red Level	2
Tracking the Caribou	Lighthouse	Ginn	White 5	10
Tracks on the Ground	Skyrider LM Chapters	Gardner	Set 2	9
Tractors	Discovery World Links	Heinemann	Stage C	4
Traffic	Lighthouse	Ginn	Pink A: 1	1A
Traffic Jam	First Stories	Gardner	Emergent D	1B
Trail Riding	Alphakids Plus	Gardner	Transitional Level 13	6
Train Race, The	Alphakids Plus	Gardner	Early Level 8	4
Training Like an Athlete	Oxford Reading Tree	OUP	Fireflies Stage 9	9
Training Ruby	Dragonflies	Gardner	Red	2
Training with Ali and Emma	Info Trail	Pearson	Emergent Science	8
Trains	Alphakids Plus	Gardner	Extending Level 21	9
Transport	Oxford Reading Tree	OUP	Fireflies Stage 2	2
Trapped!	New Way	Nelson Thornes	Orange Platform Books	9

TITLE	SERIES	PUBLISHER	SET (OR AUTHOR)	BAND
Trash or Treasure	Alphakids	Gardner	Transitional Level 14	5
Travels with Magellan	Oxford Reading Tree	OUP	Stage 8 True Stories	7
Treasure Chest	Oxford Reading Tree	OUP	Stage 6 & 7 Stories	7
Treasure Hunt	Alphakids Plus	Gardner	Transitional Level 12	5
Treasure Hunt, The	Oxford Reading Tree	OUP	Robins Pack 3	9
Treasure Island, A	PM Plus	Nelson Thornes	Blue Level	4
Tree Horse, A	PM Plus	Nelson Thornes	Green Level	5
Tree House, The	AlphaWorld	Gardner	Level 13 (trans)	5
Tree, The	Alphakids	Gardner	Early Level 6	3
Tree-House, The	Story Chest	Kingscourt	Get-ready Set A	1B
Trees	Literacy Links Plus	Kingscourt	Early D	7
Trees, Please!	Kingscourt Reading, Extension	Kingscourt	Set 9	9
Triceratops and the Crocodiles, The	PM Plus	Nelson Thornes	Orange Level	6
Tricking the Tiger	PM Plus	Nelson Thornes	Turquoise Level	7
Trip into Space, A	Kingscourt Reading, Core	Kingscourt	Level 8 Benchmark Bk	3
Trixie's Holiday	PM Plus	Nelson Thornes	Gold Level	9
Trojan Horse, The	Literacy Links Plus	Kingscourt	Fluent C	8
Troll's Hat, The	Web Guided Reading	OUP	Stage 8 (Duck Green)	8
Troop of Little Dinosaurs, A	PM Storybooks	Nelson Thornes	Purple Set B	8
Trouble at the Supermarket	Sunshine Readers	Gardner	Orange Level	6
Truck Parade, The	PM Plus	Nelson Thornes	Purple Level	8
Trucks, The	Sails Foundation	Heinemann	Pink C – You	1A
Try Again, Emma	Lighthouse	Ginn	Orange: 1	6
Try Again, Hannah	PM Storybooks	Nelson Thornes	Green Set B	5
T-shirt Triplets, The	Literacy Links Plus	Kingscourt	Fluent B	8
Tug of War	Oxford Reading Tree	OUP	Stage 4 More Stories C	3
Tug of War, The	Kingscourt Reading, Core	Kingscourt	Level 9 Benchmark Bk	4
Tug of War, The	Storyworlds	Heinemann	Stage 7 Once Upon a Time	6
Tulips For My Teacher	PM Photo Stories	Nelson Thornes	Green 12	5
Tunnel, The	Sails Foundation	Heinemann	Pink C – Are	1A
Tunnels	AlphaWorld	Gardner	Level 17 (trans)	7
Tunnels	National Geographic	Rigby	Purple Level	7
Turkey, The	Sails Foundation	Heinemann	Pink C – Come	1A
Turtle Flies South	Literacy Links Plus	Kingscourt	Fluent A	8
Turtle Talk	Kingscourt Reading, Extension	Kingscourt	Set 7	7
Turtle Who Danced with the Crane, The	Pelican Big Bks	Pearson	Cullimore, Stan	7
Turtles in Trouble	Alphakids Plus	Gardner	Extending Level 23	9
Twiga and the Moon	Storyworlds	Heinemann	Stage 7 Animal World	5
Twins	Alphakids	Gardner	Emergent Level 4	2
Twins, The	Web Guided Reading	OUP	Stage 4 (Duck Green)	4
Two Animal Stories	New Way	Nelson Thornes	Green Platform Books	6
Two Baby Elephants	Lighthouse	Ginn	Orange: 8	6
Two Brown Bears	Oxford Reading Tree	OUP	All Stars Pack 1	8
Two Eyes, Two Ears	PM Non-fiction	Nelson Thornes	Red Level	3
Two Giants, The	Storyworlds	Heinemann	Stage 9 Once Upon a Time	10
Two Little Birds	Kingscourt Reading, Core	Kingscourt	Level 1 Collection	1A
Two Little Dogs	Story Chest	Kingscourt	Ready-set-go Set D	2
Two Little Ducks Get Lost	PM Plus	Nelson Thornes	Blue Level	4
Two Little Goldfish	PM Storybooks	Nelson Thornes	Orange Set C	6
Two Little Mice, The	Literacy Links Plus	Kingscourt	Early D	5
Two Red Tugs	PM Storybooks	Nelson Thornes	Purple Set C	8

TITLE	SERIES	PUBLISHER	SET (OR AUTHOR)	BAND
Two Snakes	Alphakids Plus	Gardner	Early Level 9	4
Two the Same	Web Guided Reading	OUP	Stage 1 (Duck Green)	2
Two Tricky Tales	Skyrider LM Chapters	Gardner	Set 2	8

U

TITLE	SERIES	PUBLISHER	SET (OR AUTHOR)	BAND
Ugly Dogs and Slimy Frogs	Crunchies	Orchard	Twice Upon a Time	9
Ugly Duckling	Alphakids	Gardner	Extending Level 20	8
Ugly Duckling, The	New Way	Nelson Thornes	Violet Parallel Books	9
Ugly Duckling, The	PM Traditional Tales	Nelson Thornes	Turquoise Level	7
Ugly Duckling, The	Storyworlds	Heinemann	Stage 5 Once Upon a Time	4
Umbrella	Story Chest	Kingscourt	Ready-set-go Set AA	2
Uncle-and-Auntie Pat	Rockets	A&C Black	West, Colin	9
Under Attack	First Explorers	Kingscourt	Level 1	9
Under Sail	Alphakids	Gardner	Extending Level 22	9
Under the Sea	Alphakids	Gardner	Extending Level 19	8
Underground Adventure	Oxford Reading Tree	OUP	Stage 5 More Stories A	5
Underground Railroad, The	Oxford Reading Tree	OUP	Stage 9 True Stories	9
Ungrateful Tiger, The	Alphakids Plus	Gardner	Extending Level 20	8
Unusual Birds	Oxford Reading Tree	OUP	Fireflies, More – Stage 5	6
Unusual Buildings	Oxford Reading Tree	OUP	Fireflies Stage 6	8
Unusual Traditions	Big Cat	Collins	Purple	8
Up and Down	Kingscourt Reading, Extension	Kingscourt	Set 3	3
Up and Down	Oxford Reading Tree	OUP	Stage 2 More Patterned Stories	2
Up and Down	PM Plus Non-fiction	Nelson Thornes	Starters Two	1B
Up in the Sky	PM Plus	Nelson Thornes	Starters One	1A
Up the Amazon	National Geographic	Rigby	White Level	10
Up the Big Hill	Info Trail	Pearson	Beginner Geography	4
Up the Tree	First Stories	Gardner	Emergent A	1A
Up, Down and Around	National Geographic	Rigby	Red Level	2
Up, Up and Away	Big Cat	Collins	Red A	1B
Up, Up and Away	Lighthouse	Ginn	Pink A: 4	1A
Using Colour	AlphaWorld	Gardner	Band 8: Purple	8
Using Rocks	AlphaWorld	Gardner	Band 4: Blue	3

V

TITLE	SERIES	PUBLISHER	SET (OR AUTHOR)	BAND
Vagabond Crabs	Literacy Links Plus	Kingscourt	Early D	7
Valentine's Day	Story Chest	Kingscourt	Ready-set-go Set AA	2
Vanishing Cream	Oxford Reading Tree	OUP	Stage 5 More Stories A	5
Vegetables Make Me Laugh	Sunshine Readers	Gardner	Orange Level	6
Veronica Who Lived in a Vinegar Bottle	Alphakids Plus	Gardner	Extending Level 18	7
Vicky the High Jumper	Literacy Links Plus	Kingscourt	Fluent C	9
Victorian Adventure	Oxford Reading Tree	OUP	Stage 8 Stories	8
Victorian Seaside Holiday, A	Discovery World Links	Heinemann	Stage C	5
Video Game	Alphakids	Gardner	Early Level 7	3
Viking Adventure	Oxford Reading Tree	OUP	Stage 8 Stories	7
Village in the Snow	Oxford Reading Tree	OUP	Stage 5 Storybooks	5
Village Show, The	Oxford Reading Tree	OUP	Robins Pack 3	9

TITLE	SERIES	PUBLISHER	SET (OR AUTHOR)	BAND
Visit to the Farm, A	Big Cat	Collins	Turquoise	7
Volcanoes	Alphakids	Gardner	Extending Level 22	10
Volcanoes	Oxford Reading Tree	OUP	Fireflies, More – Stage 5	7
Volcanoes and Geysers	PM Plus Non-fiction	Nelson Thornes	Silver Level	10
Vote for Me!	Alphakids	Gardner	Extending Level 20	8
Voyage into Space	Storyworlds	Heinemann	Stage 9 Fantasy World	9
Vroom!	Rigby Star	Rigby	Blue Level	4

W

TITLE	SERIES	PUBLISHER	SET (OR AUTHOR)	BAND
Waiting	Story Chest	Kingscourt	Get-ready Set AA	1B
Wake Up!	Kingscourt Reading, Core	Kingscourt	Level 3 Little Books	2
Wake Up, Dad!	PM Storybooks	Nelson Thornes	Red Set A	2
Walk Tall	Skyrider LM Chapters	Gardner	Set 2	9
Walk, Ride, Run	PM Plus	Nelson Thornes	Yellow Level	3
Walkathon, The	PM Storybooks	Nelson Thornes	Silver Set B	10
Walking in the Autumn	PM Non-fiction	Nelson Thornes	Green Level	6
Walking in the Spring	PM Non-fiction	Nelson Thornes	Green Level	6
Walking in the Summer	PM Non-fiction	Nelson Thornes	Green Level	6
Walking in the Winter	PM Non-fiction	Nelson Thornes	Green Level	6
Walking the Dog	Dragonflies	Gardner	Red	2
Walter's Worries	Skyrider LM Chapters	Gardner	Set 1	9
Washing Our Dog	Alphakids	Gardner	Early Level 7	3
Washing the Elephant	Lighthouse	Ginn	Pink A: 5	1A
Waste	Pathways	Collins	Year 1	3
Watch Dog Who Wouldn't, The	Sunshine Readers	Gardner	Purple Level	8
Watch Out!	Pathways	Collins	Year 1	6
Watch the Birdie!	Web Guided Reading	OUP	Stage 8 (Duck Green)	7
Water and Wind	PM Plus Non-fiction	Nelson Thornes	Silver Level	10
Water Can Change	National Geographic	Rigby	Turquoise Level	9
Water Fight, The	Oxford Reading Tree	OUP	Stage 2 More Stories A	3
Water Lilies & other stories	New Way	Nelson Thornes	Violet Platform Books	8
Water Moves	AlphaWorld	Gardner	Band 2: Red	2
Water Park, The	Sails Foundation	Heinemann	Pink A – Is	1A
Water, The	Sails Foundation	Heinemann	Pink C – Go	1A
Waterfalls, Glaciers and Avalanches	PM Plus Non-fiction	Nelson Thornes	Gold Level	9
Waves	Literacy Links Plus	Kingscourt	Contemporary Stories	2
Waving Sheep, The	PM Storybooks	Nelson Thornes	Green Set A	5
Way I Go to School, The	PM Storybook Starters	Nelson Thornes	Set 1	1A
We Can Run	PM Storybook Starters	Nelson Thornes	Set 2	1B
We Can See Three	PM Maths	Nelson Thornes	Stage A	2
We Dress Up	PM Plus	Nelson Thornes	Starters One	1A
We Get Squashed!	First Stories	Gardner	Emergent A	1A
We Go Out	PM Storybook Starters	Nelson Thornes	Set 1	1A
We Go Shopping	AlphaWorld	Gardner	Band 1B: Pink	1B
We Like Fish!	PM Storybook Starters	Nelson Thornes	Set 2	1B
We Like Weddings	Spotty Zebra	Nelson Thornes	Red – Change	1B
We Love the Farm	Lighthouse	Ginn	Pink B: 5	1B
We Made a Dragon	AlphaWorld	Gardner	Level 17 (trans)	7
We Need Insects!	Four Corners	Pearson	Year 2	8

TITLE	SERIES	PUBLISHER	SET (OR AUTHOR)	BAND
We Need More Trees!	Alphakids	Gardner	Transitional Level 15	6
We Ski	Kingscourt Reading, Extension	Kingscourt	Set 1	1B
We Want William!	Crunchies	Orchard	Colour Crackers	9
Weather	AlphaWorld	Gardner	Level 22 (ext)	10
Weather	Pathways	Collins	Year 1	8
Weather in the City	National Geographic	Rigby	Red Level	2
Weather Vane, The	Oxford Reading Tree	OUP	Stage 4 More Stories A	4
We'd Better Make a List	Story Chest	Kingscourt	Ready-set-go Set DD	3
Wedding, The	Oxford Reading Tree	OUP	Stage 4 More Stories A	4
Welcome Home, Barney	Crunchies	Orchard	Colour Crackers	8
Well I Never	Story Chest	Kingscourt	Stage 5	8
Were the Old Days the Best?	Info Trail	Pearson	Beginner History	4
Were They Real?	Big Cat	Collins	Purple	9
Wet Grass	Story Chest	Kingscourt	Stage 2	6
Wet Paint	Kingscourt Reading, Extension	Kingscourt	Set 3	3
Wet Paint	Oxford Reading Tree	OUP	Stage 4 More Stories B	3
Wet Weather Camping	PM Plus	Nelson Thornes	Turquoise Level	7
Wet! Wet! Wet!	Story Street	Pearson	Step 2	2
Whacky Wheels	Skyrider LM Chapters	Gardner	Set 1	7
Whales	Alphakids Plus	Gardner	Early Level 9	6
Whales	PM Non-fiction	Nelson Thornes	Silver Level	10
Whales on the World Wide Web	Alphakids	Gardner	Extending Level 20	9
Whale's Year, The	Lighthouse	Ginn	Green: 2	5
What a Load of Rubbish	Lighthouse	Ginn	Turquoise: 8	7
What a Mess!	Genre Range	Pearson	Beginner Plays	5
What a Mess!	Story Chest	Kingscourt	Ready-set-go Set C	3
What a Week!	Rigby Star	Rigby	Yellow Level	3
What Alice Makes	Spotty Zebra	Nelson Thornes	Pink A – Ourselves	1A
What Am I For?	Web Fiction	OUP	Stage 6 (Variety)	8
What Am I Going to Be?	Kingscourt Reading, Extension	Kingscourt	Set 6	6
What Am I?	AlphaWorld	Gardner	Level 17 (trans)	7
What Am I?	Kingscourt Reading, Core	Kingscourt	Level 5 Little Books	2
What Are You?	Literacy Links Plus	Kingscourt	Emergent A	1A
What Babies Used To Wear	Pelican Big Bks	Pearson	Witherington, Anne	8
What Can a Diver See?	National Geographic	Rigby	Pink Level	1A
What Can be Recycled?	Discovery World Links	Heinemann	Stage C	4
What Can I See?	Kingscourt Reading, Extension	Kingscourt	Set 1	1A
What Can it Be?	Kingscourt Reading, Extension	Kingscourt	Set 2	2
What Can You See?	Pelican Big Bks	Pearson	Body, Wendy	4
What Did Kim Catch?	Literacy Links Plus	Kingscourt	Emergent D	2
What Dinah Saw	Lighthouse	Ginn	Gold: 6	9
What Do I Need?	First Facts	Badger	Level 3	4
What Do You Know About Dolphins?	National Geographic	Rigby	Green Level	7
What Do You Like?	Big Cat	Collins	Red B	2
What Do You Want That For?	Lighthouse	Ginn	Yellow: 4	3
What Do You Want to Be?	Oxford Reading Tree	OUP	Fireflies Stage 7	8
What Do You Want to Be?	Web Weavers Non-fiction	OUP	Stage 2 First Words NF	3
What Has Spots?	Literacy Links Plus	Kingscourt	Emergent B	1A
What is Bat?	Literacy Links Plus	Kingscourt	Early C	5
What is He?	Rigby Star	Rigby	Red Level	2
What is it?	Kingscourt Reading, Extension	Kingscourt	Set 2	2

TITLE	SERIES	PUBLISHER	SET (OR AUTHOR)	BAND
What is it?	Oxford Reading Tree	OUP	Stage 2 More Patterned Stories	2
What is it?	Spotty Zebra	Nelson Thornes	Red – Ourselves	2
What is This?	Oxford Reading Tree	OUP	Fireflies, More – Stage 2	2
What Jessie Really Likes	Lighthouse	Ginn	Pink B: 8	1B
What Lays Eggs?	Kingscourt Reading, Extension	Kingscourt	Set 2	2
What Makes Toys Move?	Spotlight on Fact	Collins	Y1 Toys and Games	4
What Mr Croc Forgot	Rockets	A&C Black	Rodgers, Frank	7
What Shall I Wear?	Lighthouse	Ginn	Pink B: 6	1B
What Shall We Have For Tea Tonight?	Info Trail	Pearson	Beginner Geography	3
What Tommy Did	Literacy Links Plus	Kingscourt	Early B	7
What Was it Like?	Oxford Reading Tree	OUP	Stage 8 More Stories A	8
Whatever the Weather	Pelican Big Bks	Pearson	Body, Wendy	5
What's Around the Corner?	Literacy Links Plus	Kingscourt	Early B	4
What's for Dinner?	Alphakids	Gardner	Emergent Level 3	2
What's For Lunch?	Story Chest	Kingscourt	Get-ready Set C	2
What's in the Cake Tin?	Dragonflies	Gardner	Red	2
What's in Your Lunchbox?	Web Guided Reading	OUP	Stage 2 (Duck Green)	3
What's Inside?	Big Cat	Collins	Red A	1B
What's Inside?	Spotty Zebra	Nelson Thornes	Pink A – Change	1A
What's Inside Me?	Oxford Reading Tree	OUP	Fireflies Stage 8	10
What's it Made Of?	Rigby Star Non-fiction	Rigby	Blue Level	2
What's That Noise?	Alphakids	Gardner	Emergent Level 4	2
What's That Sound?	Spotty Zebra	Nelson Thornes	Pink A – Change	1A
What's There?	Pathways	Collins	Year 1	2
What's This Spider Doing?	Kingscourt Reading, Core	Kingscourt	Level 9 Little Books	4
What's This? What's That?	Alphakids	Gardner	Emergent Level 2	1B
What's Underground?	Big Cat	Collins	Blue	5
Whatsit, The	Oxford Reading Tree	OUP	Stage 5 More Stories A	5
Wheelbarrow Garden, The	PM Plus	Nelson Thornes	Green Level	5
Wheels	AlphaWorld	Gardner	Band 5: Green	5
Wheels	Big Cat	Collins	Pink B	1A
Wheels	Oxford Reading Tree	OUP	Fireflies Stage 1+	2
Wheels	Sails Foundation	Heinemann	Pink B – For	1A
When Grandad Was at School	Info Trail	Pearson	Beginner History	3
When I Grow Up	Lighthouse	Ginn	Pink B: 3	1B
When I Was Sick	AlphaWorld	Gardner	Band 3: Yellow	3
When I'm Older	Literacy Links Plus	Kingscourt	Early C	5
When the Bus Was Late	Alphakids Plus	Gardner	Extending Level 24	10
When the Tide Goes Out	Kingscourt Reading, Core	Kingscourt	Level 4 Benchmark Bk	2
When the Volcano Erupted	PM Storybooks	Nelson Thornes	Turquoise Set A	7
Where are the Babies?	PM Storybook Starters	Nelson Thornes	Set 2	1B
Where Are the Sun Hats?	PM Storybooks	Nelson Thornes	Yellow Set A	3
Where Are They Going?	Story Chest	Kingscourt	Ready-set-go Set A	2
Where Did All the Water Go?	PM Plus Non-fiction	Nelson Thornes	Yellow Level	4
Where Do All the Puddles Go?	Rigby Star Non-fiction	Rigby	Orange Level	7
Where Do These Go?	Spotty Zebra	Nelson Thornes	Pink B – Change	1B
Where Does Food Come From?	PM Plus Non-fiction	Nelson Thornes	Green Level	5
Where is Curly?	Rigby Star	Rigby	Yellow Level	3
Where is Hannah?	PM Storybooks	Nelson Thornes	Red Set B	2
Where is it Safe to Play?	PM Plus Non-fiction	Nelson Thornes	Red Level	3
Where is My Spider?	Story Chest	Kingscourt	Stage 4	7

TITLE	SERIES	PUBLISHER	SET (OR AUTHOR)	BAND
Where is Patch?	Rigby Star	Rigby	Pink Level	1B
Where Is Sam?	Dragonflies	Gardner	Red	2
Where is Skunk?	Story Chest	Kingscourt	Ready-set-go Set CC	4
Where is the Wind?	Big Cat	Collins	Red B	2
Where is White Rabbit?	Skyrider LM Chapters	Gardner	Set 2	8
Where's Cheep?	Web Guided Reading	OUP	Stage 5 (Duck Green)	4
Where's Daddy Bear?	Web Fiction	OUP	Stage 2 (Variety)	2
Where's Our Car?	Rigby Star	Rigby	Yellow Level	3
Where's the Baby?	Alphakids	Gardner	Early Level 6	3
Which Animals Lay Eggs?	Web Weavers Non-fiction	OUP	First Non-fiction: Pack B	2
Which Home?	Info Trail	Pearson	Beginner Geography	5
While We Sleep	Kingscourt Reading, Core	Kingscourt	Gold	9
Whistle Tooth, The	Kingscourt Reading, Extension	Kingscourt	Set 5	5
White Horse, The	Literacy Links Plus	Kingscourt	Fluent D	7
Who?	Kingscourt Reading, Extension	Kingscourt	Set 2	2
Who Can See the Camel?	Story Chest	Kingscourt	Ready-set-go Set AA	2
Who Did it?	Storyworlds	Heinemann	Stage 5 Our World	4
Who Did That?	Oxford Reading Tree	OUP	Stage 1+ More Patterned Stories	2
Who Goes on the Bonfire?	Info Trail	Pearson	Emergent History	9
Who is it?	Oxford Reading Tree	OUP	Stage 1 First Words	1B
Who is the Tallest?	Alphakids	Gardner	Early Level 7	3
Who Lives Here?	Kingscourt Reading, Extension	Kingscourt	Set 4	4
Who Lives Here?	Spotty Zebra	Nelson Thornes	Red – Ourselves	2
Who Lives on a Farm?	Kingscourt Reading, Core	Kingscourt	Level 1 Little Books	1A
Who Looks After Me?	National Geographic	Rigby	Pink Level	1A
Who Made This Mess?	Web Fiction	OUP	Stage 3 (Variety)	3
Who Took the Cake?	First Stories	Gardner	Emergent C	1B
Who's Coming For a Ride?	Literacy Links Plus	Kingscourt	Emergent A	1A
Who's in the Shed?	Literacy Links Plus	Kingscourt	Contemporary Stories	4
Who's That Knocking at My Door?	Alphakids Plus	Gardner	Early Level 10	4
Whose Egg is This?	Kingscourt Reading, Core	Kingscourt	Level 7 Little Books	3
Whose Footprints?	Lighthouse	Ginn	Red: 10	2
Why Do You Need to Read?	Web Weavers Non-fiction	OUP	First Non-fiction: Pack A	4
Why Does the Moon Change Shape?	Badger NF Guided Reading	Ticktock	Stepping Stones	8
Why Elephants Have Long Noses	Literacy Links Plus	Kingscourt	Early D	6
Why Flamingoes Have Red Legs	New Way	Nelson Thornes	Violet Parallel Books	9
Why Frog and Snake Can't Be Friends	Literacy Links Plus	Kingscourt	Traditional Tale	8
Why Rabbits Have Long Ears	Literacy Links Plus	Kingscourt	Fluent D	9
Why Recycle?	First Facts	Badger	Level 4	9
Why the Sea is Salty	Literacy Links Plus	Kingscourt	Fluent C	8
Why Tortoise Has a Cracked Shell	Storyworld Bridges	Heinemann	Stage 10	10
Wibble-Wobble	Kingscourt Reading, Extension	Kingscourt	Set 4	4
Wide Mouthed Frog, The	Literacy Links Plus	Kingscourt	Early B	5
Wiggle! Woggle	Spotty Zebra	Nelson Thornes	Pink B – Ourselves	3
Wilbur's Wild Ride	Kingscourt Reading, Core	Kingscourt	Level 6 Collection	3
Wild Cat Guide, The	Lighthouse	Ginn	Purple: 8	8
Wild Easts and the Wild West, The	Kingscourt Reading, Extension	Kingscourt	Set 8	8
Wild Nature	Kingscourt Reading, Core	Kingscourt	White	10
Wild Weather	Oxford Reading Tree	OUP	Fireflies Stage 6	8
William and the Dog	Oxford Reading Tree	OUP	Robins Pack 2	9
William and the Pied Piper	Oxford Reading Tree	OUP	Robins Pack 3	9

TITLE	SERIES	PUBLISHER	SET (OR AUTHOR)	BAND
William's Mistake	Oxford Reading Tree	OUP	Robins Pack 2	9
Willow Pattern Plot, The	Oxford Reading Tree	OUP	Stage 6 & 7 More Stories B	7
Wind and Fire, Part 1	Story Street	Pearson	Step 5	7
Wind and Fire, Part 2	Story Street	Pearson	Step 5	7
Wind and Sun	Literacy Links Plus	Kingscourt	Early D	6
Wind and the Sun, The	Rigby Star	Rigby	Green Level	5
Wind Blows, The	First Stories	Gardner	Emergent D	1B
Wind Power	National Geographic	Rigby	Orange Level	6
Wind, The	Big Cat	Collins	Yellow	3
Windy Day, A	Web Guided Reading	OUP	Stage 1 (Duck Green)	1B
Wings	AlphaWorld	Gardner	Band 5: Green	5
Wings	Rigby Star Non-fiction	Rigby	Pink Level	1A
Winning	Oxford Reading Tree	OUP	Citizenship Stories Stage 9/10	9
Winter	Kingscourt Reading, Extension	Kingscourt	Set 6	6
Winter on the Ice	PM Plus	Nelson Thornes	Purple Level	8
Winter Woollies	Kingscourt Reading, Extension	Kingscourt	Set 8	8
Wiz	Web Guided Reading	OUP	Stage 5 (Duck Green)	5
Wizard's Hat, The	Web Fiction	OUP	Stage 4 (Variety)	5
Wobbly Tooth, The	Literacy Links Plus	Kingscourt	Early B	4
Wobbly Tooth, The	Oxford Reading Tree	OUP	Stage 2 More Stories B	4
Wolf and the Kids, The	Storyworlds	Heinemann	Stage 5 Once Upon a Time	5
Wolf Whistle, The	Web Guided Reading	OUP	Stage 7 (Duck Green)	7
Wolves	PM Non-fiction	Nelson Thornes	Silver Level	10
Woman and the Tiny Bird, The	PM Gems	Nelson Thornes	Green 12	5
Woman Who Fooled the Fairies, The	Big Cat	Collins	Gold	9
Wonders of the World	Oxford Reading Tree	OUP	Fireflies Stage 5	9
Woodcutter and the Bear, The	Rigby Star	Rigby	Star Plus	8
Woody's Week	Big Cat	Collins	Red B	2
Woof!	Literacy Links Plus	Kingscourt	Emergent C	2
Woolly, Woolly	Literacy Links Plus	Kingscourt	Early B	4
Work Helicopter, The	PM Plus	Nelson Thornes	Orange Level	6
Working Dogs	First Facts	Badger	Level 3	5
Working in the Film Industry	Oxford Reading Tree	OUP	Fireflies Stage 10	10
Working with Dad	Alphakids Plus	Gardner	Early Level 7	3
World Atlas	Four Corners	Pearson	Year 2	10
World Instruments	Oxford Reading Tree	OUP	Fireflies Stage 4	6
World of Dummies, The	Skyrider LM Chapters	Gardner	Set 2	9
World of Sport, A	Rigby Star Non-fiction	Rigby	Turquoise Level	8
World's Largest Animals	Discovery World Links	Heinemann	Stage D	9
Worm Looks for Lunch	Big Cat	Collins	Green	3
Worm Song	Alphakids	Gardner	Early Level 10	4
Worms at Work	Alphakids	Gardner	Extending Level 21	9
Would You Be a Bee?	Info Trail	Pearson	Beginner Science	7
Writing	Web Weavers Non-fiction	OUP	First Non-fiction: Pack A	4
Wrong Colours	Web Weavers Non-fiction	OUP	Stage 1 First Words NF	1B

X-Rays	Alphakids Plus	Gardner	Extending Level 18	8

TITLE	SERIES	PUBLISHER	SET (OR AUTHOR)	BAND
Y				
Yasmin and the Flood	Oxford Reading Tree	OUP	Stage 4 Sparrows	4
Yasmin's Dress	Oxford Reading Tree	OUP	Stage 4 Sparrows	3
Yawn, Yawn, Yawn	Sunshine Readers	Gardner	Purple Level	7
Year at Duck Green, A	Web Guided Reading	OUP	Stage 7 (Duck Green)	6
Year With Mother Bear, A	Kingscourt Reading, Extension	Kingscourt	Set 6	6
Yellow	Literacy Links Plus	Kingscourt	Emergent C	1B
Yellow Overalls	Literacy Links Plus	Kingscourt	Fluent C	8
You Are Special	First Explorers	Kingscourt	Level 1	9
You Can't Catch Me	Lighthouse	Ginn	Red: 5	2
You Can't Park an Elephant	Pathways	Collins	Year 2	8
Youngest Giraffe, The	PM Plus	Nelson Thornes	Orange Level	6
Your Amazing Body	Alphakids Plus	Gardner	Early Level 11	6
Yo-Yo a Go-Go	Rigby Star	Rigby	Green Level	5
Yum and Yuk	Story Chest	Kingscourt	Stage 3	5
Yum! Yum!	Storyworlds	Heinemann	Stage 2 Animal World	2
Yummy Scrummy	Oxford Reading Tree	OUP	All Stars Pack 2	10
Z				
Zac and Chirpy	PM Photo Stories	Nelson Thornes	Red 3	2
Zac and Puffing Billy	PM Photo Stories	Nelson Thornes	Magenta 2/3	2
Zac and the Ducks	PM Photo Stories	Nelson Thornes	Red 4	2
Zac's Train Ride	PM Photo Stories	Nelson Thornes	Yellow 7	3
Zac's Train Set	PM Photo Stories	Nelson Thornes	Magenta 2/3	1B
Zala Runs for Her Life	PM Storybooks	Nelson Thornes	Purple Set A	8
Zoo Dinners	Sails Foundation	Heinemann	Pink C – Get	1A
Zoo Overnight	Skyrider LM Chapters	Gardner	Set 2	9
Zoom In!	Kingscourt Reading, Extension	Kingscourt	Set 10	10